Lassoing the Sun

Lassoing the Sun

A YEAR IN AMERICA'S NATIONAL PARKS

*

Mark Woods

Thomas Dunne Books
St. Martin's Press
New York

THOMAS DUNNE BOOKS.
An imprint of St. Martin's Press.

LASSOING THE SUN. Copyright © 2016 by Mark Woods. All rights reserved. Printed in the United States of America. For information, address St. Martin's Press, 175 Fifth Avenue, New York, N.Y. 10010.

www.thomasdunnebooks.com
www.stmartins.com

"Embracing Sound of Silence Was One of Mother's Gifts" column (May 6, 2012) is reprinted by permission of *The Florida Times-Union*.

Designed by Donna Sinisgalli Noetzel

The Library of Congress Cataloging-in-Publication Data is available upon request.

ISBN 978-1-250-10589-9 (hardcover)
ISBN 978-1-250-10590-5 (e-book)

Our books may be purchased in bulk for promotional, educational, or business use. Please contact your local bookseller or the Macmillan Corporate and Premium Sales Department at 1-800-221-7945, extension 5442, or by e-mail at MacmillanSpecialMarkets@macmillan.com.

First Edition: June 2016

1 3 5 7 9 10 8 6 4 2

To loved ones who are gone
and beloved places that remain

Lassoing the Sun

PROLOGUE: BEFORE DAWN

*M*ama was dying.

I didn't know this when I pulled off California's Highway 101 just before the bridge crossing over the Klamath River.

We were about an hour away from our destination, a campground in Redwood National and State Parks. Temporary signs along the road had alerted drivers to be prepared for what was ahead: a whale jam.

I pulled the rental car into a dirt parking lot. My wife, daughter, and I got out and joined the people walking toward the two-lane bridge to see Mama—a forty-five-foot-long female gray whale who had entered the river in late June 2011 along with her calf.

Thousands of people had been pulling over every day, standing on the edge of the bridge, taking pictures, oohing and aahing as Mama shot air and water out of her blowhole while her calf swam by her side.

In late July, the calf returned to the ocean.

Mama stayed.

When we got there in mid-August, she still was in the river, still swimming circles under the bridge, still creating whale jams on Highway 101. But she also was drawing more concern by the day. I didn't know this at the time, but flotillas of kayaks, canoes, and stand-up paddleboards had tried to coax her out of the river and back into her natural habitat, the salt water of the ocean. Members of the Yurok tribe hopped in a small boat and tried drumming and singing. Others tried flutes, violins, and ukuleles.

Mama stayed in the river.

Scientists tried fear, playing recordings of killer whales farther upriver, hoping the sound of a predator would make Mama head back to the ocean.

Mama stayed in the river, swimming her circles under the bridge.

When we arrived, it was an overcast day, the sky almost as gray as the whale.

We walked onto the bridge, sticking close to the railing on the left to stay out of the way of the traffic coming from the north. My daughter, Mia, spotted Mama first. She hurried to get out her camera and turn it on, worried that she was going to miss the shot.

Mia was nine. The camera had been a Christmas gift the previous year.

When I was her age, I had a Kodak Hawkeye Flashfun II. I loved photography for the same reason I loved baseball. Because Dad did. When we made family trips, Dad and I both brought our cameras. When I grew up, I wanted to be Ansel Adams, play shortstop for the Detroit Tigers, and go to the moon. So I suppose giving Mia a camera was another example of parents trying to re-create their own childhood. And as with many such attempts, it hadn't worked as hoped. Mia hadn't used her camera much.

But now she seemed intent on getting a shot of Mama. Not that she needed to worry about Mama suddenly heading off to sea. The whale didn't get far from the bridge before she turned around and swam back toward us. When she passed under the bridge, the crowd shifted to the other side. Back and forth, back and forth.

On one pass, Mia took a picture, glanced at the back of her camera, and said, "Look!"

I explained that once upon a time, back when there was something called film inside cameras, we didn't know until long after the trip whether we had captured the moment. She didn't roll her eyes. We were making progress.

Mia had been complaining nonstop ever since we left our home in Jacksonville, Florida, flying to San Francisco and heading north. She didn't care if we were going to a national park. She didn't want to be doing a long drive or camping or pretty much anything else I had planned. She wanted to be at home, sleeping in her own bed, watching her familiar TV shows, enjoying the final week of summer before school started again.

"I don't want to go," she said repeatedly, as though if she said it often enough we might change our minds and head back to Florida.

The only time she wasn't complaining, she was watching movies. As I drove north, there was one point, as the redwoods seemed to be growing taller by the minute, that I tried to point out the trees. I got no response. Mia was busy watching *Rio*. My wife, Toni, was checking something on her iPhone.

I was frustrated and annoyed. Pissed off at the electronic devices. Pissed off that this wasn't turning out like I had envisioned—which is to say, a remake of the trip I made to the redwoods when I was nine years old.

MOST OF THE details from childhood are hazy and jumbled. Many are gone completely. I've tried to recall specific Christmas and birthday gifts. Other than the Kodak camera and a red baseball glove, I just come up with vague memories of sweaters, model rockets, and vinyl albums.

This isn't simply because my parents didn't give us extravagant gifts. Although in a monetary sense, that certainly was true. During my childhood, Dad was a missionary on an Indian reservation in Nevada, a minister at a couple of midwestern churches, and a chaplain at a hospital. Mom stayed at home to raise three children, then got her master's and became a social worker and—much to my chagrin when she showed up in my high school—a substitute teacher.

But even on their limited income, my parents managed to give us some epic family trips.

Before our trips I would ride my bike with the banana seat to a nearby Shell station and get maps—actual folded paper maps—so I could plot out the route. I remember being excited whenever we spotted a sign saying that we were entering a new state. But the most magical of signs—brown, with an arrowhead logo, snowcapped mountains, a bison and a sequoia tree—announced that we were entering a national park.

We went to Yosemite, Lassen, Rocky Mountain, Grand Canyon, and later, on a trip to the East Coast, a series of historical sites from Philadelphia to Washington. The years have jumbled the timeline a bit. But I think my first national park was at that time, in the late 1960s, one of America's newest national parks: Redwood National and State Parks.

More than forty years later, I could close my eyes and imagine our campsite. Not only could I picture the pop-up camper that we pulled behind the station wagon, but I could hear it being set up—a mix of metal rails sliding, canvas popping open, and Dad's swearing. Whenever I watch *A Christmas Story* and hear Ralphie's dad fighting with the malfunctioning furnace, I think of my dad and the camper.

It slept four, room enough for my parents and my two sisters. I set up my pup tent maybe twenty feet away. I was closer to my parents there than I was in my bedroom at home. And yet being in that tent was liberating, frightening, and exciting.

The tent was made of thick canvas, a material that when it rained seemed to do a better job at soaking up water than repelling it.

I'd fall asleep to the sounds of the woods. Rustling trees, snaps of branches. I'd wake up to birds chirping, pots and pans clanging, the poof of the camp stove, and the sizzle of breakfast.

I remember walking back to the campsite after ranger talks, shining a flashlight into the trees, turning it off, and getting a glimpse of so many stars that it made the planetarium at home suddenly seem understated.

I remember the smell of the redwoods.

I didn't realize just how deeply this scent was embedded until we got out of the rental car at the bridge over the Klamath River and I took a deep breath.

Even though I hadn't been in this part of the country since I was nine, I think I could have closed my eyes and told you where I was.

It smelled familiar, like walking into a childhood home and instantly being transported back in time.

I HAD JUST turned fifty.

At thirty, I got married. At forty, I became a father. At fifty, I guess I had my version of a midlife crisis.

It didn't involve a sports car. I was quite content with a 1994 Volvo 940 with dents and scratches all over its faded dark green exterior, and small burn marks from a previous owner on its tan cloth interior.

In a way, the Volvo *was* my midlife crisis vehicle. I used driving it and avoiding having to make a car payment as an excuse to plan adventures and continue a lifelong pattern of never quite appreciating the moment, of always searching for something—a place, a job, a quest—that would make me happy.

The year I turned fifty, I planned three trips to national parks. And each, I realized at some point, involved an attempt to turn back the clock, or at least pretend like it wasn't moving forward.

There was an anniversary trip with my wife to Cumberland Island National Seashore in Georgia, a weekend to rekindle the spark of twenty years ago. There was a buddy road trip, not to Vegas for a wild weekend, but to the Grand Canyon for a run I thought would prove to myself that age wasn't slowing me down. But the most significant of the three trips was the final one: to the redwoods, to my childhood.

When my family—my mother in Arizona; a sister in Reno, Nevada; another sister in a Detroit suburb—asked what I wanted to do for my fiftieth birthday, I decided I wanted us to go to a national park, the one I went to when I was Mia's age.

As I was planning the trip, an e-mail popped in my inbox, saying entries were being accepted for something called the Eugene C. Pulliam Fellowship for Editorial Writing. I deleted it the first time. But when it came again, I read the details. It was established to enable one "mid-career" editorial writer or columnist to break away from daily responsibilities to "broaden his or her horizons."

I figured I at least fit the basic requirements. I was the Metro columnist for *The Florida Times-Union* in Jacksonville. I was mid-career. Or at least I hoped I was. My paper, and pretty much every other one, had gone through waves of layoffs. I had survived. But even when you weren't one of the people to get a tap on the shoulder, you were left feeling a mix of guilt and relief and depression. The idea of getting away, broadening some horizons, sounded pretty appealing.

But if I could immerse myself in any topic for a year, what would it be?

I already had the national parks on my mind because of the trips when my daughter, who loves Disney World and knows I believe it's a torture chamber with lines, asked, "What is your Disney?"

I thought about her question and ran through some ideas in my head. A baseball stadium on a perfect summer day. Rolling country hills for biking. A trail. A river, woods, mountains, a canyon. Yeah, that's it.

"Not a theme park," I said. "A national park."

The National Park Service was gearing up to celebrate its centennial in 2016. Many people, from John Muir to Ken Burns, had beautifully documented the history of the parks. But what about the future? What if I spent one calendar year, a year not far from the eve of that centennial, trying to answer questions about the future of the national parks?

The proposal was much more detailed. But that was it in a nutshell. I mailed it, never expecting to win. Then one day I got a call from Todd Gillman, Washington bureau chief for *The Dallas Morning News* and chairman of the Pulliam judging panel.

I was going to my Disney.

THE FAMILY TRIP became sort of a prelude. Or at least that's how I thought about it then. As is often the case with family vacations, we don't realize the significance of them until later.

After watching Mama at the bridge, we continued on to Jedediah Smith Redwoods State Park, one of the state parks that partners with the national park.

In the spring, I had talked to a ranger about what campground he'd recommend for families.

"You can't go wrong with the Jed," he said.

I had reserved campsites 30, 33, and 35, side by side, away from the highway, not too far from the River Beach Trail and the Smith River. I didn't know it when we arrived, but months and years later, if you told me I could instantly be transported to any place on earth at any time, I might have started there. Those campsites, that week in the redwoods.

I expected Mia to stay glued to some electronic device until her three cousins arrived. But within minutes of getting out of the car, she was running around, exploring. We walked down to the Smith River. A narrow wooden footbridge crossed the shallow, clear river, leading to the rocky beach and the old-growth redwoods in Stout Memorial Grove.

There were several boulders—much taller than Mia—near the footbridge. To my surprise, my daughter, the same girl who typically was nervous about trying anything new, scrambled up one without any prompting. When she reached the top of the rock, she stood there, arms outstretched in victory.

If I had tried to script a scenario that illustrated the power of the outdoors on children, I couldn't have done any better than this. And it happened repeatedly during the week.

One day we went to the beach. The kids complained the whole way there, saying they wanted to stay at the campground. But once we were there—even though it was cold and foggy, with a damp wind blowing off the ocean, and even though they were wearing short-sleeve shirts—we couldn't get them to leave.

They designed an obstacle course in the sand and made everyone run it. I watched my mom running it and wondered how many grandmothers would do that.

At one point, Mom grabbed a stick and started doing something that she did whenever we went to a beach, something Dad used to do. She wrote haiku in the sand.

> *Pacific Ocean*
> *Seals barking, brisk waves*
> *Woods family here.*

Mia looked at this and started counting out the syllables with her fingers. Then she grabbed a stick and began writing her own poem in the sand.

> *Fun and family*
> *Camping at the Redwoods Park*
> *Being together*

She already had figured out one of the great truths about the national parks. The beauty wasn't just the towering trees or rugged ocean. It was in being together, away from the concerns of work and school and daily life.

We played card games. We cooked meals over stoves and campfires. We sat around the embers, toasting marshmallows and listening to Mia's cousin Ben sing, "Beans, beans, the musical fruit, the more you eat . . ."

Mom bought souvenirs for the grandkids in the gift shop. Not trinkets or T-shirts. Books. One afternoon I looked around and all four cousins were scattered around the campsite, reading. Mia was sitting on the picnic table, buried in her copy of Gary Larson's *There's a Hair in My Dirt*. She seemed to like it partly because it had a couple of cusswords.

Mom also bought and read aloud *Everybody Needs a Rock*, by Byrd Baylor.

"'Everybody needs a rock,'" she began. "'I'm sorry for kids who don't have a rock for a friend.'"

After she finished the story about how to pick out a rock—not just any rock, a special rock that fits just right in your hand, a rock that you find yourself and keep as long as you can, maybe forever—the kids spent the rest of the week searching for their rocks.

Near the end of the week, we decided to do a roughly six-mile round-trip hike to the Boy Scout Tree.

"Okay," Mom said at the trailhead. "Let's try something. Let's all be quiet for five minutes."

Good luck with that, I thought.

But we started walking and everyone was quiet. I focused on what I could hear. The scuffling of boots on the trail, the rustling of the trees shifting far overhead, the chirping of birds. And more. But even if I described all the sounds, it wouldn't really explain what the place sounded like. There was a sense of space.

I recalled what the Grand Canyon sounded like when a friend and I started down a trail into it at four A.M., pitch black, silent. Our headlamps illuminated just a few feet at a time. Still, we knew the canyon was there. And not just because we had seen it in daylight. We could sense that on one side of us there was a rock wall and the other side massive open space.

I'm sure there are scientific explanations for this, how you use your senses to calibrate space in ways you don't even realize. All I know is that *feeling* the canyon was every bit as awe-inspiring as seeing it. And that as we began silently hiking the trail to the Boy Scout Tree, this didn't feel like just another walk in the woods.

When Mom announced that the five minutes were up, the kids

started talking, giggling, and pushing ahead, on a mission to make it to the Boy Scout Tree.

It was one of those August days in the Pacific Northwest, before the rainy season arrives. The sun was shining, the air cool and dry. The trail meandered through woods, gently rising and falling, twisting and turning, eventually opening up and letting shafts of sunlight stream diagonally through the redwoods down to the ferns. It felt like something out of a fairy tale.

Throughout the hike, Mom kept falling behind, which was unlike her. We always half joked that we had to train for a vacation with Nana. But I didn't think much about this. She was seventy-three years old. It was about time she started slowing down a little.

"I'll walk with you, Mom," I said.

We let the others go ahead. Mom kept apologizing when she had to stop and catch her breath after short hills. I kept telling her it was okay, it was a beautiful day to be in the woods.

She was resting on a giant log alongside the trail when I recalled coming to the redwoods when I was about Mia's age, camping at Prairie Creek Redwoods State Park, playing in the tide pools, taking pictures of the elk, going for hikes like this.

"I don't know if I appreciated that then," I said. "But I do now."

On the last morning of the trip, I took a photo of Nana and the four grandchildren sitting on a fallen tree near our campsite. Afterward, as I helped Mia get off the end of the log, she was upset about something. She said through clenched teeth, "You, me, the footbridge."

We walked to the footbridge, down the path that had now become familiar, to the view of the river and Stout Memorial Grove. We stood there and she vented a bit about something someone had said about her being the smallest. Then we got quiet.

I was so happy. Not happy that she had been upset. Happy that when she was upset, she came to this spot. I scribbled something in a notepad I was carrying, preparing for the year in the parks.

Mia
footbridge
solace of nature

On the drive back to San Francisco, Mia fell asleep almost instantly. I was debating whether to wake her when we approached the Klamath River bridge.

The temporary signs were gone. So were the traffic jams and, I realized, the whale.

We had been isolated from the news that week. I assumed Mama finally went back out to the ocean.

That's what happened when a whale entered the Klamath in 1989. It's what had happened with other whales in other spots along the California coast. Humphrey. Delta and Dawn. All returned to the ocean.

It wasn't until I got back home that I found what had happened to Mama.

We saw her on a Sunday. She beached herself Monday evening. She died Tuesday, before the sun rose over the Klamath River.

The stories said her health deteriorated in her last two days. In other words, when we watched her swimming her circles, she was dying.

The media coverage, blogs, and press releases gave the scientific reasons for why this happened—basically she had spent seven weeks outside of her saltwater habitat. They also quoted people talking about what it meant. Some of the locals said Mama was sending a message. They pointed to *The Inland Whale,* a book containing a selection of native stories.

The title story was told by Fannie Flounder, a Yurok tribe member, to anthropologist Theodora Kroeber. The Associated Press report about Mama's death quoted Janet Wortman, a relative of Flounder, explaining what the late tribal member believed this meant: "She said when the whale is in the river, it means the world is out of balance . . . things aren't the way they should be. Fannie said, 'You all need to get together and pray and dance and beat your foot on the ground and that will tilt the earth back the way it is supposed to be.' "

I later read the story "The Inland Whale" from that collection of native tales. It did tell the story of the earth being tilted out of balance, tipping so far that the ocean came flowing into the river, bringing with it all kinds of fish and sea life that didn't belong there. And with dancing and praying and stomping, balance was restored and the fish flowed back into the sea. All except for a female whale.

But that was only part of the story.

The rest of it—the part that wasn't in any of the news coverage—involved another reason for the whale being in the river.

"The Inland Whale" isn't so much about a whale as it is about a boy and his mother. The whale is there to comfort the boy, to make him strong, to prepare him for life without her.

In the story, the boy named Toan grows up, becomes a man, and loses his mother. The tale ends by saying the mother taught her son that it is wrong to grieve too much for the dead, that it is dangerous to even think too much about the one who has died.

Toan remembered this teaching. He passed his mother's grave whenever he went to the river, and sometimes he took his carving and sat near where she lay while he worked; as he had sat near her all his life. He cried to her sometimes, but for the most part, her tender smile and the shu-shu-shu-shu rustle of her step came into his memory and out again, soft and passing as a river breeze.

Mama was dead.

I knew this as I prepared to begin my year in the national parks. But there was something I didn't know yet, something that would change how I looked at rocks, how I listened to river breezes, how I chased the sun from one end of America to the other.

My mom was dying.

1

*

JANUARY: ACADIA NATIONAL PARK

$\mathcal{M}$y alarm went off at four A.M.

I hit my watch and took a few seconds to remember where I was and why I was there.

I was in Maine for New Year's Day. It was dark, 30 degrees outside.

The first light of another year in America was about eleven miles and three hours away—7:09 A.M., atop Cadillac Mountain in Acadia National Park, the highest mountain in Maine and on the whole North Atlantic seaboard.

WHEN PEOPLE HEARD about my chance to spend a year in the national parks, they inevitably had two reactions. First, they asked if I needed someone to help carry my luggage. Second, they made a suggestion.

You have to go to . . . Glacier, Crater Lake, Zion. Whichever park was their favorite.

I explained there were a lot of places I wasn't going to make it to in one year. When the National Park Service was created by an act of Congress in 1916, there were fourteen national parks and twenty-one national monuments. By the time I headed to the parks, the park service was on its way to passing four hundred sites, which fell into more than twenty different designations. National

seashores, national monuments, national lakeshores, national bat-
tlefields, and on and on. The park near where I live in Florida has
a one-of-a-kind designation—Timucuan Ecological and Historic
Preserve.

They all are pieces of our National Park System, managed by
the National Park Service. But when we talk about national parks,
most people think of the places with the grandest designations, with
"National Park" as their surname. There were fifty-eight at the
time. A fifty-ninth was in the works. Pinnacles National Monument,
south of San Francisco, was on its way to becoming Pinnacles National Park.

When people said I had to go to a specific park, I explained that
my goal wasn't to see the most beautiful parks or to visit as many as
possible. My goal was to go to twelve parks—one a month, each sym-
bolizing a different issue facing the national parks in the next hundred years.

This, of course, was in some ways impossible. It's hard enough
to see a hundred minutes into the future, let alone a hundred years.
In 1916, kids were building miniature wooden forts with a new toy
that Frank Lloyd Wright's son had created: Lincoln Logs. And actual
homes were taking advantage of the latest technological advance:
a toggle switch to turn on lights.

In 1916, who could have imagined some of the changes and
challenges that the first hundred years would bring to the park service? Kids carrying around telephones in their pockets? Traffic jams
on the floor of Yosemite Valley *and* on its rock walls?

And for all the talk about people loving their parks to death, the
National Park Service heads to its next century facing a much bigger threat. People *not* loving their parks to death. Apathy. Or, if you
prefer the word I heard used over and over, starting with NPS
director Jonathan Jarvis: relevancy.

"We exist only upon the wishes of the people," he said when I
met with him in Washington, D.C. "Remaining important to society
is critical to our future."

In the last hundred years, America has changed, becoming less rural, more diverse, and—for better and worse—more attached to technology. America will continue to change. And in another hundred years, will Americans still care passionately about the national parks?

To start the year-long search for answers, I decided to start in one symbolic spot: Cadillac Mountain in Acadia National Park.

When a new year dawns in America, this is where it begins— with first light hitting the 1,530-foot summit on Mount Desert Island in Maine.

Maybe. In America, we seem to debate everything, even the site of our first sunrise. In 1999, the town of Lubec protested after the U.S. Naval Observatory declared that the summit of Cadillac would be the first place to see the sun rise on January 1, 2000. Lubec, located in Maine's Washington County (billed as "Sunrise County"), argued that while its Porcupine Mountain is only 210 feet, being sixty miles east of Cadillac gave it a thirty-second edge.

The U.S. Naval Observatory redid the calculations and—saying that the refraction of light in the atmosphere can cause fluctuations in how quickly light arrives at a spot—conveniently declared it a tie. Siasconset, Massachusetts, also claimed to be first. And if you want to get technical, St. Croix in the U.S. Virgin Islands beats all the New England sites. And it is trumped by Guam ("Where America's Day Begins"). And there's a small island managed by the U.S. Air Force . . .

Suffice it to say: While it was tempting to begin the year in St. Croix, first light atop Cadillac seemed fitting.

The park was created in 1916, just weeks before the park service, when President Woodrow Wilson established it as Sieur de Monts National Monument. It was the first national park east of the Mississippi River. It became Lafayette National Park in 1919 and Acadia National Park in 1929. And as both the park and the park service headed toward their centennials, Acadia seemed like a 47,000-acre microcosm of the future.

In many ways, it is a model park, a place that with the help of partners such as Friends of Acadia is better off today than it was several decades ago. But it has dilemmas about technology and infrastructure, cell phone towers and parking lots. It is intertwined with towns, creating a mix of cordiality and conflict. It has something the park service is trying to preserve here and in other places: stunningly dark night skies. It straddles geographic zones, making it a place to watch the effects of climate change. And in the last century, the summit has become such a popular destination that one of the park's biggest dilemmas is how to handle the traffic and crowds.

"It's our Old Faithful," park planner John Kelly says.

Compared to other iconic national parks, Acadia is a compact park. Yellowstone is 3,472 square miles and attracts about 3.4 million visitors a year. Acadia is 73 square miles and attracts about 2.4 million visitors a year. Many of them, including President Obama and his family in 2010, go to the summit of Cadillac. On a typical late summer day, the road and parking lot are packed with cars and tour buses.

There was another reason to start the year atop Cadillac. Long before any of this—before today's cruise ships and tour buses, before yesterday's cog railway and hotels, before anyone was arguing about the location of America's first sunrise, before there even was an America—this was a place where the original locals gathered.

Ancestors of several modern-day tribes, collectively known as Wabanaki ("People of the Dawnland") came to the top of this mountain.

They came to greet the sun.

So with all of this in mind, I circled New Year's Day on my calendar, contacted several people in Maine, and asked if they knew of anyone who started each year by watching sunrise atop Cadillac. More than one gave the same answer.

"Lili Pew," they said.

They said Lili, a former board chair of the Friends of Acadia, was very active in the park. And by active, they didn't just mean raising funds. She was in the park nearly every day. Biking, hiking, cross-country skiing.

They gave me her contact information. They wished me luck trying to keep up with her.

STATE ROAD 3, heading toward Bar Harbor, was quiet. I passed motels and cottages, signs for putt-putt golf and glider rides, lobster pounds, antiques shops, handcrafted wood cupolas, and homemade hard ice cream. All closed.

I could picture this two-lane road bustling with activity in July. But with January around the corner, it felt like I had dropped into a Stephen King novel. And not the first few chapters when everything is almost normal. The end, after some sinister force has taken a quaint corner of New England and wiped out all but a few humans.

It had been an unseasonably warm start to the Maine winter. The lakes and ponds weren't covered with ice yet. But the fall leaves were long gone, and they seemingly had taken with them most of the other colors. Even though it was not much past noon, the sun was low and muted.

It was both bleak and beautiful.

It was six weeks before the New Year. I was headed to Maine to meet Lili and plan for the first sunrise. At this moment, though, I was trying to make it to a campground before the rapidly approaching sunset.

I inadvertently ended up on the Park Loop Road. This twenty-seven-mile, mostly one-way road is one of the iconic stretches of pavement in the national parks. At certain times of the year, cars are lined up bumper-to-bumper. On this day, I drove the loop without seeing a single vehicle in front of me or in my rearview mirror.

By the time I made it around the loop and to the Blackwoods Campground, it was nearly dark. The booth at the entrance was empty. A sign said to find an available site and self-register in the brown box on the porch.

There are more than three hundred sites in the campground. A few months earlier, every single one of them would have been full, the campground buzzing with more than a thousand people. Now one section was open. And when I drove into Loop A, the light dimming even more under the trees, I didn't see another person.

There was a tent set up in one site, a motorcycle in another. But as best as I could tell, that was it.

I picked out a site, decided it wasn't right, picked out another, changed my mind again, and then finally realized how silly this was. I took one that seemed nice and flat, not too far from the one lone open bathroom. I pulled my tent out, and as I started to set it up, it began to rain. A cold rain.

I'm sure if someone had been there and had been watching me, they would have been shaking their head. I eventually got the tent set up, crawled inside, and looked up.

The rain fly was inside out.

This was hardly backcountry camping. I had a rental car twenty feet away, a bathroom nearby. And the temperature, while chilly, was above freezing. Still, this felt foreign and unnerving. I felt like a camping virgin.

I had decided that when I traveled during the year I would camp as much as possible. This was partly to stretch money as far as possible, partly because you have a different experience in a park if you sleep on its ground.

Or at least that's what I told myself. The truth was that I hadn't done much camping since I was a kid. I still was outside nearly every day. Running, biking, paddleboarding. But after I moved away from home at age eighteen, I had stopped camping. Not on purpose. It just happened. I tried to think of when I had camped since I was a child. I came up with four times. Each involved friends or family. On this trip, and most of the ones that would follow, I was alone.

I sat in my tent and listened to the rain.

This wasn't a pitter-patter of water. It sounded more like someone was hurling giant water balloons. I kept waiting to get soaked. But at some point I dozed off. And when I woke in the middle of the night, I was dry and it was quiet. When I unzipped the tent, I realized why I didn't hear rain anymore.

It had snowed.

It was still dark, still hours before sunrise, but I couldn't sleep. And while my new Big Agnes tent was doing its job, my old sleeping bag was not.

I grabbed it, climbed into the car, started the engine, and sat there, doubting myself, doubting my plans for the year.

THE NEXT DAY I met Lili Pew in Bar Harbor. From the moment she greeted me, I liked her. She had the traits that seemed to be standard issue for many of the year-round residents—down-to-earth, outdoors-loving, independent-minded, funny.

And she seemed as excited about my project as I was.

"How was last night?" she asked.

"Great," I said, deciding not to mention that I had ended up sleeping in a rental car.

We went to the Thirsty Whale, one of a handful of restaurants still open. She ordered her usual, fish tacos and an Arnold Palmer. Then she told me the story of how she ended up living here.

It's a story that begins before she was born, before the park itself was born. She grew up in Philadelphia. But her family has deep roots in Maine, houses that go back to a time I had read about, when so many families from her hometown vacationed here that it was known as "Philadelphia on the rocks."

"I used to summer here," she said.

When she said that, the use of "summer" as a verb jumped out. For me, summer had always been either a noun or an adjective. I had taken vacations in the summer. I had gone to summer camps. I never had summered anywhere. But the area around Acadia has a long history of people summering in it. And when Lili Pew mentioned this, I probably should have realized her roots were attached to one of the iconic American family trees. But I didn't.

For every detail that should have confirmed this—a mention of a godmother who helped found a nature center in the park, a friendship with one of the Rockefeller descendants—there were five others that defied whatever preconceived notions I had. I'm not sure what I expected. I guess some sort of stereotype. Maybe someone who was a little soft. And long before I returned for New Year's Day, I knew who was going to be the soft one atop Cadillac Mountain. It wasn't someone named Pew.

But if there were any doubts, Lili called shortly before the new year and asked when I was arriving. She said she had a great opportunity, a chance to get on a boat that was going twenty-some miles off the coast. She was going to go for a dive. She added that she was going to wear a dry suit, as if this somehow made the idea—diving into water that even in the middle of summer was icy—seem like no big deal.

She was looking forward not only to what she'd see while in the water, but what she'd see on the boat ride back: the view that Samuel de Champlain saw. Sixteen years before the Pilgrims landed at Plymouth Rock, the French explorer saw these rocky summits and named it île des Mónts Deserts.

She wondered if I'd be there in time to join her.

"No," I said, not sure whether to be disappointed or thankful. "I won't get there until that night."

I didn't even bother to tell her about my New Year's Day tradition. A polar plunge. In Florida. When friends in Wisconsin heard about this, they mocked the idea of anything in Florida being called a polar plunge. If you don't have to cut a hole in some ice, one of them said, it doesn't count.

ONE EVENING, BEFORE going back to the campground and losing cell service, I called home. Mia was busy with homework. One of her fourth-grade projects had been to chart the phases of the moon for a month.

So each night she did what, to her, made perfect sense. She went online.

"Let's go outside and look at the real thing," I had said one night when there was a nearly full moon.

Not only didn't she want to do that, but she didn't see the purpose. She had the answer. It was right there on the computer screen. Why would she go outside?

When she got on the phone this night, I told her that once I got to the campground I wouldn't have any access to the Internet; in fact I wouldn't even have a cell signal. To her, this sounded like a nightmare.

"It's actually really nice," I said.

I said good night and headed to my campsite. In a matter of a few days, I was starting to feel comfortable there—and starting to feel very fortunate to live in a time when we not only have cell phones but also have places where we lose cell phone service.

While starting a campfire, I thought about how it's only a matter of time—likely a shorter time than any of us imagine— before there will be nowhere on earth where we won't have phone service, Wi-Fi, or whatever else is around the corner. I don't look forward to that day.

In theory, I always could leave my phone behind or just turn it off. And maybe I would do that for a while. But if there had been a signal here, I'm sure that eventually I would have looked at e-mails, listened to voice mails, and at least mentally headed to another place.

Instead, I did something I've never been good at.

I stayed right there, in that moment, with the campfire crackling and the trees rustling overhead.

When the fire died out, I turned on my headlamp and headed to the east edge of the campground, following a short trail that led to the deserted Park Loop Road, then to some rocks on the rugged coastline and something that made me freeze.

The stars.

The trees perched along the rugged coastline were visible not because they were illuminated by anything, but because they were silhouetted by skies so dark that they had turned milky.

In 1916, when people were flipping those first toggle light switches, they would have laughed at the idea of light pollution. But in the last century, we've reached a point where most of us forget what it feels like to stand under a sky like this.

A *National Geographic* cover in 2008 featured a photo of a cluster of skyscrapers and the headline: "The end of night. Why we need darkness." It pointed to scientific studies that show how the proliferation of man-made light has affected many forms of life, including ours.

The idea of trying to preserve night skies is a relatively new one for the park service. In the late 1990s, it established a Night Skies Team, a group of scientists in Colorado headed by Chad Moore. When I traded e-mails with Moore, below his e-signature and title—Night Skies Team Leader—was a quote from Chinese philosopher Lao-Tzu: "When darkness is at its darkest, that is the beginning of all light."

When the park service director unveiled his "Call to Action" in 2011, it included thirty-six goals for the second century. No. 26 was labeled "Starry, Starry Nights." And while it focused on establishing "America's first Dark Sky Cooperative on the Colorado Plateau," one of the models of existing cooperation was here in Maine.

One afternoon in his office, John Kelly, the Acadia park planner, had pulled up a series of images on his computer, maps with splotches of color, bringing to mind weather radar. But in this case, the colors represented the amount of light on the East Coast of America.

"You can actually see the creep of light coming up the coast with the growth of population," Kelly said. "We're in this little pocket where it's clear."

The pocket was partly the result of lighting ordinances in the towns that share Mount Desert Island with the park. And while there was some initial resistance to the regulations, businesses had realized that the lighting changes not only saved money but brought in more business. The latest issue of the chamber of commerce magazine had a photo of a starry sky on its cover and information about the third annual Acadia Night Sky Festival.

Nearly 1,500 people attended events during the weekend—a cloudy, rainy weekend—that included a concert with songs about night skies.

Some scientists predict that, at the current rate of light pollution, those songs eventually will be about something that no longer exists—night skies that look like this.

I thought about that while standing on the rocks, looking at the stars above the Maine coast.

We don't use the night skies to navigate any more. We have GPS and Siri. But nothing orients you quite like looking up and seeing countless stars.

For thousands of years, people have been doing this and trying to use words and music and art to describe what they're feeling. If something happened to Vincent van Gogh's *The Starry Night* tomorrow, if we couldn't go to New York's Museum of Modern Art and gaze at the original, there would be a worldwide outpouring of sadness and loss. And yet as we lose the inspiration for that painting, the night skies that Van Gogh saw in the 1880s, the world shrugs.

Maybe that's because most of us have never seen truly dark skies. Or even if we have, we forget what they look like.

At home in North Florida, on a clear night with a new moon, I can look up and see stars. But not like this. Never like this.

ALTHOUGH I DID not sample the Ben & Bill's lobster ice cream— created to prove to customers that the local business does indeed make its own ice cream—I did have several other flavors. It was Lili's nightcap of choice.

"Does it ever get too cold for ice cream?" I asked.

"Never," she said as if that were a silly question.

I quickly realized that it also rarely was too cold—or hot or wet or any weather condition you can think of—to keep Lili out of the park.

For a few days, she played tour guide and ambassador, driving me around the park in her Subaru, planning a hike, and taking me for a bike ride that was part sightseeing, part workout, part history lesson.

When we biked to a stretch on Sargent Mountain, Acadia's second-highest mountain, with a spectacular view, Lili pointed to a rock next to the carriage road that looked like a chair.

"That's my office," she said with a laugh.

She said she comes there when she wants to just sit and think. She came there after 9/11. Like everyone else, at some point she wanted to get away from the images on the television, the loop of planes hitting towers again and again. So she came to the chair. There weren't any planes flying overhead that day. The skies were blue and empty. There was solitude.

We got back on the bikes and, as the light began to fade, headed back to the parking lot.

She was busy as a real-estate agent, taking phone calls and trying to resolve issues, and she also had a part-time job at Home Depot. When I asked her about that weekend shift at Home Depot, she said that part of what she loved about it was the sense of completion. Everything else in her life was a long-term project. That was different. She started a task and finished it. The only other thing that gave her that sense of immediate accomplishment was an athletic workout.

When she was younger, she said, she trained in the park and could tell you the exact distance between Point A and Point B, but she couldn't tell you much about what was in between. After a divorce, she moved here as a year-round resident. That's when she truly began to appreciate the park.

She quickly grew to love winter here. The crowds were gone.

And to her the park didn't feel cold and empty. It felt pristine and inviting.

"You get to see the park at its rawest, its purest," she said. "When I made the decision to live here, I tried to look at everything as if I were visiting for the first time."

Before I saw Acadia for the first time, truth be told, I was more excited about some of the places I would make it to after first sunrise. This was just the somewhat gimmicky opening scene. After just a few days in the park, I changed my mind.

When you look at America's national parks, Acadia doesn't have the most acres, oldest trees, deepest canyons. What it does have is something that can't be quantified with numbers, something more subtle but equally profound—like the trails and paths and roads themselves, all carefully designed to blend into the landscape.

As Lili drove me through the park one day, she pointed out not only the meticulous details—the protective stones alongside the road often referred to as "Rockefeller's teeth"—but also the big-picture design of George Dorr and John D. Rockefeller Jr.

They didn't just acquire land and then donate it to the American people. Rockefeller, reluctant at first to be a part of Dorr's plans, eventually became the driving force, overseeing the construction of the carriage roads and stone bridges. The materials, the sight lines, the experience they would create.

"Start incorporating this into your mind-set," Lili said as we dipped into a valley and then gently climbed around the ocean side of the next mountain. "He wanted everything to be a passageway from one part of the landscape to the next, with slow rolling curves rising up to a vista. All of these passages were considered to be episodes of a journey. He uses that phrase many times. It's an 'episodic journey of discovery.'"

I scribbled that phrase down and underlined it.

It was both an apt description of what it still felt like to explore and a summary of what I hoped would begin with first light of the New Year.

One big episodic journey of discovery, starting with the four A.M. alarm.

I WOKE UP and stumbled out of the spare bedroom. Lili and Carol were already up and starting to get ready.

Carol Bult, a close friend of Lili's, had graciously offered to let me stay in her house in Seal Harbor for the New Year's Day trip. And as much as I had enjoyed camping a few weeks earlier, after the cold, rain, and snow I was more than happy to take her up on that offer.

Carol is a geneticist and computational biologist at the Jackson Laboratory, a research institution that was established on Mount Desert Island in 1929. Her job involves improving the use of the genome to tailor cancer therapy options to individuals. She also volunteers for search and rescue in the park. In other words, I was in the company of two smart, tough locals.

The three of us were going to start the year by biking to the summit of Cadillac Mountain.

When I had first contacted Lili, she had said that maybe we'd cross-country ski or snowshoe to the top. But with no snow on the hills of Maine, we were going to ride mountain bikes, with metal-studded tires for the ice on the roads.

We left the house at five, riding about a quarter mile on Carol's street before dropping down onto one of the carriage roads.

The beams of light from our headlamps danced along the path. When I glanced up, I caught glimpses of what was visible between the trees—so many stars that it almost felt fake, like someone got a little carried away with Photoshop.

Our tires crunched on the crushed stone. Climbing quickly washed away the initial chill. Lili and Carol pointed out some of the landmarks we passed. Jordan Pond, Day Mountain, Bubble Pond. In the dark, it wasn't so much what I was able to see, though. It was the exhilarating feel of the place, the reminders of what it was like to be a kid moving through woods at night. And then we got on a paved road and started climbing toward the turnoff for the road leading to the summit of Cadillac Mountain.

As we reached the gates—the 3.8-mile road closes to vehicles each winter—the black sky was starting to turn gray.

In the distance, we could see a string of headlamps. We weren't going to be alone. But it also wasn't going to be like January 1, 2000, when local resident Martha Stewart announced plans to start that year atop Cadillac.

Stewart did a trial hike and decided it was too difficult to reach the summit in time for sunrise. She announced that she was canceling the original plans and would instead drive to the beach, hike to a ledge overlooking Frenchman Bay, then have a big breakfast at her home in Seal Harbor. The Associated Press reported that the guests, dressed in fuzzy bathrobes, would find their names written on egg-shaped rocks borrowed from the park to serve as placards. They would eat fruit from candied grapefruit shells, drink from giant café au lait mugs, and wipe their fingers on fine Irish linen.

A couple of thousand other people went ahead with their plans to start the year wearing fleece and Gore-Tex, standing on the rocks atop Cadillac Mountain. And with the road clear of snow, the park service opened it to vehicles, leading to a scene that's normal for the middle of summer but a rarity on January 1.

This year, though, the gate was closed. No vehicles. Just a few dozen people walking and, as best I could tell, three people biking.

The road had patches of ice. But the studded tires worked, gripping the surface and making a sound that reminded me of being a kid, with baseball cards in my spokes.

"Happy New Year!" Lili shouted as we passed people.

"Happy New Year!" they shouted back.

When we reached about the two-mile mark, Lili said we were coming up on the waterfalls, which during the winter sometimes become icefalls.

"We'll see which it is on the way down," she said.

Maybe. Visibility was quickly fading. Wisps of clouds had turned to dense fog. The stars were gone. The only lights visible were the dim headlamps farther up the mountain.

We rounded a couple of bends, continuing to climb.

A family was headed down. It still was about an hour before sunrise, but apparently they were giving up on watching from the summit.

"Last stretch," Lili yelled out. "Quarter mile to the top."

We pushed up the final few hundred yards, reaching the top about 6:15 A.M., more than forty-five minutes before sunrise.

We took off our backpacks. The women ducked behind the closed Cadillac Summit Center to change into dry base layers. I pulled out the shirt I had packed, took a deep breath, then started shedding layers—Gore-Tex shell, fleece, wicking base—until I was standing there, shirtless, sweaty, and suddenly aware of the wind.

I had heard stories about the wind, about how even in the summer, when the sun rises before four A.M., the wind can make things downright chilly. But it wasn't even so much the temperature. It was the sound.

I had ridden out hurricanes in Florida and heard the wind howl. I had been in canyons where the wind whistled. This wind sounded unlike anything I had ever heard.

It crackled, ripped, and snapped.

It still wasn't clear what the sunrise was going to look like, but it obviously was going to have a memorable soundtrack.

There were about forty people at the top, many huddled next to large rocks, hoping to block the wind gusts coming from the west. On a clear morning, you could see chains of islands dotting miles and miles of the Atlantic Ocean. On this day, as it gradually got lighter, you could barely see the rocks fifty feet in front of you.

The vegetation, coated in a layer of rime ice and swaying in the wind, reminded me of corals underwater in the Florida Keys. Only in this case, not only weren't there any fish swimming past, there weren't any bright colors. It felt as if we were standing in the middle of a black-and-white photo.

I wandered around, trying to capture this scene with my camera, tucking my gloves in a pocket so I could adjust the settings. And before I knew it, my teeth were chattering.

"Are you okay?" both Lili and Carol asked.

"I'm fine," I said.

My teeth kept chattering. I tried to tighten my jaw and make it stop. This only muffled the chattering.

"Here," Lili said after a while. "Get in this."

She handed me a bivy sack. They poured some tea from a thermos and we huddled behind a rock. I kept telling myself it wasn't really that cold. I had spent many a day growing up in Wisconsin playing for hours in single-digit temperatures. My chattering teeth kept telling me that after twenty-some years in the Sunshine State, I was a Floridian.

Between the tea and the bivy sack and body warmth, I eventually stopped shaking.

We couldn't actually see the sun, but everything was getting lighter, the increases coming in fits and spurts, as if every so often someone turned a dimmer switch.

The black-and-white landscape turned pinkish.

Pink fog, pink vegetation, already pink granite turning even pinker.

I thought of the Nick Drake song, "Pink Moon," and how it was used in a Volkswagen ad. Some friends in a Cabrio driving along moonlit roads pull up to a house party, look at each other, then back up and return to the road and the pink, pink, pink moon.

Down the mountain, at Martha Stewart's place, perhaps people were wearing fuzzy bathrobes, drinking giant mugs of café au lait and sitting in front of egg-shaped rocks in an old estate. I wouldn't have traded places. At this moment, there was no place I'd rather have been than sitting in a polyethylene bag, sipping tea, leaning against one of the rocks on this old mountain.

At 7:09 A.M., with still no sign of the actual sun, Carol counted down the seconds, as you would at the previous midnight.

"Ten, nine, eight, seven . . ."

"Happy New Year!" we yelled loud enough to hear the sound of our voices over the snapping of the wind.

To our left, three twentysomething guys cracked open beers. And when the sun did appear ever so briefly—or at least the distinct glow of something beyond the fog—people pointed and cheered.

First light was more like first glow.

Someone apologized, saying you never know what you're going to get atop Cadillac Mountain. I told them I had seen many chamber of commerce sunrises that I couldn't remember.

"This sunrise I will remember," I said.

We got back on our bikes and headed down the hill. The wind had faded. The sound of the studded tires on the icy roads was now cranked up a notch.

We stopped at the overlook and got a second sunrise. This time it wasn't just a hazy glow. A big bright-red ball came up over the summit of Cadillac. It lit up the clouds behind it and covered stretches of the landscape below in a warm light.

I thought about something Lili had told me earlier. She talked about how the light changes. In winter, the sun doesn't just rise late and set early. Instead of passing high overhead, it stays closer to the horizon. And the result is the light that many a photographer has fallen in love with. It cuts through trees and across the mountains, highlighting details, emphasizing patterns.

"It's like a skipping stone of light," she said.

Lili had said that if we were lucky, we'd see some of her favorite things about the park on New Year's Day—the waterfall on the side of the road turned to an ice sculpture full of turquoise blues and greens, the top of the mountain shimmering in a way that makes her feel close to her mother.

"There's this wonderful poem 'Do Not Stand at My Grave and Weep,'" she said. "It talks about the diamond glint of snow on top of the mountain. I read that at my mother's funeral. And every time I come up here and see the light skipping across the mountain, with the diamond glint on the snow, I think of my mom."

When we got off the bikes, I looked across the road and saw the waterfall for the first time. It was an icefall. And when the sun came out for a brief moment, I saw the light skipping across the mountain.

Lili's mother died in 1986 at age forty-nine. She was the first woman to head the National Association of State Racing Commissioners. She had breast cancer, discovered way too late. She died in a hospital in Lexington, Kentucky.

Lili had told me that much. When I got back home, I found some of the obituaries. The story in *The Philadelphia Inquirer* said that Joan Ferguson Pew-Hickox, known to her friends and many acquaintances simply as "Joanie," brought to the Thoroughbred industry "a seemingly limitless energy, a quick intelligence and a great impatience, an impatience directed at its resistance to change and its fragmentation."

I read that and smiled. It reminded me of the woman who had taken me to the summit of Cadillac.

I also found several versions of the poem Lili read at her mother's funeral. It generally is traced to Mary Elizabeth Frye in 1932. The most common final two lines are: "Do not stand at my grave and cry. I am not there; I did not die." But I was drawn to one that ended differently. With a sunrise.

> *I give you this one thought to keep—*
> *I am with you still—I do not sleep.*
> *I am a thousand winds that blow,*
> *I am the diamond glints on snow,*
> *I am sunlight on ripened grain,*
> *I am the gentle autumn rain.*
> *When you awake in the morning's hush*
> *I am the swift, uplifting rush*

Of quiet birds in circled flight.
I am the soft stars that shine at night.
Do not think of me as gone—
I am with you still—in each new dawn.

From the comfort of my warm Florida home, I read that and thought about Maine. The blowing wind, the diamond glints, the shining stars and the new dawn.

I thought about how my parents went to Acadia for one of their anniversaries and watched a sunrise atop Cadillac.

I thought about how Dad sometimes made statements about death that were half joking, half serious. "When I'm gone . . ." he'd say.

When he was gone, he told Mom, he wanted her to find someone else. When he was gone, he also wanted her to know he was still with her. He said it would be like the love letter Union soldier Sullivan Ballou had written to his wife. He would be in the wind. ("I shall always be near you . . . if there is a soft breeze upon your cheek, it shall be my breath.")

Ken Burns featured a reading of the letter in his *Civil War* series, along with a violin playing "Ashokan Farewell."

After Dad died, I noticed that Mom had a cassette tape of that song in her car.

A couple of years later, for her sixtieth birthday, Mom decided that she wanted the rest of the family to do a rafting trip through the Grand Canyon. At one point, as we drifted along a calm stretch of the Colorado River, deep in the canyon, our guide—a small woman with ripped arms—stopped rowing and pulled out what looked like a musical instrument case.

She unlatched it and, sure enough, she had brought a violin with her.

She rested it on her shoulder and began to play. A few notes into it, I realized what she was playing.

"Ashokan Farewell."

As the music carried through the canyon, a soft breeze blew upon our cheeks.

So many people in this world have so many beliefs, things they seem to know with absolute certainty. Sometimes I'm envious. I have so many questions and doubts that I often don't know what I believe.

I do know that, as this year began, I already believed that it was possible to find comfort in dark skies and pink landscapes. And that if Dad was with us when a breeze blew through the canyon, he really must have been with me when a wind whipped across a mountain in Maine. And Mom? She was waiting at the next stop.

2

*

FEBRUARY: SAGUARO NATIONAL PARK

$\mathcal{B}$y the time I landed in Tucson, the sun had set.

Even in the dark, though, I could see the outlines of the desert, the jagged ridges of the mountains, the silhouettes of cacti standing near the road leading toward Gates Pass, some with arms raised as if welcoming me back to Arizona, back to the place my mom now called home.

The cacti and Mom. These were the two reasons I was here.

The first can produce 40 million seeds in a lifetime and, if everything falls into place, have one grow up to be a symbol of the American West. The second is from a generation that willingly piled the kids into a station wagon and drove across the country to see such symbols. I wasn't sure which one faced bigger threats in the next hundred years, the cacti or the cross-country family vacation.

I just knew that to look into the future it helps to be able to look into the past. And in a one-square-mile piece of Saguaro National Park—an area called Section 17—rangers, scientists, and volunteers were continuing one of the longest-running vegetation studies in the park system.

They were doing a saguaro census, counting and measuring the cacti that often are viewed in humanlike terms. Edward Abbey, the author who referred to saguaros as "planted people," once wrote that when nobody else was around he talked to cacti.

"On simple subjects, of course," he said.

Saguaros grow in only one place on earth—a desert that includes much of southern Arizona and stretches into a corner of southwestern California and across the border into Mexico.

Shortly after the park was established in 1933, originally as Saguaro National Monument, rangers noticed that an area east of Tucson known as the Cactus Forest was losing its cacti. To try to figure out why saguaros were dying, the park service started counting and measuring the cacti in Section 17. Some subsections were counted every year. Others were counted as a sample every ten years.

As I headed there, the park was in the middle of resurveying the entire Section 17 for the first time in seventy years. They were asking for volunteers to help out, to be citizen scientists. So I flew to Tucson, planning to spend a week in the desert, part of it counting and measuring cacti.

Driving in the dark, looking at the outline of the desert, inhaling its distinctive scent, I remembered the first time I came here. I arrived after sunset on that trip too. Even in the dark, perhaps especially in the dark, it was one of the most beautiful places I had ever seen.

This was about fifteen years earlier. The previous winter Mom and Dad had driven from Wisconsin to Kentucky, where I had started a new job and my wife and I had bought our first house. On their way home, Dad lost control of their Saturn sedan in the rain on I-64 between Lexington and Louisville. The car flipped at least once. I got a call telling me to come to the Frankfort hospital.

Toni and I zipped along the back roads of Kentucky, past the horse farms, not saying a word. When we arrived at the hospital, I was told that Mom was fine. But the woman at the information desk couldn't seem to figure out where my dad was. Eventually, she said to go to a room on a lower floor.

There Dad was—bruised, banged up, groggy, but very much alive.

I broke into tears.

"I'm okay," he said.

"I know," I said.

The doctors told me to go ahead with a work trip I had planned—to Anchorage to cover the University of Kentucky basketball team in the Great Alaska Shootout.

A few days later, before leaving, I stopped by the hospital to say good-bye. As I was leaving the room, I glanced back. Mom was trying to lean over the hospital bed to kiss Dad. Her neck had been stiff since the crash. So she was awkwardly and painfully twisting one way. And he was awkwardly and painfully twisting another way.

Together, they managed a peck on the lips.

If you're going to have a final image of your parents together, it's not a bad one.

Dad was released from the hospital while I was in Alaska. He and Mom returned home. He went back to work as chaplain at Theda Clark Medical Center in Neenah, Wisconsin. But shortly after I got back to Kentucky, Mom called. Dad had collapsed while at work. By the time I got there, he was dead.

They led us into his room so we could say good-bye. A few nurses stood in the hallway outside the room, crying. That's when I started to realize that, as chaplain, he not only had helped many patients deal with tough times but had been there for the staff as well.

I stayed in the room after everyone else had left. I leaned over to kiss Dad. His forehead was cold.

A few days later, as I sat in the living room of my parents' house, only partly listening to the funeral home representative talking about plans for the service, I kept looking at what was on the coffee table. Glossy brochures from companies selling shiny new camper vans littered the table's surface.

He was just a few months away from retiring. He and Mom had big plans for the future. They were going to move somewhere warmer, perhaps Tucson, and travel the country, crossing off all the national parks they hadn't been to yet.

There were all kinds of things in the house that made me sad. Family photos. Notes in Dad's handwriting. Puzzles he used to do. But I think the saddest things of all were those brochures.

I would think about those brochures and their plans, when I started a sentence with "someday . . ."

Mom easily could have stayed in Wisconsin, their home for more than thirty years. She had a large network of friends there. She had their house. She had a church. Two, actually. After Dad became chaplain at the hospital, he didn't want to stay at the Baptist church where he had been minister and make the new pastor feel like he was always looking over his shoulder. So he and Mom had started going to a Lutheran church down the street.

At the Sunday service there after his death, instead of singing a hymn, the pastor said, "Let's all whistle."

Dad couldn't sing even close to the right key. But he could whistle beautifully. One time he was in an airport concourse, walking behind Mary Travers of the group Peter, Paul and Mary. Instead of doing what most fans would do—starting a conversation, asking for an autograph—he started to whistle "Puff, the Magic Dragon." And she began whistling along. They never said a word, never even looked at each other.

I never could whistle. But at that service, I tried. And as everyone in the church tried, for the first time in days, we smiled and laughed.

Not long after that Mom decided to sell the house and move to Tucson.

Some people move from the Midwest to Arizona and try to make the place adapt to them. They fill their homes with reminders of where they came from. They try to grow grass and plant familiar flowers. Not Mom. She embraced everything about Tucson—the architecture, the food, the literature, the arts, and most of all, the desert.

She learned about the desert, volunteering at the visitor center in the western piece of Saguaro National Park. And when we came to Arizona, she passed that knowledge along to her children and grandchildren. If I go for a hike in Florida, a place I've called home since the 1980s, I often struggle to identify trees and birds. But in the Sonoran Desert, I can do okay at a game of Name That Cactus. The prickly pear, cholla, barrel, and, of course, saguaro.

All of this is why I chose to make Saguaro National Park the second stop on the journey. Because of the cacti and Mom. And because after Maine in January, I wanted to be somewhere warm.

WHILE PACKING FOR the flight, I got a call. Mom wasn't feeling right. She had gone to the hospital and they had decided to admit her and do some tests. She said she didn't really feel that bad. Mainly just tired. And her skin itched.

"I'm glad I'm coming there," I said.

"Me too," she said. "I love you."

"I love you too," I said.

When I was growing up, we never said those words. I knew my parents loved me. I'm pretty sure they knew I loved them. But I can't remember us ever saying this out loud. Not once. So when I first heard those words from a girlfriend in college, it was like a jolt of something. I wasn't sure whether to be giddy or scared. I think I decided to be both.

When I landed in Tucson, it was late, too late to go to the hospital. Abe picked me up at the airport.

Mom had met Abe Valenzuela at Southside Presbyterian Church. Located less than a mile from downtown, the church itself was unlike any I had ever been in.

It was built with local materials—pine logs, saguaro ribs, flagstone—and had a circular sanctuary modeled after Native American kivas. On a typical Sunday, traditional Presbyterian hymns mixed with gospel music, prayers in English and Spanish, blessings in Tohono O'odham. Worshipers wore everything from suits and ties to jeans and T-shirts. And their backgrounds were as diverse as their clothes. Native American descendants from the church's beginnings, Latinos, African-Americans, transplanted retirees like my mom.

Abe was a retired Tucson firefighter with roots in Mexico and the Zapotec. He sang in the choir and had a deep, booming voice. After they were dating for a while, Mom decided to sell her house in Sun City—she said she didn't like living in a retirement community, so far north of town—and buy one near Gates Pass. She told me Abe was going to move out of his house and live with her. I told her I was happy for her. And I meant it.

Abe became a part of our family. And whenever we went to Tucson, we became a part of his big family.

On the way to the house we talked a little about Mom, then made small talk about how warm a winter it had been so far and how it looked like it was going to be a beautiful week to be in the desert.

The next day I had a series of interviews lined up with people associated with the park. But first I headed down the hill to St. Mary's Hospital.

The hospital was undergoing renovations. And it felt like it was time. Maybe past time. I wound my way through some of the construction, eventually finding Mom's room.

She was awake, lying in bed. She smiled. The first thing I noticed was how her skin looked almost golden. When I gave her a hug, I noticed that her eyes also were quite yellow.

"And I can't stop itching," she said, scratching her legs as we talked.

She had been told she wasn't going to get the test results that day. So she told me to stick to my plans.

"Are you sure?" I asked, knowing that I didn't want to cancel what had taken a while to arrange.

"Yes," she said.

I DROVE TO the other side of Tucson, to the part of Saguaro National Park that abuts the east edge of town. I took a picture of the entrance sign, went into the visitor center, and found a rubber stamp with the name of the park and the date.

For all the talk of technology and the future of the parks—I could sit at my computer and watch bears in Alaska or virtually hike to the bottom of the Grand Canyon—one of the most wildly successful programs of the last twenty-five years is decidedly old-fashioned: the Passport to Your National Parks.

The beauty of the passport isn't necessarily the pocket-size, spiral-bound notebook, or the maps inside. It's the blank pages, ready for ink stamps that can be found only in each of the national parks.

Once upon a time, if you had a souvenir from an event or someplace, it meant that you, or someone you knew, had actually been there. Not anymore. It was 2012 and I could already go online and order 2016 Rio Olympic pins.

The national parks passport was different. The only way to get it stamped from a park was to visit that place. More than a million passports had been sold. And they weren't just for kids. When I met with Dayton Duncan, the writer behind the PBS national parks series, he asked if I had one yet.

"You have to get one," he said.

I got one in Acadia. I wanted to get it stamped on New Year's Day, but the visitor centers weren't open. So this was my first stamp of the year.

February 7, 2012.

It felt like this was the day the year really began. First sunrise was the national anthem. This was the opening pitch.

I met with Darla Sidles, the superintendent of the park. She grew up in Texas and recalled going to Big Bend National Park as a teenager, taking a boat across the Rio Grande to Mexico, back in the days before 9/11 changed so many things. She had worked at nine national parks. Her most recent stop was an urban park, Independence National Historical Park in Philadelphia, so she was glad to be back in a place with wilderness and sparkling night skies.

We started talking about the power of the desert and she suggested I might want to meet Ross Zimmerman. His son, Gabe Zimmerman, was an aide to U.S. representative Gabrielle Giffords and was killed in the 2011 shootings. To honor Gabe, his family and friends started an event that focused on getting people out into public lands.

I wrote that down, thinking it might fit in somewhere.

After meeting Kevin Dahl of the National Parks Conservation Association (NPCA) for lunch, I headed toward the western half of the national park. On the way, I called Mom to see how she was doing. From the moment I heard her voice, I knew something was wrong.

She said a doctor had stopped by her room.

"He said I'm dying," she said. "He came in and said . . ."

"What?" I said. "That can't be right."

She said that the doctor had matter-of-factly told her she wasn't going to live much longer, that they could make her comfortable or do some treatment that might give her a couple of extra months.

I flashed back to arriving at the hospital where Dad had been chaplain, walking down a hall, seeing Mom crying and hearing her saying Dad was already dead.

"That's not right," I had said all those years ago.

I didn't mean that it wasn't fair. I meant that it was flat-out incorrect. Had to be. He wasn't dead. He couldn't be. He had driven home from Kentucky and gone back to work.

It turned out he was dead. But Mom's diagnosis obviously was a mistake.

"That's not right," I said. "I'll be there in a few minutes."

I pulled over into an apartment parking lot at the top of a hill. Flags advertising move-in deals flapped in the wind. I just sat there for a few minutes, thinking this couldn't be right. Mom's diet was beyond healthful. It was annoyingly so. She'd take a bite of something and say, "Oh, that has way too much sugar." She walked several miles every day. When Dad was alive, he certainly had his share of health issues. But Mom? She seemed to defy aging. I always pictured her being the ninety-year-old woman who still walked around the block with her dog every morning.

AT ABOUT FIVE P.M., the doctor came in. He was a different doctor from the one who had talked to her earlier in the day, a gastroenterologist with a bedside manner Mom immediately appreciated.

He wheeled in a stool, lowering it before sitting down. "I don't want to tower over you," he said, smiling.

Mom motioned to the nurse. "Will you shut the door, please?"

The nurse closed the door and the doctor looked at Mom.

"Okay, you've had a lot of doctoring in the last days, a lot of X-rays . . . are you comfortable that I talk to you with all of these people in the room?" he said.

"I'm very comfortable with it," Mom said.

In addition to me, there was Abe, the pastor at their church, one of Mom's best friends and—eventually via two phones we held up in front of the doctor—my sisters in Nevada and Michigan.

"So, um . . ." the doctor said, pausing and no longer smiling. "So how everything started is that I got to know you in December."

The doctor recalled their first meeting. He had thought maybe she had an ulcer. But when they did an endoscopy and it didn't show anything, he started to get concerned. Her liver function tests were too high. So they did a CAT scan.

"And the CAT scan showed a big . . ."

He paused again.

"A growth, a tumor, a cancer," he said. "And likely not a good cancer."

He said they didn't have the tests back yet, but it likely was bile duct cancer, cholangiocarcinoma. I had never heard of it. When I googled it later, I found out that February was Cholangiocarcinoma Awareness Month. Seven days into the month, we were quite aware, thank you.

We kept asking basically the same questions over and over, as if maybe one of these times they'd lead to a different answer. The doctor was patient. Eventually he took out his pen, flipped over a green piece of paper that contained some of Mom's medical records, and started to draw on the blank side.

"Think of a tree," he said. "A big oak tree, with no leaves, in the middle of winter."

The room was quiet. Just the rhythmic hum of the hospital bed and the scratching of pen on paper. After he left the room, I would remember that as much as any words. The oak tree in the winter; the scratching that seemed amplified as he drew a circle in the middle of the trunk and filled it in, making the circle bigger and bigger, darker and darker.

"You've got a huge tumor, the size of a grapefruit, sitting in the middle of your liver, right there where all the branches of the tree are going into the main duct that drains all the juices from the liver," he said, tapping his pen at the spot on the paper. "Right smack there."

That, he told Mom, is why she was jaundiced, itching, her urine dark. The tumor was blocking everything.

The doctor repeated there were no good options. She couldn't have surgery. She couldn't have chemotherapy at this point. Her bilirubin levels were too high. Maybe she could have a procedure done to try to bring the bilirubin levels down. But his sense was that the tumor was too big, that no doctor in town would be willing to try it. If anyone would do it, he said, it would be a doctor over at University of Arizona Medical Center.

He called the other doctor. For most of the call, we could hear only half the conversation. But when he mentioned the size of the tumor—about 9 centimeters—we could hear the reaction on the other end of the line. A loud groan.

After the call, he turned back to Mom and summarized the "tough questions" she needed to ask her oncologist and discuss with her family.

"So that's it," he said. "Let me get down to radiology. It's getting late. Nothing happens after six. . . . You think about it with your family."

"I'm not ready to give up," Mom said.

"Well, there you go," he said, standing up. "You've given your answer."

Mom, sitting there quietly for most of this, looked at the doctor and said, "I have grandchildren I want to see."

THE NEXT MORNING, the skies were overcast. Not just patches of clouds. There wasn't any blue sky in sight. I couldn't ever remember seeing a sky like this in Tucson.

Then it started to drizzle.

Rain in the desert typically is a beautiful, almost magical thing. I had heard about monsoon season, people celebrating the arrival of the summer rain. In this case, though, it just felt dreary. But maybe that was because the most magical part of rain in the desert is how it smells of the creosote bush. And if we took a deep breath, all we smelled was the antiseptic scent of a hospital room. Room 3123 at St. Mary's Hospital.

I spent the night in a chair in the corner of the room, tossing and turning, waking up disoriented, wondering for a split second where I was, then hearing the hum of the hospital bed and the beeping of equipment. It wasn't just a bad dream.

Mom's room had plain tan walls. On the wall at the foot of her bed, below a clock and a small cross with Jesus, were two white eraser boards that had the room number, phone number, date, physician's name, nurse's name, tech's name, and two open-ended statements.

"Daily goals: Today I'd like to . . ."

"It's okay to ask. My questions are . . ."

I wasn't even sure where to begin with the questions. But I looked at the first one and thought, Today I'd like to . . . turn back the clock a few days, to when everything seemed so perfect. Or better yet, to last August and the trip to the redwoods when Mom was complaining about not feeling right and I kept thinking she was in her seventies, she was supposed to slow down a little.

Mom's daily goals were much simpler. They didn't involve time travel, just a short drive up the nearby hill.

She wanted to go home. To her house, her dog, and her desert.

As a nurse checked on Mom, I opened up the *Arizona Daily Star* and read the news of the day. Rick Santorum had won three Republican primaries. In Tucson, at the annual gem show, someone had stolen $1 million in "precious stones."

Presidential politics and precious stones.

Both seemed absurdly meaningless.

A steady stream of Mom's friends stopped by, talked and played a dice game, Farkle. We tried to explain what the doctor had told us. We talked about what we were going to do next.

We were there nearly a week and Mom turned on the television only once, for one of the few TV shows she watched. *CSI* somewhere. It always surprised me that my mother, who hated anything and everything violent, was hooked on a show that started every episode with a murder.

But most of the time, her room was quiet. I'd walk down the hall and hear TVs blaring. When I returned to Mom's room, it was just the sound of people talking, dice rolling, cards shuffling, or more often than not, nothing other than the slight hiss of the heater, the hum of the bed, and the beeping of medical equipment.

At one point, when it was just the two of us, Mom brought up something I had been thinking about—something I felt guilty thinking about. What did this mean for my year in the national parks?

I had canceled everything I had planned for February. But what about March and beyond? Should I still go to the Dry Tortugas? That wasn't just a matter of going back to Florida. It involved taking a ferry seventy miles from Key West to an island without a cell signal.

"I want you to go," Mom said. "And I still want to go to Denali with you."

Mom had a tradition of doing a trip to a national park each year with a group of girlfriends. She had wanted to go to Denali this year, but it looked like they were going to skip a year. So when I won the fellowship and began planning my year, I told her we would go to Denali.

"I still want to do that," Mom said. "And I want to go to the Grand Canyon with Lauren."

She had begun another tradition with her grandchildren. When they turned twelve, she took them on a trip. A few years earlier, when Sophie—the daughter of my middle sister, Lisa—had turned twelve, Mom had taken her to the Grand Canyon. This year she planned to do a similar trip with Lauren, the daughter of my youngest sister, Beth.

"Let's see how you feel," I said.

We talked some more about national parks. I asked Mom which was her favorite.

She thought about it for a while. She said she couldn't pick one. But then she started talking about the Grand Canyon. She said she wanted to see it again.

The room was quiet. We sat there, not saying anything, looking out the window.

Everyone who had stopped by talked about what a blessing it was that I had been in Tucson the day Mom was given her diagnosis. One of Mom's close friends, a woman Mom met after moving to Tucson, said it was a "God thing."

"Baloney," said another friend, someone who had gone to seminary with Dad.

The two quickly got into a friendly argument. Not so much

about the existence of God things, but about how such things work. One believed one thing. Another believed something else.

As her friends debated, Mom didn't say anything. She smiled, as if she had heard this before. Eventually she did what she often did during that week. She was too tired to read. She didn't want to watch TV. So she just gazed out the window.

Right below her window was the hospital chapel. Atop it was a brilliantly white tower with three bells, topped by a cross. There were times when the shadows crept across the buildings, leaving only the cross lit up by the sun. Behind it, visible in the space between other parts of the hospital, was a piece of the downtown skyline. And beyond that, in the distance, were the mountains.

I wondered whether Mom was looking at the cross or the mountains.

WHEN MOM FINALLY was released from the hospital after a week, we went back to her house. In the hospital, she kept saying she wanted to get out and get some fresh air. But when she got a chance, she said first she just wanted to sleep.

I thought about taking a nap too. But instead I decided to take her Jeep and go for a drive.

I left her subdivision, turning onto Gates Pass, climbing a favorite route for local cyclists. On the right-hand side of the narrow road, the hill is thick with saguaros. I remembered how when I first visited here, Mom taught me one of the first of many lessons about the local vegetation. The saguaros typically are more plentiful on the warmer, south-facing slopes.

After the crest, the road makes a big, swooping descent down the other side of the mountain, away from Tucson and into an undulating straightaway. The first time I drove that—and, for that matter, pretty much every time after that—it felt like I had been dropped into the setting for a Western. In a way, I had.

If you turn left at the T at the end of the road, a few miles to the south is Old Tucson Studios, a tourist attraction where parts of dozens of movies were filmed, from the original *Gunfight at the O.K. Corral* to *¡Three Amigos!*

I turned right and headed north, riding the waves of the road toward the visitor center for the western district of Saguaro National Park. This is where Mom had been volunteering for several years.

Instead of paying a single-use fee, I decided to buy an annual pass for all the national parks. As I was paying, the ranger asked if this was my first time to Saguaro.

"No," I said. "I've been here many times. My mom actually volunteers here."

She looked at me and—maybe because of the name on the credit card, or maybe because of a resemblance to my mother—said, "You're Nancy's son, aren't you?"

Another ranger came out. I recognized him right away. Richard. Years ago, when Mia wasn't much past being a toddler, she and her cousins had done the Junior Ranger program here with him.

"Tell your mom that when she feels better, we're going to continue our winter tradition of going for soup," he said. "Not that we're having much of a winter."

I told him I would. I said I wanted to go for a hike. Nothing too long, just something to get out in the desert.

"I'd do King Canyon," he said.

He pulled out a map and said there should be flowers blooming in the wash, the rocky floor of the canyon that remains dry until the rare rainstorm fills it with water.

When I got to the trailhead, I looked around and took a deep breath before starting. It felt like the first real breath I had taken in a week.

As I walked through the wash, the rocks crunching under my feet, everything seemed magnified. The yellow of the flowers growing in places that you wouldn't think anything could grow. The buzzing of a few bees. The chirping of birds. The smell of the desert.

I passed two tall saguaros with arms linked.

I thought about a Time-Life coffee table book called *Cactus Country* that Kevin Dahl had pulled off a shelf in his office and handed to me, shortly before I called Mom and found out she was dying. The book was written by Edward Abbey.

When people look back at Abbey's writing, they rarely refer to this book. Maybe that's because finding Abbey's prose in a Time-Life book is kind of like turning on the TV and hearing Bob Dylan's voice selling Chryslers. But while people still talk about *Desert Solitaire* (nonfiction in Arches National Park) and *The Monkey Wrench Gang* (fiction at Glen Canyon), in *Cactus Country* Abbey beautifully explains why, out of all the deserts he knew, he loved the Sonoran most.

"For all its harshness, loneliness, cruelty and cunning, one desert haunted me like a vision of paradise," he wrote.

I thought about Abbey talking to the saguaros when nobody was around. On simple subjects, of course. I didn't talk to these saguaros. But as I walked past them, I couldn't help but think about some complex subjects. What this week meant. What this place meant.

I sat down on a rock. The air was cool, dry, and still. It was the time of year when the blindingly bright sun felt good.

On a nearby ridge, not far from a tall saguaro with three arms raised skyward, stood the skeletal ribs of a dead saguaro.

It is no wonder that artists are drawn to these skeletons. Set against a deep blue sky, they are oddly, ruggedly beautiful. Looking at this one, I recalled things I had learned while hiking with Mom and listening to ranger talks.

Saguaros can live to be more than two hundred years old. And they often die how they grew. Slowly. The arms sag, an infection sets in, the green skin rots away, creating a thriving ecosystem for the bugs and microbes. If you look near one of the skeletons, you might find younger cacti, in various stages of life.

This isn't just an ending. It's part of a cycle. It's a beginning.

I stood up, took a swig of water and walked briskly back toward the parking lot.

A couple of hours in the desert didn't wash away a week in the hospital. But it made me feel hopeful. It was a bad cancer. But Mom wasn't your ordinary seventy-three-year-old. While soft-spoken and slim, she was surprisingly strong and tough. If plants can thrive here, then anything is possible, right?

I got in the Jeep and headed back up over Gates Pass and down the hill toward Mom's house, noticing the shadows of the saguaros, a landscape full of natural sundials.

Mom was sitting on her back patio, looking out across the desert toward downtown and the distant mountains.

Most places you watch sunsets by looking to the west, following the sun's path. Not here. At the end of the day, we would inevitably look to the east and watch what the sunlight did to the Catalinas. A gradual, spectacular evolution of colors. From browns and tans to oranges and reds to pinks and purples.

In the hospital room, we had been able to see a sliver of this show every evening. But we couldn't smell the desert; we couldn't hear it.

So we sat there, not saying a word as the sun set behind us and the mountains in front of us changed colors. In the beauty and silence hung one obvious eternal question: How many more sunsets do we have?

3

MARCH: SAGUARO REDUX

*D*on Swann joined the four people standing out of the rain, underneath the roof in front of the Saguaro East visitor center.

"I don't know how many people are going to show up," Swann said. "We'll wait a little bit longer. Does everybody know each other?"

Swann, a wildlife biologist at Saguaro National Park, led the introductions. There was Dennis, a white-bearded man who was a saguaro census veteran; Siria, a student intern; and Chantal, an Arizona State University student. A few minutes later, Theresa, a University of Arizona graduate student, arrived.

We were headed to Section 17, a one-square-mile section in the foothills, to continue a kind of scientific scavenger hunt. A saguaro census.

The three women all put on ponchos. Dennis pulled the hood of his sweatshirt over his head and put on a rain jacket. A few days earlier I had been looking at my rain gear and thinking, "Why did I even bother bringing this to Tucson?"

Now I was quite happy to have it with me, and happy to be heading into the desert to count and measure saguaros.

After February, I had rearranged my plans, trying to find ways to be there for Mom and yet still be in the parks. Instead of going to the Dry Tortugas in March, I would go later in the year and stay in Arizona for now, making some trips to northern Arizona and returning to Tucson, Mom, and, on an unusually wet and cold spring day, the counting of cacti.

We waited for a while at the visitor center before Swann said, "Well, I guess this is it."

The census had kicked off about six months earlier during the National Geographic BioBlitz, an annual event held at one national park. For a typical weekend count, two dozen volunteers might show up. This time there were five of us.

We got in a couple of cars and headed north on Cactus Forest Drive, a one-lane, one-way paved road that loops through eight miles of the park. After a few minutes, we veered off it and went down a dirt road leading toward Section 17.

The story of how scientists ended up monitoring this piece of the desert begins with President Herbert Hoover creating Saguaro National Monument on March 1, 1933, citing outstanding scientific interest because of the exceptional growth of cacti, especially the "so-called giant cactus." Shortly after the monument opened to the public, park staff noticed that the giant cacti were dying. Researchers found that a large number of the saguaros were rotting, oozing a black liquid. They hypothesized a contagious bacterial infection was not only killing the existing saguaros but threatening to wipe out their future.

"At the time they were seeing chestnut blight and Dutch elm disease," Swann said. "And they thought that potentially by removing the diseased individuals it might help the survival rate of those that weren't showing signs of it."

They picked one square mile—Section 17 of Range 16 East, Township 14—and divided it into sixty-four subplots. In the northern half, they did nothing with the unhealthy cacti. In the southern half, unhealthy saguaros were either removed or treated with antibiotics. They followed every single saguaro for five years, then a subset of those for ten years.

And after ten years they found . . .

"No difference," Swann said. "We now are pretty certain that the mortality was caused by freeze, which allowed the bacteria to come in and start eating the tissue as it died."

When we got out of the cars, Swann pulled out a poster board with two photos taped to it.

Both photos were taken from a spot not far from where we stood, looking north, across the Cactus Forest and toward the mountains.

The top photo was taken in 1935, two years after the park was established. The bottom one was taken in 1998.

Even a rookie citizen scientist could instantly spot the most obvious difference: the size and number of saguaros.

In the 1935 photo, there were hundreds, maybe thousands, of saguaros. Most were tall, with long, impressive arms. They filled the foreground and beyond, only growing smaller as they faded into the distance.

One cactus, not in the photo but part of the forest at the time, was estimated to be about 250 years old. By the 1990s, it had fifty-two arms. When the tallest of those limbs toppled in 1992 and stuck between two other arms, the news made *The New York Times.*

"Granddaddy," as the cactus was dubbed, was dying. And it wasn't alone.

By the time the 1998 photo was taken, there was one cactus in the foreground. It wasn't as tall as most of the cacti in the 1935 picture, its short arms were nothing like the candelabra-like saguaros that used to stand there, and its nearest visible saguaro neighbor was in the distance.

Comparing the two photos and taking a guess, I estimated that there were maybe a tenth as many saguaros in the same space.

While Glacier National Park was losing its glaciers, Saguaro National Park was losing its saguaros. Or so it seemed.

"But if you notice here . . ." Swann said.

He pointed out what else had changed dramatically in the two photos: what was in the space between the saguaros.

In the 1935 photo, there was mostly bare ground. In the 1998 photo, the space between the cacti was packed full of vegetation. The only bare ground visible was a narrow road.

"Before the park was established, probably from the 1870s to 1940 or so, the trees were cut down for fuel," Swann said. "Mesquite makes a really nice fuel. Paloverdes make a nice fuel. We had commercial logging. We had industry. There was heavy cattle grazing."

And those trees—many of them nurse trees for saguaros—were essential to the growth of young wannabe giant cacti.

In other words, we now know that when Saguaro National Monument was created, and when the census began in 1941, the biggest problem facing the saguaros wasn't bacterial infection or freeze or even that generations of old cacti were dying.

It was that future generations weren't growing.

Talk about symbolism.

WE WALKED A short distance. The air smelled like desert rain. One of the first times I visited here, Mom had us cup some of the shiny leaves of the creosote bush in our hands and blow on them. The moisture in our breath was enough to bring out the scent.

That wasn't necessary this morning. The clouds were doing the trick.

We stopped walking. Swann bent over and drew a map in the dirt. We planned to stake the boundaries of the subplot with flags, split up, and methodically search the space—200 meters by 200 meters—for saguaros.

We had several GPS devices and walkie-talkies. When we found a cactus, we were to record its location, measure it, and put a flag in it so we didn't count it twice.

Swann was a few years older than me. He had been working at this national park since 1993. Earlier in his career, he had studied Blanding's turtles in Maine. That's when he became interested in long-term studies. He talked about what we can learn from a long, scientific timeline—how it can give us the wisdom to understand when something is part of a natural cycle and when it's reason for panic.

"Our world is changing, and as humans, we are influencing it," he said. "On the other hand, not everything that seems to be a problem is as much of a problem as it seems when you first encounter it. I think the saguaro story is a good example of that."

When he told a little of that story—and answered questions about the future—he often added a caveat: It's complicated.

I liked that he kept using those two words. With all the information available today—perhaps partly *because* of all the information available—we don't want things to be complicated. We want them to be simplified. We want absolutes, good or bad, right or wrong, hero or villain. And the truth typically is that . . . it's complicated.

"Any questions?" Swann asked before we began.

We started to walk toward our subplot and someone pointed at a tall saguaro nearby. How are we going to measure one like that?

"We're going to use some high school math and a clinometer," Swann said with a smile, holding up a device used to measure angles of elevation.

We eventually split up into a couple of groups and began searching, weaving between trees and cacti, trying to avoid getting caught on something.

We walked with our eyes mostly trained on the ground. The biggest challenge of the morning wasn't going to involve counting and measuring the tall, old saguaros. They were easy to spot and, with a quick math refresher, not too difficult to measure. The hard part was spotting the young saguaros.

Saguaros don't just shoot out of the ground. Although it is the largest cactus found in the United States—one grew to be seventy-eight feet tall—a saguaro starts off as a small tuft, maybe only a quarter-inch high after its first year, and continues to grow very slowly. It can take ten years for a saguaro to reach an inch in height.

And without the arms, additions that might not come until the cactus is seventy-five years old, young saguaros resemble some of their desert neighbors.

This explains why one of the volunteers excitedly called Swann over to look at what he had found tucked under a paloverde tree—and why Swann got more excited about this cactus than anything else we found.

It was a plump little thing, barely above ankle-high. And it was indeed a saguaro.

No clinometer necessary to measure it. After we recorded what turned out to be our smallest find of the day—eighteen centimeters, or about seven inches—Swann talked in scientific terms, estimating the cactus to be less than twenty years old, before adding an unscientific opinion.

"Pretty cool," he said.

Finding this one small cactus raised an obvious question: Isn't there a possibility we're missing more like it?

"Yes," Swann said.

He said it was indeed likely that we were missing some young cacti in this census. But part of the beauty of such a long-term study is that researchers can take data and work backward, figuring out everything from germination dates to percentages of saguaros overlooked.

Shortly after spotting the little saguaro, we passed a tall one that clearly had seen better days. Its midsection had turned from green to brown. It seemed to be tilting to one side. I thought about Edward Abbey's observation: Life and death often are found side by side in the desert.

"Is that cactus dying?" I asked.

"That main stem has been badly damaged and is going to fall off," Swann said. "It remains to be seen how the whole saguaro will do. It takes several years after the freeze to see the whole effects. . . . You see that brownness; then it starts to ooze that black stuff. That's the bacterial necrosis we were talking about."

MARCH: SAGUARO REDUX   57

For decades, sights like this caused dire predictions. In the early 1960s, some respected experts on plant pathology were saying that by 2000 there wouldn't be any living saguaros in Saguaro National Monument—which is part of the reason the saguaro-thick land on the other side of town was added to the park by President John F. Kennedy in 1961.

And here we were, more than fifty years later, walking through Section 17 and finding not only saguaros of the past, but ones that could be standing in another hundred years.

I saw an old saguaro on a ridge in the distance, one arm extended, resembling a Wild West gunslinger. It reminded me of a man vs. cacti story I'd heard. Back in the early 1980s, two men had decided to wander into the desert near Phoenix and, just for fun, start shooting saguaros. The first man shot a small one so many times that it toppled to the ground. Not to be outdone, his buddy chose a larger target—about twenty-five feet tall, with at least one large arm.

The second man fired away until a four-foot arm fell from the saguaro and killed him. The man was twenty-seven. The cactus was estimated to be more than a hundred. I don't know whether the saguaro survived. I want to believe that it did, that it grew a few more arms, as if daring someone to challenge it to another shootout.

After we reached one end of the subplot, we started back-tracking, pulling out the flags on the saguaros we spotted, looking for ones we might have missed.

We posed for a group photo, hopped in the cars, turned on the heaters, and circled around the Loop Drive back to the visitor center. Swann thanked everyone for coming out, then led me back to his office to try to explain what our findings—what they have been finding for months and years—meant for the future of the saguaro.

"This is what Section 17 looks like from the air," he said, pointing at a photo. "We were in this subsection today, B8. That's the trail that runs through it. This is the wash. . . . What we found today is pretty consistent."

He pointed to a graphic that broke down the census not only by numbers but by size. It basically confirmed what the photos had illustrated. There weren't nearly as many tall saguaros as in the early 1940s, but there were many more young ones.

"So it's not all doom and gloom?" I said.

"There are so many times in the history of the saguaros in this park that people have predicted their extinction," Swann said. "By 1962, there were major scientists saying we don't think there will be any saguaros in the park by the year 2000. Well, sorry, but there are more saguaros in the national park than there have been in decades."

He quickly added that almost all of the small saguaros date to before the mid-1990s. Since then, there has been a major drop-off in their numbers, presumably caused by recent droughts. If those droughts continue, it could lower the long-term survival rate. And combined with buffel grass—an African grass brought to the United States in the 1930s for livestock—taking over the desert and serving as kindling for fires, it could be doom and gloom.

So when you take all of this—the trends and cycles, the seventy years of data, the buffel grass, the years of drought, the rain falling on this spring day—the future of this place and its namesake cactus clearly is . . .

"Like I said, it's complicated," Swann said.

As I headed to the parking lot, I realized that I found myself clinging to the positive notes of the morning.

When I began the year, I was focused on finding reasons to be concerned about the future. While I still wanted to sound alarms about the risk of losing some of America's natural and historic treasures, I also wanted to find hope, the life alongside the death. With the thought of losing my mother, I needed to find it now more than ever.

I pulled out of the park, thinking about something I had asked Swann when we all had been standing there before the census. I wondered whether the rain might have a fairly immediate effect, causing some desert plants to bloom while I was in Arizona. He said it could.

"What it will do is give these plants sort of renewed life," he said.

The windshield wipers slapped back and forth. This wasn't just rain. It was drops of renewed life falling from the sky.

If only I could bottle some of that. It sure sounded better than chemo.

THE NEXT MORNING the skies were clear. I got up, went outside, and watched the sun come up over the mountains, then headed back into the kitchen to make coffee. Mom came out of her bedroom wearing a bathrobe and gave me a big hug.

She felt frail, bony. But she squeezed me tightly. I squeezed back for a few seconds, then relaxed. Mom kept squeezing and squeezing. When she finally let go, she dabbed her eyes.

"All you kids live too far away," she said.

It was a Sunday. Mom was going to church. I was going for a hike.

I headed over Gates Pass, down the rolling road, pulling into the dirt parking lot at the King Canyon trailhead, the same trailhead I came to at the end of that week in February, shortly after my mom was released from the hospital.

Ross Zimmerman had suggested doing a hike here.

He and his wife, Pam Golden, pulled into the parking lot, got out of their car and introduced me to three other people who would be joining us for all or part of the eight-mile round trip to Wasson Peak, the highest point in the western part of the park.

"It's a beautiful morning for a hike," I said as we started up the trail.

I first heard about Ross when I met with park superintendent Darla Sidles in February, a few hours before I called my mom and she said she was dying. Darla had explained that Ross was a local ultrarunner with a passion for connecting people to public lands.

When one of his sons, Gabe, was killed in the shootings at a Gabby Giffords event, Ross had turned to that combination of activity and the outdoors to help grieve and commemorate, both privately and publicly.

They had just passed the first anniversary. And while there had been many somber memorials, Ross and others had come up with the idea for a different kind of event to be held every January, something that involved getting people outside, in their parks and on their trails.

They called it BEYOND—as in moving beyond the morning of January 8, 2011.

"Commemorate, celebrate, commit," said the promotion for the first event. "Out of tragedy, our community came together. Let's come together again."

Thousands of people did, including Giffords. The day before participating in a memorial event at the University of Arizona, she made an unscheduled trip to a piece of the Arizona Trail, an 817-mile path that runs from the Mexico border to Utah. Several years earlier, Gabe's mother, Emily Nottingham, had helped the trail join the likes of the Appalachian Trail and Pacific Crest Trail as National Scenic Trails.

Giffords chose that particular spot, east of Tucson, because of the trailhead. The Gabe Zimmerman Davidson Canyon Trailhead was renamed after the community outreach director who, her husband had said at the memorial service, was like a little brother to her.

Even their names sound familial.

Gabrielle and Gabriel.

Gabby and Gabe.

She walked about three hundred yards onto the trail, then turned around and walked back. News stories said that the surprised hikers and horseback riders who saw her on the trail later said she looked healthy and happy. And while that certainly was one of the more dramatic moments of the first anniversary weekend, it was but one example of the basic goal of BEYOND: a healthy and happy community.

I e-mailed Ross and asked him if he'd be up for meeting, maybe going for a hike somewhere in the national park and talking about the power of public places. I attached a column I had written shortly after the shootings. It was about how I had often gone with my mom to the corner of Oracle and Ina Roads in Tucson. Not the southeast corner, which had been pinpointed on news graphics ever since the shootings. The northwest corner and Tohono Chul, a forty-nine-acre urban oasis that *National Geographic Traveler* named one of the top "secret gardens" in North America.

This was the Tucson I knew and loved to visit. It was the antithesis of the act of violence it was being linked with. It was peaceful, natural, spiritual.

We traded a few e-mails, as much about running as anything.

Once upon a time, if you had asked me what kind of athletic feat I wanted to be able to do, I would have said I wanted to hit a baseball like Al Kaline. Now I wanted to be able to run like Ross Zimmerman had for decades.

He was heavily involved in more than thirty years of the Tucson Trail Run series. And while the rest of the running world seemed to be moving toward glitz and gimmicks, I liked how these runs remained a decidedly old-school mix of hard-core and low-key. No entry fees or medals. Just show up and run into the mountains.

Ross had done so many double crossings of the Grand Canyon—from one rim to the other and back—that he made it sound like just another long training run. I had done it once. Favorite run of my life. And one of my last ones, I feared. I now had searing groin pain every time I tried to run. And when I wasn't running, I was miserable to live with.

You would think knowing my mom might be dying would have snapped me out of this, making whether I could run seem meaningless. It didn't. If anything, it made me want to run even more. I had a feeling Ross could understand.

When Ross suggested I meet him and Pam for a run in the

national park, he promised we'd go only a little faster than hiking pace.

We met at a trailhead on the edge of Saguaro East. And even if I hadn't known that they were runners, I would have guessed it the second I saw them get out of their car. Ross not only had the look of someone who had logged thousands of miles—late fifties, lean, tan, a cap over his gray hair, and a stride that made it seem as if he were ready to start down a path at a moment's notice—I quickly got the sense that he also had the personality of an ultrarunner. And I mean that as a compliment. Most of the ultrarunners I know are a little different, and not just because they consider a 26.2-mile marathon a nice warm-up. They are low-key, intelligent, tough, obsessive, analytical, and quirky.

Ross's career was in computers, but his education was in biology. He had come to Tucson to complete a Ph.D. He stayed partly because of the abundance of inviting trails in every direction.

The one he chose for our run was near Section 17. As promised, we started out slowly, zigzagging through the desert vegetation, dipping in and out of the washes.

When we weren't talking about running, Ross was talking about oil. His vision of the future was a bleak one. Soaring prices for nearly everything, lower standards of living for nearly everyone.

When I got back home, we traded e-mails again and Ross elaborated on what he had said about the end of oil. He recommended a book by Jeff Rubin that he said he had been reading when he started talking to Gabe about this topic. He sent me a link to a website he created, but said he hadn't done a good job of updating it.

"Gabe was my main reviewer, and it's been harder to spend time on it without him to talk to about things," he wrote. "See you before long."

I read that and shook my head, frustrated with myself for trying to steer the conversation on the run away from oil. For starters, oil was relevant. From a long-term view, energy could profoundly affect pretty much everything in our world, including travel to national parks. Beyond that, I realized, this wasn't just some wonkish, impersonal look at the future. It was a very personal piece of the past, a conversation a father had been having with a son, a conversation they never got to finish.

Thinking about that made whatever was happening with my mom seem almost natural, like seeing an old saguaro in the desert.

It's one thing to lose your parents sooner than you had hoped. But to lose a child. And to have it happen so suddenly, so violently, so inexplicably. How do you move beyond that?

When we began the hike on the King Canyon Trail, heading toward Wasson Peak, that was one of the questions I had.

Ross and Pam introduced me to Mark Kimble, Jennifer Boice, and Tom Alston.

MARK AND JENNIFER, a married couple, had spent decades working at newspapers. Jennifer had been the editor of the *Tucson Citizen* when the paper was shut down in 2009. Mark had been editor of the editorial page. I was glad to hear that both had landed on their feet, finding life beyond newspapers. Mark became communications director for Gabrielle Giffords. He was at the Safeway the day of the shooting.

Giffords had recently announced she was resigning. Ron Barber, a staffer who was wounded in the shootings, was preparing to run for the seat.

Tom Alston also was on the Barber staff. He was the solar outreach and policy coordinator. But that wasn't necessarily why Ross had invited him. Tom grew up in national parks. His father, Joe, had been assistant superintendent at Yellowstone and superintendent at Glacier Bay National Park and Preserve, Curecanti National Recreation Area, Glen Canyon National Recreation Area, Rainbow Bridge National Monument, and for the final six years before he retired in 2007, Grand Canyon National Park.

"So what's your favorite?" I asked.

Tom thought for a moment. He said there were things he liked about a lot of different parks. But if he had to pick one . . .

"I'd have to say Yellowstone," he said,

Some of it, he said, was the time of his life. He was a teenager. And to go through your teen years in Yellowstone creates some pretty powerful memories. Some of it was the place itself. He described going to Lamar Valley, finding a good spot, and just watching the wildlife appear.

We climbed gradually for about a mile. We started to talk about current events, debating whether Arizona or Florida had wackier news—and I was just about to play the trump card of hanging chads—when Pam called out.

"Look at this," she said.

She pointed to something tucked next to the side of the trail.

It appeared to be a small, dead plant. I wasn't sure why she was excited about it.

"It's the night-blooming cereus," she said. "The Queen of the Night."

As she began to explain that all these cacti bloom just once a year, for one evening, I realized I did know about them. Mom had pointed them out before, telling me about sometimes going to Tohono Chul for their annual bloom party. No one ever knows exactly when the bloom will occur, just that it will be sometime between late May and late July.

Barbara Kingsolver, the author who grew up in rural Kentucky before studying biology at the University of Arizona, included the bloom of one Queen of the Night in *The Bean Trees*. It was the kind of detail that was discussed in book clubs and high school classrooms. What did the bloom mean? Beauty emerging when things are darkest? A reminder to appreciate the moment?

Whatever the symbolism and message, because of the abundance of rain in recent months, a particularly spectacular bloom was expected at some point this summer.

Looking at the forlorn plant in front of us, it was hard to imagine.

"We could wait until it blooms," Pam said with a laugh.

We decided we probably should continue on. We reached the saddle of the ridge, the first place where we could see what was on the other side of the mountain, and took a break. Standing there, we found it hard to decide which way to look. Ahead of us, we could see part of the city of Tucson and, beyond the development, the Catalinas in the distance. When we turned around, we could see where we had just come from, the trail, the open desert beyond, and more mountains in the distance.

Someone suggested that we take a picture.

We posed for a few shots, the city and the sun at our backs. Mark and Jennifer headed back down the trail, toward the parking lot, and we continued up the final mile or so toward Wasson Peak.

Just short of the summit, the temperature dropped suddenly, turning the breeze refreshingly chilly. We were high enough that there were no big saguaros around us. But Pam noticed a small one on the south-facing slope.

"They usually stop at four thousand feet," she said. "What's our elevation?"

Ross glanced at his GPS: 4,560 feet.

"They'll get up here," he said. "They'll get up to five thousand sometimes."

If the future brings rising temperatures, it's conceivable that the saguaro population also will rise to higher elevation. In the eastern section of the national park, with a high point of 8,664 feet, there is plenty of room for that kind of migration. Here in the western part, though, the highest peak is 4,687 feet.

We continued the short distance to the top of Wasson Peak.

"We have to apologize for the substandard view," Ross said.

The typically rich blue sky had a milkiness to it. But even at this relatively modest elevation and with this haziness, it still was quite the view.

Ross pointed out Mount Wrightson, at 9,453 feet the highest peak visible from Tucson.

We stood there for a while, enjoying a day when the sunshine actually felt comforting, not stifling. When we turned and looked north, we could see I-10 making its way in the distance toward Phoenix. This stretch of the interstate is mostly straight and downhill, the landscape mostly flat and bland. But Tom pointed to the one rocky formation, forty-five miles from Tucson, that appears to rise out of nowhere, like a sand castle built on a beach.

"Mark, see that kind of scraggly looking . . ." he said.

"Is that Picacho Peak?" I said. "We climbed it with my mom."

"I'm impressed," he said.

The word *picacho* means peak in Spanish. So Picacho Peak is a redundant name, and with an elevation under 2,000 feet, it might seem like a presumptuous one too. But getting to the top of the rocky spire involves using some cables, crossing catwalks, and dealing with a bit of exposure.

Mom did it shortly after moving to Tucson, and decided she wanted to do it every year for her birthday, albeit not on her actual birthday in June. It would be too hot by then. Winter or maybe spring, when the poppies bloom in the foothills.

She ran out of friends willing to climb Picacho with her. So one year when her children visited her, we did it. Afterward, I told her I'd gladly come back and do it again. I hadn't done that yet. I kept saying "next year."

I thought about this when I looked at the peak in the distance. It wasn't just the site of some American history, the place where the westernmost battle of the Civil War had been fought 150 years earlier. It was the site of a hike with Mom, one that all of a sudden felt too much like family history.

We headed back down the trail. Ross continued the biology lesson, explaining how southeastern Arizona has some of the highest biodiversity of anywhere in the United States. As he was pointing out some of the stands of vegetation, Pam spotted something.

"A tarantula hawk," she said.

I looked to the sky, expecting to see a bird. I realized she was talking about a wasp.

"They alight on these beautiful fuzzy tarantulas and inject a paralyzing toxin," she said. "And then they lay an egg inside the tarantula."

"And when the egg hatches?" I asked.

"The tarantula gets eaten alive," Ross said.

Up until this point, I had been trying to find meaning in the examples of life and death side by side around every bend in the desert. The story of the tarantula hawk had the opposite effect. It made me think maybe I should just try to enjoy the hike. And avoid tarantula hawks.

Tarantula hawks rarely sting people, and when they do, the pain lasts only a few minutes. And while they don't lay eggs in people, apparently the pain is still overwhelming. Justin Schmidt, a Tucson entomologist, had been stung by enough insects in his life that he created something called the Schmidt Sting Pain Index. The sting of a tarantula wasp was a 4. Schmidt described it as "an immediate, excruciating pain that simply shuts down one's ability to do anything, except perhaps scream."

One of Ross's degrees is in entomology. And at one point he picked up a beetle and tried to identify it, apologizing that his insect knowledge was deteriorating. I figured as long as he could identify a tarantula hawk, that was good enough for me.

As we headed back down the mountain, we quickly came to a fork in the trail, and instead of veering back to the left and the King Canyon saddle, we headed right to a descent that would loop around to where we had started.

"So," I said, "tell me how you decided to do a trails tribute for Gabe."

"It started with my cousin in Boston," Pam said. "You need to talk to him at some point."

Steve Golden had spent more than thirty years working for the National Park Service. Long before the park service began articulating a vision for the second century that included "bringing the parks to the people," he had been doing exactly that, helping communities save their natural places as part of the NPS Rivers, Trails, and Conservation Assistance Program.

After the shootings, he and one of his children came to Tucson for the memorial service.

"Then he went home and started thinking about what to do to honor Gabe," Pam said.

He wasn't alone. In Washington, in a rare display of bipartisanship, the House voted unanimously to name a meeting room in the U.S. Capitol Visitor Center after Gabriel Zimmerman. It was the first time a room in the Capitol complex had been named for a congressional staffer. When it was dedicated, Vice President Joe Biden recalled how Gabe reportedly had responded to the gunshots by rushing toward the shooter. And standing not far from a plaque bearing a bronze relief of his son's smiling face, Ross Zimmerman said, "An echo of Gabriel will persist, perhaps for centuries. It isn't worth the loss, but the echo is good and true."

While that was a touching and fitting tribute, Gabe's family and friends wanted his legacy to do more than echo in the polished stone walls on Capitol Hill. They wanted it to be heard on the dusty trails all over Tucson, in the canyons and on the mountains, in the sounds of running shoes, hiking boots, trekking poles, bicycle tires, conversation and laughter, hearts beating and lungs breathing.

The annual communal event was Gabe's echo.

The trailhead on the Arizona Trail was Gabe's echo.

This hike, I eventually realized, was full of Gabe's echo.

As we headed down the trail, back to the elevation where giant saguaros covered the hillside, Ross talked about how Gabe wasn't hard-core outdoorsy—he gravitated toward sociology, not biology—but he grew up in a family where being outside was just a normal part of life.

"Unlike his father, he had actual coordination," Ross said. "He played on a soccer team that won the state championship. I can't do sports to save my life."

Gabe eventually did decide to follow in a few of his dad's footsteps and run across the Grand Canyon, north rim to south rim. And while clearly his father was proud of this, he seemed equally as proud when he talked about Gabe settling into a job that seemed made for him.

"He was very gifted at what he did," he said. "Even as a child, he had amazing interpersonal skills."

He became a part of Gabrielle Giffords's first campaign team in 2006. When she was elected, she said she wanted to have the best constituent services program that ever existed. She put that task in Gabe's lap. Some people would dread the idea of spending their days trying to solve constituents' problems. Gabe loved it. He could talk to anyone. Or perhaps even better, he could listen to anyone, no matter how irate.

In the office, they dubbed him the "constituent whisperer."

He eventually became Giffords's community outreach coordinator. He had organized dozens of Congress on Your Corner events before the one on January 8, 2011.

We were rounding a bend, Ross walking in front of me, Pam behind me, when they took turns telling me a story about something that happened on this trail.

In August 2010, Gabe's girlfriend, Kelly O'Brien, was training for her first marathon.

"Gabe took her up here for a run," he said. "They stopped at the saddle."

Pam continued the story, reminding me how the saddle where we stopped earlier had beautiful views in both directions. When Gabe stopped there with Kelly, he said to her, "Which direction do you think is most beautiful?"

"And then with her facing that way, he proposed," she said.

I almost stopped walking. I didn't see this coming when the

story started. Maybe I should have. I had read a newspaper story that said shortly before the shootings, Gabe had been talking to a colleague about wedding plans.

I realized now that when we had stopped at the saddle and taken pictures, it wasn't just another spot on another trail. It was a place where Gabe's echo was especially loud.

"They were probably within a couple of days from setting the actual date for the wedding when the shooting happened," Ross said.

I glanced back at Pam. She was wiping her eyes. I wanted to say something. But all I could manage to do was mumble, "I'm sorry."

So here I had been thinking of this as my special trail because I had come here after my mom was released from the hospital. Whatever I was dealing with then and now seemed so ordinary in comparison. What they had experienced, what they undoubtedly were continuing to experience a year later, seemed so unfathomable. Like getting stung by a tarantula hawk, again and again.

We continued hiking and talking. About Gabe, Kelly, the Grand Canyon, the future of the parks. But when we paused a few minutes later, I tried to say what I had been thinking. I was grateful they were taking the time to show me the park and tell me about Gabe and BEYOND. It would fit nicely into the story of the parks. But I'm sure part of the reason I was drawn to them was purely personal.

Mom was still alive. But if the doctors were right, if this was the end, at least she had lived a full life, at least her family was getting a chance to say good-bye.

"You didn't get that," I said.

"We try to cherish the thirty-one years," Pam said.

"And we're pretty sure he died instantly," Ross said.

"That's helped," Pam said.

We started to walk again, steadily descending, passing a picnic area built in the 1930s by the Civilian Conservation Corps and heading down into the wash leading back to the trailhead.

It was less than a mile back to the parking lot.

As we scrambled over some rocks, Tom wandered over to the nearby walls.

"Do you see the petroglyphs?" Ross said.

A lot of human history was recorded here, some of it going back centuries, some of it much more recent. On their second date, Gabe brought Kelly here to show her the petroglyphs. After the shootings, they came to this trail to scatter his ashes.

Tom called out. He had found some of the petroglyphs on a nearby wall. We went over to look at the drawings.

"Early journalism," Ross said. "Maybe these were Mark's predecessors."

"News of the day," I said, wondering what the writing on the walls said. Probably something about a bleak future.

Worry about what lies ahead hardly is a new activity. I have no doubt that shortly after some caveman invented the wheel, a neighbor lamented that once everybody had a wheel or two, the entire place would be ruined. (And there have been times, particularly while I was driving in South Florida, when I've thought the neighbor was onto something.)

I grew up with school reading lists that included heavy doses of dystopia in *Animal Farm, Fahrenheit 451,* and *1984.* The year I went to college, the post-apocalyptic world of *Mad Max* was in theaters. Still, the doom and gloom seemed to be ramped up even higher in the new-millennium, post-9/11, recession-mired decade leading up to this year in the parks.

From tween literature (*The Hunger Games* and *Divergent*) to Disney/Pixar movies (*WALL-E*) to the doomsday drumbeat of television news, the future looked grim. And when it came to the national parks, report after report illustrated that there were plenty of reasons to be concerned about the future.

Saguaro National Park and its namesake cactus made it into several reports. So when I had arrived here in February, I thought the saguaro could serve as a symbolic piece of vegetation—one that already was in danger and, if we weren't careful, could be wiped out in the future.

What I had found out was, in a word, complicated.

And yet there was one point near the end of our hike in King Canyon—a hike that had included talk about all kinds of complicated subjects—when Ross Zimmerman boiled something down to a simple truth. I had said I didn't know how he moved forward after the kind of loss he experienced.

He shrugged. You don't have much choice, he said. You just do.

The sun rises. A new day dawns and you head out into it.

4

*

APRIL: THE GRANDEST CANYONS

*W*hen Grand Canyon river guides hold their version of an annual convention, they gather at a remote warehouse in northern Arizona, just down Highway 89A from Marble Canyon and Lees Ferry, the starting spot for most canyon rafting trips.

This was my first destination other than Tucson since Mom's diagnosis. In March, she had the surgery to put in a stent. Her bilirubin level dropped enough to start chemo, which at least seemed like a positive step. But the prognosis was still grim.

While I was back in Florida, Abe and my sisters gave me updates. They said the drugs were taking a toll on her, both physically and mentally. She had fallen a few times. When I talked to her on the phone, she seemed confused.

I knew that Mom wanted to return to the Grand Canyon, and that she probably wanted to go with me on this trip. At this point, that seemed out of the question. Still, with all of that in mind, I felt guilty that after landing in Phoenix, instead of heading a couple of hours south, I pointed the rental car north and drove almost to the Utah border. But Mom kept telling me to go ahead, to continue with my plans. And I told myself that at least I would be in the same state, spending time near something that made me think of her: the Colorado River and its canyons.

On a series of trips, all after her sixtieth birthday, she had rafted nearly 400 miles of it, including nearly the entire 277 miles of the Grand Canyon.

Long before my mom's diagnosis, the Colorado River was in my plan for the year. Partly because it runs through some of my favorite places on earth. Partly because the 1,400-mile blue line on maps of America's West—beginning in the Rocky Mountains and wriggling its way southwest, passing through a string of national parks and national recreation areas, plummeting 14,000 feet before reaching its delta as little more than a dripping faucet—represented one of the biggest issues for the future. Water.

In his book *A River No More,* Philip Fradkin called the Colorado "the most used, the most dramatic and the most highly litigated and politicized river in the country, if not the world." And although that was based on Fradkin's reporting in the 1970s, a few decades hadn't changed the description. If anything, they only punctuated it.

As I headed to Marble Canyon, the beautiful prelude to the Grand Canyon, the West was heading for another year of drought. The National Climatic Data Center reported that 7,000 daily record-high temperatures were broken or tied in the previous four weeks, a stretch the National Oceanic and Atmospheric Administration dubbed "Meteorological March Madness." And when scientists looked into the future and saw a combination of higher temperatures, less precipitation, and more evaporation, they predicted that the Colorado's flow was only going to continue to decrease.

Not that you needed to be a scientist to be aware of this concern. All you had to do was visit Glen Canyon Dam, look at Lake Powell behind it—the reservoir that was created in 1963 and took seventeen years to fill—and see the growing white ring between the red rock and the blue water.

BEFORE REACHING PAGE, the town that sprung up as the dam was being built, I took Highway 89A and headed toward the last bridge to cross over the Colorado before it begins its gradual descent into a canyon that, by the time it reaches its heart, is a mile deep and ten miles wide.

There are two bridges side by side, the steel arches beneath them making them look like mirror images. The first opened in 1929. Before that, the only way for automobiles to cross the river, other than making an 800-mile drive, was on the ferry operated a few miles upriver by John D. Lee. In 1995, a new forty-four-foot-wide bridge opened—and the old Navajo Bridge became one of the grandest pedestrian bridges you'll find anywhere.

I drove across the new bridge, pulled into a parking lot, and walked out onto the old bridge.

Looking down at the river, I remembered passing under these bridges when we began our rafting trip through the Grand Canyon for Mom's sixtieth birthday. The arches high overhead had felt like a gateway, the spot where we left behind not only roads and cars but jobs and everyday worries.

I headed up a slight hill to Marble Canyon Lodge, the lettering and style clearly designed to evoke thoughts of the Old West. The lodge was located a short distance from where the Colorado River flows from the southwest tip of Glen Canyon National Recreation Area to the northeast tip of Grand Canyon National Park. When I had called to make a reservation, I was told it would be thirty-eight dollars a night. I thought maybe I had heard wrong. But sure enough, when I checked in, that was my room rate.

I got my key—not a plastic card but an actual key—unlocked the door next to a window A/C unit, used a little extra muscle to push it open, and walked into a musty room.

Some of the online reviews trashed the lodge. I liked it. I felt like I had gone not only to another place but to another time. Maybe the 1920s, when the lodge opened. Maybe the 1970s, when we made family treks that included stops at places that felt a bit like this.

So it was dated and worn. It also was thirty-eight dollars a night. During the day I could walk a few hundred yards to the old bridge, spot juvenile California condors, and watch the river. At night I could return and look up at the stars.

WITH A DAY to kill before the gathering of the river guides got under way, I decided to drive to Lees Ferry, touch the river, go for a short hike, and then head to Glen Canyon Dam.

On the drive to the dam, I stopped and made a short walk to an overlook—a vantage point that gives you a clear sense of the lake behind the dam and what remains of Glen Canyon in front of it.

A couple, probably in their seventies, was standing there.

"It's something, isn't it?" the man said.

"Yeah, it is," I said. "I'm not sure exactly what it is. But it's something."

He nodded. "I know what you mean," he said.

I wasn't even exactly sure what I meant. Just that I had mixed emotions about what was in front of us. Even nearly fifty years after it was completed—a period when man had gone to the moon and created the Internet—the 710-foot-high structure wedged into the middle of the canyon walls remained an impressive display of engineering and man-made power. And Lake Powell behind it was indeed striking. But I couldn't help but think about something Wallace Stegner wrote about the reservoir.

Stegner was a writer and historian whose description of the national parks—"the best idea we ever had, absolutely American, absolutely democratic"—led to the title of the PBS series. In the late 1960s, he wrote of America's newest lake: "Though these walls are lower and tamer than they used to be, and though the whole sensation is a little like looking at a picture of Miss America that doesn't show her legs, Lake Powell *is* beautiful. It isn't Glen Canyon, but it is something in itself."

Others had trouble seeing the beauty. Some looked at it and saw death. Edward Abbey wrote, "The difference between the present reservoir, with its silent sterile shores and debris-choked side canyons, and the original Glen Canyon is the difference between life and death. Glen Canyon was alive. Lake Powell is a graveyard."

That was 1981. Abbey predicted that the dam would be gone within a generation. Thirty years, he said. And here we were, more than thirty years after that essay, and dams across America—most notably in Olympic National Park in Washington—were indeed being torn down.

Glen Canyon Dam, however, was still standing. The water behind it was dwindling, though. As I drove toward the dam, I thought about the first time I saw Lake Powell.

I CAME AT it from the other direction, from the north, on the river, at the end of a rafting trip with Mom a few years earlier.

Mom was doing trips with each of her children. I was in my mid-forties. If you had suggested this when I was younger—a vacation with just my mother?—it would have sounded like a nightmare come true. And while it still had moments that felt like a bad road-trip comedy, it was remarkably pleasant.

We drove her camper van from Tucson to Moab, Utah, spent a couple of nights in Arches National Park, then spent four days rafting through Cataract Canyon and Canyonlands National Park before finishing in Glen Canyon National Recreation Area.

There were two big differences between this trip and the one we did in the Grand Canyon a few years earlier: The boats had motors and the water wasn't icy.

As much as we appreciated water being warm enough to take occasional dips in, we quickly realized that when the motors were cranked up, it changed the experience. Some of my strongest memories of the Grand Canyon trip involved the sound. Not just the roar of the rapids, but the quiet between them.

We'd be coasting down a flat stretch of the river, listening to the rhythmic creak of the oar strokes, the lapping of water against the side of the raft, and then we'd hear it. At first it would just be a steady whisper, a soft *shhhh* in the distance. But it would gradually get louder and louder and louder until we were in the middle of it, a frenetic cacophony of water and oars and shouts. Then we'd emerge and the noise would fade surprisingly quickly, the whisper staying with the rapids, the quiet returning.

This cycle would continue all day. And if we camped near rapids—not too close but not too far away either—we were blessed with, I'm still convinced, the best white noise on earth for sleeping.

But even with the air temperature topping a hundred, the temperature of the water in the Grand Canyon didn't make you want to jump in it. Before the dam was built, the river changed with the seasons—in size, color, and temperature. After the dam was in place, the water in the Grand Canyon, emerging from Lake Powell's depths, stayed in the forties. This has all kinds of effects, including making a spectator sport out of bathing on river trips. When people decided their body odor had reached the point that they needed to rinse off, they'd put on a swimsuit, lather up with biodegradable soap, and run screaming into the water.

Above the dam, it was different. In our Cataract Canyon trip, the water was so pleasant that we repeatedly made stops to swim in calm stretches. And on the final day of the trip, we came to small rapids that our guides told us would be perfect for hopping out of the rafts and floating down.

Well, that is, if the guide company—let's just call it Acme River Expeditions—condoned such a thing. And, as our guides said, Acme River Expeditions absolutely prohibited such an activity. But, they added, if you were going to accidentally fall overboard, this would be a delightful place to do it. Oh, and if you *did* happen to fall overboard, please make sure to do it on the upriver side of the boat and then to float on your back, with your feet in front of you.

As people in other rafts began toppling into the small rapids, Mom decided she was going to stay in our raft. I said I was going to try it. Only apparently I wasn't paying close enough attention to the directions for accidentally falling overboard. I fell in just fine. But I didn't pop back up to blue skies, red rock, and most important, oxygen.

I came up and felt the bottom of the raft over my head and water all around me.

For a split second, I also felt panic.

My closest brush with death as a child came when we lived in Reno and made a winter trip into the mountains. As my parents set up a picnic, a friend and I wandered over to where a stream flowed into a frozen lake. We started playing a game, tiptoeing onto the ice toward where it got thinner and thinner, then scampering back when it started to crack. Only one time it didn't just start to crack. It broke.

I plunged down into the dark, frigid water. And when I came up, my hands hit something solid. The current had carried me under the ice. I instinctively swam back into the current as hard as I could. After a few strokes, I popped back up, gasping for air, probably as much out of fear as need. We headed back to the picnic area, our jeans and jackets soaked, our fear replaced by a sort of post-adventure giddiness. We were laughing. When we told my parents why, they did not find it amusing.

Although what happened in the Colorado River was nowhere near as perilous—in an instant I pushed off from the raft and popped up alongside it—I could hear Mom frantically saying, "He's underneath!"

"I'm fine," I said. "I'm fine."

The guide looked at me in the water next to the raft, shook her head, and said something about falling out of the boat to my *other* upriver side. I apologized, stuck my feet out, and floated downriver, hooting and hollering with the rest of the people who had accidentally fallen overboard.

At the end of the rapids, the water slowed and we climbed back in the rafts. Shortly after that, the water slowed even more. Eventually it seemed to stop. It was a strange, disappointing feeling. And not just because it meant the end of the trip was near. During our little speck of time on the Colorado, it felt as if the river was always in control—we were just along for the ride—and that it had been this way for aeons. The river was the driving force in everything around it. The landscape, the vegetation, the wildlife.

At the end of our trip, that no longer was the case. The river was no longer in control. It no longer was even a river. We had reached the northern edge of Lake Powell.

FIVE YEARS AFTER that trip, I was at the southern edge of Lake Powell, the place where a river was turned into a reservoir.

"This first elevator will take us a hundred and ten feet below the visitor center," the tour guide said. "Is everyone having a good day so far?"

When the elevator doors opened, we walked through a tunnel and out into the bright sunlight and the top of the dam. Looking downstream, our guide gave a history of the dam and its construction. How 10 million tons of concrete were poured ("that's enough to make a four-lane highway from Phoenix to Chicago") using six thousand tons of shaved ice. How the city of Page rose out of nothing ("back then it was the world's largest trailer park with a thousand mobile homes"). How two thousand men worked on the project (and eighteen died). How when it was finished, it had a base thicker than a football field.

"Based on the way it was designed and constructed," she said, "Glen Canyon Dam has a life expectancy of two thousand years."

As we moved to another part of the top of the dam, I kept thinking about this detail. Not how tall it was or how thick part of it was. Hearing the dam described in terms of its own life. It was forty-nine years old. If the engineers who built it were right, it had only about another 1,951 years left.

By man-made standards, two thousand years certainly was impressive. But there were redwoods already that old. Some bristlecone pines in Great Basin National Park were five thousand years old. And the rock that the Colorado cuts through in the Grand

Canyon is like a vertical timeline from the Kaibab at the top (200-some million) to the dark Vishnu Schist (1.7 billion) at the bottom. A grand geological library, John Muir called it.

After our guide gave us the history of the dam, we had a few minutes to look around. I wandered over to the other side of the dam with several others and looked at Lake Powell. One of the men got excited when he spotted a large fish.

"This is the deepest part of Lake Powell, so we tend to see a lot of big fish in this area," our guide said. "We have largemouth bass, smallmouth bass, catfish, walleye, bluegill, and others. I think there are twenty different species of fish in the reservoir. And there also are freshwater jellyfish, believe it or not. The biggest fish ever caught was a striper . . . 48 pounds and 11 ounces, right behind Glen Canyon Dam that's 560 feet when full."

She emphasized the words "when full," then answered the obvious question—the elephant-sized bathtub ring in the room—before anyone even asked it.

"If you look on the Navajo sandstone you can see a white color," she said. "That's a calcium deposit left from the water. Because of the drought we've been in for about twelve years, the reservoir is about 65 feet below full."

We eventually headed back to the elevator, this time dropping 528 feet to the bottom of the dam. Our guide led us through a sort of sensory whiplash. From the chilly, drab hallway out into sunshine and a surreal sight—two acres of green grass at the base of the towering walls—and back inside, to the hum of a room with a view of eight large generators.

We took the elevator back up. I walked out into the bright light and warm air, got in the car, and before leaving the parking lot, dialed Mom's home number.

LISA PICKED UP. "You should talk to Mom," my sister said.

She handed the phone to my mom.

"Hi, Mark," she said.

"How are you doing?" I asked.

She sighed. "We took everything out," she said.

At first I didn't understand what she was trying to tell me. As she elaborated, it quickly sunk in. The chemo wasn't working. It was destroying a lot of things in her body, but not the large tumor in her bile ducts.

She said she wanted to be home with her dog, looking at the desert, not stuck in hospital rooms.

She had decided to stop chemo, to have the ports taken out, to start hospice care.

I put the car in park and sat there. "I'm really not ready to lose you," I said. "But I also really don't want you to be miserable and it not to make one bit of difference."

I told her I would start driving to Tucson. I could be there that evening.

"No," she said. "Stay there. Do what you're doing there."

We didn't talk much longer. It's hard to downshift from that conversation to small talk. Instead we just said we loved each other, then said good-bye.

I sat there in the parking lot above Glen Canyon Dam, looking at that blue water and red rock.

It was midday. The sun felt blindingly bright. The colors felt wrong. Too saturated. All of a sudden this landscape felt overwhelmingly gloomy. It was, I decided, the saddest place I'd ever been. Not because they built a dam here and it reminded those who knew it before of a graveyard. Because this would forever be the place where the idea of not having a living parent stopped being a hypothetical, sometime-in-the-future kind of thing. Now it was only a matter of when.

MY ROOM AT the lodge no longer felt quaint and charming. It felt old and depressing. I ate dinner in the restaurant, had a beer, then took a walk down to Navajo Bridge.

Now what?

That's what my daughter was in the habit of saying a lot. It was sort of an everyday version of what kids used to say on cross-country trips. *Are we almost there yet?* Standing on the bridge, looking at the stars, that's what I thought. Now what?

I got up early the next morning and headed a few miles down the road to the Hatch River Expeditions warehouse. The dirt parking lot was full of dusty old cars and bumper stickers that said things like "Drain Lake Powell."

I thought about what a ranger had said to me when I had stopped at Lees Ferry. I told him what I was doing and why I had come here—to meet with some river guides and get their perspective on the river.

"Those river guides wouldn't have the business they do if it weren't for the dam," he said.

The dam and the altering of the river certainly were full of examples of how for every action there are myriad reactions. And one of those reactions was indeed that, for better or worse, the river was more controlled and more predictable. It had become, some said, a push-button river. Guides who arrived for this seminar could be fairly confident that they had months full of trips ahead of them. Not that I blamed them for simultaneously longing for the old, untamed river.

Some two hundred people show up for the annual preseason gathering. When I first arrived to check in the day before, a few dogs ran around outside. The first few people I saw were wearing flip-flops, shorts, and floppy hats—all weathered from years of use.

It reminded me of the rafting trip in the Grand Canyon. All of the guests, including me, showed up looking as if they had just gone to REI and plopped down their credit cards. The guides had on clothing that actually had been used, and they didn't carry around the latest and greatest gear. One of the veteran boatmen led us on hikes up side canyons, walking barefoot, carrying his version of a water bottle—formerly a plastic gallon jug of milk.

The scene in front of the warehouse brought to mind a classic car show. Only in this case, instead of shiny old cars, there were shiny wooden boats, their bright colors popping out against the reddish landscape, each bow bearing a name full of meaning for the guides who gathered around them.

Celilo Falls, Surprise Canyon, Betty Boop, Tatahotso, Julius.

Inside the warehouse, the floor was cleared for the gathering. Rolled-up rubber rafts and bright-colored kayaks were stored in the rafters overhead. Around the edges of the room, tables were set up for organizations.

I was drawn to the one for Mom's Stuff. This is a salve made by Lee Udall Bennion, an artist from Utah. I started chatting with her and her husband, Joe. Her calm, down-to-earth vibe reminded me of my mom. And when she started telling me about all the different ways that people used Mom's Stuff, I couldn't help but think, Yeah, but can it cure Mom's cancer?

Joe had a pottery studio, but at age fifty he started a second career—river guide. He said he grew up avoiding the national parks, thinking they had too many rules. About ten years earlier, he had been invited to do a noncommercial river trip on the Colorado. He took it and was hooked. He had done forty-five trips and counting.

When I called home later, I told my wife that I had decided to quit my job and become a river guide. I said I was joking. Sort of.

It seemed like hard work, with an abundance of physical and mental challenges, low pay, and lots of long-term uncertainty. It also seemed idyllic, better than any antidepressant that came in a bottle. Being in a place like the Grand Canyon puts life in perspective. It boils the moment down to its basics—what matters is staying warm, keeping cool, eating, drinking, breathing—making you and your life feel incredibly small and insignificant. While this might sound demoralizing, anyone who has been deep in the canyon knows it actually is liberating, uplifting, and addictive. And river guides get to experience it again and again.

When I signed up for the event, officially called the Guides Training Seminar (GTS) but open to the public, I was told to bring two things: a folding chair and a coffee mug.

For two days, a steady stream of speakers—guides, park service staff, nonprofit leaders, historians, scientists—stood up in front of the group and gave updates and information about a wide range of topics. Condors and bighorn sheep, the tamarisk leaf beetle, norovirus prevention, uranium mining, the ongoing battle over air tours, the plans for development near the South Rim. The program included talks that ranged from "Springs and Travertines in the Grand Canyon Region and What They Tell Us About Hydrology, Paleohydrology, and Canyon Cutting" to, midway through one afternoon session, "Stretching Clinic."

In the evening, a band played, a keg was tapped, and people milled about, catching up, telling stories about past adventures, planning for future ones.

Outside the warehouse, people lined up to look through a telescope that Jim MacKenzie brought from his home in San Luis Obispo, California.

MacKenzie worked thirty years for California's state parks, starting in maintenance and finishing in historic restoration. At home, he sometimes took his telescope and set it up on street corners. The same thing happened there. People lined up.

"A lot of people have never looked through a telescope," he said. "They can't believe what they're seeing. In Monterey I would get street people and I'd get people who'd pull up in the Mercedes. . . . I get paid in oohs and aahs."

I waited my turn and put my right eye on the telescope. Once upon a time, about the time we snaked an extension cord into our backyard and watched Neil Armstrong on a small black-and-white TV, I could have told you all about the moon and its craters. But when I put my eye on the telescope, I realized it had been a long time since I had looked at the moon like this.

I might have oohed and aahed.

AS THE OUTGOING president of the Grand Canyon River Guides, Nikki Cooley had started the event by welcoming everyone—and then quickly letting them know where she stood on some recent news.

Six weeks earlier, the president of the Navajo Nation and a Phoenix-based development group had signed a memorandum of understanding to move ahead with something they were calling Grand Canyon Escalade.

The 420-acre development on the East Rim of the canyon would include a hotel, RV park, restaurants, a Navajo "cultural center," and—the most controversial piece to all of this—a gondola tramway down to the confluence of the Colorado and Little Colorado rivers.

"I want you to know that as a Navajo person, a Navajo woman, I am totally against it," Cooley told her peers.

The guides broke into applause, punctuated with a few yells of approval.

"We need your voices, too," she said. "It's a very sacred place to the Hopi, the Zuni, the Paiute, and numerous other tribes. We need your voices to tell the president of the Navajo Nation you're against what they're doing."

She shook her head.

"He used to be against it," she said. "Now he's for it."

When we broke for lunch—she announced that members of the Hualapai tribe were serving elk and deer meat on the south side of the warehouse—I found Cooley. She said that there was no question her people were desperate for ways to make money, to lift themselves out of poverty. But this was the wrong way. And she had her doubts whether such a project would actually lead to money making it past the hands of the developers and the tribe leaders, who had gone from being against the proposal to all for it.

"They brought them lots of goodies and made their eyes real big," she said.

Cooley, in her early thirties, grew up on reservations in Blue Gap and Shonto, east of the Grand Canyon. She was raised primarily by her paternal grandparents. Like most of the people on the reservation, they didn't have running water or electricity.

She was especially attached to her grandfather. He was a sheepherder, a kind and patient man who would sit and tell her and her brother and sister stories, impressing upon them the connections between all living species and the earth.

In the summer of 1992, his body began to deteriorate. By the next summer, he was dead. She was twelve years old.

She later learned that her grandfather had died of cancer— and that her grandmother believed it was because of the years he had spent working in the uranium mines in southern Utah. Her grandmother also was eventually diagnosed with cancer. They all thought about how night after night, when her grandfather came home from work, her grandmother washed his flimsy work clothes by hand so he'd have something to wear the next day.

Cooley told this story at a congressional field hearing held on the South Rim in 2010. She said it was part of the reason why she was opposed to continued uranium mining. Beyond that, though, there was what had happened during the time her grandparents were battling cancer.

She went on a Grand Canyon river trip.

She had graduated from college, earned her master's in forestry, and begun working on her doctorate. But on her first trip on the river she found her calling. She became a guide. When she spoke at the congressional field hearing, she explained that to the Navajo and to other tribes, "Water Is Life" isn't just some catchy slogan.

———

I HAD TWO epiphanies on this trip. In hindsight, both should have been obvious.

The first was that the Grand Canyon wasn't preserved for future generations the day that Teddy Roosevelt picked up his pen and created a national monument, or the day Congress finally voted to make it a national park, or any single day since.

The preservation and protection have to happen *every* day.

Three months before the gathering of river guides, Interior Secretary Ken Salazar issued a twenty-year ban on all new uranium claims on public land surrounding Grand Canyon National Park.

Before signing the document that made it official, Salazar said, "Every generation of Americans faces moments when we must choose between the pressures of the now and the protection of the timeless. Today, we know that we can no longer afford to turn our backs on . . . iconic landscapes like the Grand Canyon."

The ban gave Nikki Cooley and many others reason to celebrate. The Grand Canyon Trust led a four-year battle, rallying what it called an "unprecedented and formidable coalition." But as Roger Clark of the Trust told the river guides, this didn't mean that they could stop worrying about the mining. It just meant that they had a few years to start preparing for the next battle.

And in the meantime, there were all kinds of other concerns.

When I met with Dave Uberuaga, who had become superintendent of Grand Canyon National Park the previous year, he talked about basically being handed the keys to one of the most protected places on earth.

"And what do I spend every day doing?" he said. "Trying to protect it. . . . Each day I sit there trying to outsmart somebody else who wants a piece of the canyon."

John Muir once said that "nothing dollarable is safe." And although the Spaniards who stumbled upon the canyon in the sixteenth century declared it to be worthless, that view certainly had changed. Now all the world, it seemed, looked at the place and saw money. From Russia's state atomic energy corporation, one of many foreign stakeholders who wanted to mine for uranium near the canyon, to the Italian developer who wanted to build thousands of homes and millions of feet of commercial space just outside the park boundary in Tusayan (population 550).

The grand plans for that development left many unanswered questions, the biggest being: Where will the water come from?

Water was only one ongoing battle, though. It seemed as if people were lined up, trying to get every conceivable piece of Grand Canyon National Park. Not just the 277 miles from one end to the other. Not just from rim to rim. From the water beneath the canyon to the air above it.

When I met with the park superintendent on the South Rim, one of the most pressing issues on his desk involved finalizing a plan for overflights—basically how many air tours would be allowed, where they would be allowed, and when they would be allowed.

In 1919, when Congress finally got around to designating the Grand Canyon as a national park, this obviously wasn't a concern. At the time, Emile Berliner, a German-born American inventor, was celebrating building a helicopter that rose several feet in the air.

But by 1987, what was happening above the canyon was indeed an issue. And not just because one year earlier a helicopter and a twin-engine plane collided, killing twenty-five people. Hikes in the canyon were too often disturbed by the thump-thump-thump of helicopters and the buzz of small planes. One of the people at the forefront of fighting for a law to create "substantial restoration of natural quiet" of the canyon was Arizona senator John McCain. At the time, he said that the Grand Canyon "does not exist for anyone's financial benefit."

By 2012, McCain was on the other side of the issue, siding with the air tour companies, a conversion that brought the rolling of eyes at the river guides gathering. People pointed out that when McCain ran for president, Elling Halvorson, chairman of Papillon Group, had raised more than $100,000 for the campaign. And now McCain was pushing for what Halvorson—whose company came to the canyon in the 1960s to build the water pipeline and ended up creating the largest air tour provider—and other air tour operators wanted.

The air tour industry had taken off to the point where there were more than twenty companies in five states, doing 130,000 flights a year.

It was the sound of a bipartisan sellout. While McCain was leading the charge in Arizona, Democrat Harry Reid led the push from Nevada.

All of this paid no attention to, or at the very least underestimated, the value of quiet. Not just from an ecological standpoint, from an economic one. If more than 400,000 people take air tours each year, this means that more than 99 percent of the canyon's visitors *don't* take an air tour. They are on the rim, hiking on trails, rafting the river. Many of them go to the canyon—and spend money there—partly because of the solitude.

It is one of the most protected places on earth. But the preservation and protection has to happen *every* day. That was true a hundred years ago. It's true today. And I have no doubt it will be true in another hundred years.

That was the first epiphany.

I LEFT THE warehouse, crossed the Navajo Bridge, and headed south toward Tucson.

I didn't turn on the radio. I just watched the landscape gradually change from red rock cliffs to saguaro-covered hills to the sprawl of Phoenix, all the while in my mind going back to one day at the warehouse.

Nikki Cooley introduced Dan Hall by saying, "A little quiz for you. What is six-four, weighs a little more than 110 pounds, and waddles? If you said Dan Hall, you are correct. This man needs no introduction, but he is the director of the Whale Foundation. It's a foundation that is very dear to me and my husband. We've been sober for four years. And we would not . . ."

She paused for a moment, swallowed, and then said the foundation had saved her life. She pointed to her daughter and husband.

"If you see that cute little girl running around with my husband, our recovery is the reason why she is here today," she said.

Hall was executive director of a foundation started in the 1990s after boatman Curtis "Whale" Hansen, a legendary character among the guides, committed suicide. The foundation's mission was to provide confidential access to support for river guides.

He walked to the front of the room and, after giving some updates about the foundation, talked about what had happened seventy-five years earlier on the Green and Colorado rivers.

In 1937, Haldane "Buzz" Holmstrom, a gas station attendant from Oregon, took a wooden boat he built by himself and became the first person to do a solo run of a thousand miles of water from Wyoming to Nevada. After Holmstrom's feat, much to his dismay, he became famous. And after his apparent suicide nine years later—at age thirty-seven, of a gunshot wound to the head—he became forgotten.

As Hall noted, one of the guides in the warehouse was trying to change that.

Brad Dimock didn't just go back and read Holmstrom's diaries and coauthor a book that was published in 2004 (*The Doing of the Thing: The Brief, Brilliant Whitewater Career of Buzz Holmstrom*). He built a replica of Holmstrom's boat, the *Julius*. He took it through the canyon. And with the seventy-fifth anniversary approaching, he brought it to the gathering. It was in the row of boats sitting outside the warehouse, part of what Dimock quipped was "a small breeding population of nearly extinct species of old wooden boats."

When I saw photos of Holmstrom, I realized why Dimock was wearing a worn white captain's hat, tilted slightly back and to one side. Buzz had.

"He's a really, really remarkable character," Dimock told those gathered in the warehouse. "But . . . Buzz Holstrom had some serious things going on. The demon that drove him to incredible brilliance is likely the one that took him out in the end."

The final sentence of a five-paragraph Wikipedia entry on Holmstrom merely said, "The motivation for his apparent suicide is not known." After spending years studying Holmstrom, reading his words, building his boat, rowing his rivers, Dimock felt like he knew some of the motivation. It almost certainly started with clinical depression.

He read aloud entries in Holmstrom's diaries, noting the patterns of self-deprecation and self-denial.

"He's beating himself up," Dimock said. "What seems humble at first, you realize, 'Wow, if somebody called my friend what he's calling himself, I'd slug 'em.' . . . A lot of depression is based on one implausible fact. You're worthless, unlovable. You're never enough. You can't do enough. So you have to prove yourself. Over and over again."

He spoke faster and faster. "Every day, every minute. Guilt, shame, loneliness."

He said there's a counselor in Flagstaff who summed it up. Holmstrom couldn't even be a human being. He had to be a human doing.

"If he couldn't do," Dimock said, "he couldn't be."

The room was full but quiet. Quieter than it had been the whole weekend. Nobody was talking to the person next to him or her. Even the dogs were still, perhaps taking their cue from their owners.

Dimock repeated that we don't really know what happened, adding that what matters is they lost a friend.

"Any of those patterns sound familiar?" he said. "They're not healthy. If you have those thoughts, or you see people beating the hell out of themselves, it's time to take action now, okay?"

He took a deep breath and exhaled.

"That was hard, huh?" he said. "Let's lighten it up a little bit."

He set the stage for a viewing of *Conquering the Colorado,* a short film made the year after the original journey. As the movie played, living up to its billing—cheesy voice-over, melodramatic music—I sat there, thinking about what Dimock had said.

I was still thinking about it a couple of days later on the drive to Tucson.

I bought a copy of *The Doing of the Thing.* I read the diary entry that led to the title. Holmstrom wrote it on one of the final nights of the journey, after he had made it through Lava Cliff, the "bad rapid" he had been thinking about getting through for nearly a thousand miles.

> I had thought once past there my reward will begin, but now everything seems kind of empty and I find I already have my reward—in the doing of the thing. The stars and cliffs and canyons, the roar of the rapids, the moon, the uncertainty, worry, the relief when thru each one, the campfires at night, the real respect and friendship of the rivermen I met.

When I had arrived at the guide training seminar, I felt like I had stumbled upon a group of people who already had found the secret to life. Not necessarily a fountain of youth. More like a river of happiness.

They didn't care about having things. They cared about doing things. And the doing of these things in places like the Grand Canyon kept them healthy and happy.

If I followed their lead, I figured I had a certain degree of immunity from what was ahead. I believed the parks were going to get me through this year and beyond. As I headed to Tucson, I still believed that. But I realized it wasn't that simple.

That was the second epiphany.

———

MOM WANTED TO throw a party.

This was somewhat of a surprise, not just because of the circumstances, but because Mom never was a party person. She was more likely to run away from places where people gathered, maybe go for a hike or curl up with a good book.

But she said she wanted to thank all the people who had supported her since February. She looked at it pragmatically. She didn't have the energy to have people stopping by all the time. So why not invite them all over at once?

It was shortly after Easter. All of us—my wife and daughter, my two sisters and their children—had been there for the holiday. And it turned out to be a wonderfully normal weekend. We played card games in the kitchen, watched movies, took her dog, Wally, for walks in the neighborhood, ate meals at an outdoor table with a view of the mountains, and went to part of Easter-morning church service.

We left before the end of the service and headed to the airport. Toni and Mia were heading back to Florida. Mom hugged them a little longer than usual, then said good-bye. The drive back to Mom's house was quiet. And when we walked into the kitchen, I saw the drawing Mia had made. Mom had taped it to the pantry door.

"Happy Easter!" it said above an oval with blue and pink stripes. "Dear Nana, I hope you feel better soon. I love you! Love, Mia!"

I had debated what to tell Mia before she came to Tucson. I eventually settled upon something along the lines of "Nana is very sick." I wasn't sure if it was the right decision. This might have been an age-old dilemma, but it was new territory for me. And so was the party.

It was a sunny and warm afternoon. But Mom said she was chilly. Wearing a purple sweater that looked a couple of sizes too big on her shrinking body, she shuffled outside to a chair in the sun, next to the pool, with a view of the desert and the mountains in the distance. She sat down and draped a blanket over her legs.

The guests started to arrive. We greeted them and told them Mom was outside. One man introduced himself to me, said he used to live in my mom's old neighborhood. I thanked him for coming. Then there was an awkward silence.

"I'm not sure what to say," he said. "I've never been to a party like this."

It turned out to be a wonderful party. Conversations inevitably led to stories about the things we all seemed to have in common. Hikes with Mom. Trips to favorite places. Funny moments. I absorbed it all in a way I wouldn't have a few months earlier. Realizing that there weren't going to be new stories, I clung to the old ones.

One of Abe's grandsons, Dalton, broke out his acoustic guitar and played. Mom seemed happy. Eventually, though, she said she was getting tired. She left her own party and went into her bedroom. Nobody blamed her.

I was glad that, even though she never was a party person, she had thrown this one.

JOHN FIFE, THE former pastor of her church, stopped by another day.

I had been to a few services when he was still preaching. He was an interesting character, an avid outdoorsman and a human-rights activist who had spent decades diving headfirst into immigration issues. He was tall and often wore cowboy boots, jeans, and a large belt buckle.

We sat down at one end of the long table in the kitchen.

John asked how she was. She said okay. He looked her in the eyes, smiled, and said, "What you're doing takes a lot of courage."

I could tell she appreciated this.

Our society teaches us that we should fight until the very end, exploring every possible option, spending every last penny, enduring every pain.

I think Mom sometimes felt that by stopping the chemo, she was being weak, the antithesis of the never-quit mantra. We told her otherwise. The hospice staff told her otherwise. But John took it one step further. He said that not only was she not quitting, but she was showing a kind of strength that most people didn't have.

The room was quiet for a few seconds.

"I don't want a big funeral in the church," she said.

John looked at her, smiled, and patted her hand. "Nancy," he said, "it's not for you."

She thought about this for a moment and nodded.

We started talking about her funeral. I promised her it wouldn't be something formal in the church. She suggested something out-side, maybe in her backyard, maybe like the party.

I remembered years ago when Mom and Dad gave me their wills. I tucked them in a file cabinet, unopened. I didn't want to read what they wanted to have happen when they died, let alone talk about such things. And now I was sitting there, talking to Mom about how she didn't want a big service, how she wanted to be cremated, how she wanted her children and grandchildren to continue to get to-gether when she was gone.

It was a conversation neither one of us really wanted to have but both knew we needed to. Afterward, sitting on her deck, looking at the desert, I thought about how coming of age, transitioning from a child to an adult, supposedly is something that happens when you're young. But as I thought about all the other moments in my life that made me think I was all grown up, I decided I was wrong. This was the moment when the internal needle moved from child to adult.

I HEADED NORTH from Tucson again, this time toward the South Rim of the Grand Canyon.

I still couldn't run more than a few feet. But I could walk. So I hiked down the South Kaibab Trail. That's where I met a boy named Blue.

I heard his parents call him that as he excitedly ran down the trail not long after getting off the hiker's express shuttle to the trailhead. He had blond pigtails and was wearing a blue headband and little green puffy jacket. And when I started chatting with his mom and dad, I realized why they called him Blue. His eyes were the color of the day's milky sky.

Blue was four. He was excited about the day's adventure, a 7.5-mile hike to the Bright Angel Campground. I asked why he was excited about something I pictured my daughter, and many other children, dreading.

"I'm going to the bottom," he said.

His parents, both guides for an adventure company, had enormous packs. But when Blue took off running, and they hoisted the packs onto their backs and followed, they all had big grins on their face.

If you were looking for the future of the national parks, you'd be hard-pressed to do better than a boy named Blue.

When I crossed the footbridge and watched the river rushing underneath it, I thought about the rafting trip with Mom. How at one point one of the guides had asked if anyone wanted to "ride cowboy." My mother raised her hand. I was in another boat, so I heard about it only when we reached our next stop and everyone was still talking about how she had gotten up on the front of the raft, held on to the rope . . . and promptly gotten bucked off into the river.

The guides quickly scooped her up and pulled her into a raft. She was still dripping wet when I saw her. And grinning. And I remember feeling oddly like the parent, glad I hadn't actually witnessed any of this because it probably would have sent me into a panic.

I know that trip helped Mom. It was in May 1998, a year and a half after Dad died. She never forgot him. Sometimes, seemingly out of the blue, she'd mention missing him. But that trip helped her move forward. She was sixty at the time. She had done a lot of living after that. And I gave the canyon—and places like it—a lot of the credit for that.

We save rivers and canyons and mountains, and they save us.

While crossing the river on the footbridge, I thought of John Daggett.

What Daggett and an old college buddy, Bill Beer, did is part of canyon lore. In April 1955, before the dam was built, they jumped into the water at Lees Ferry and spent twenty-six days swimming through the Colorado River. And while they had a variety of reasons for doing it—some of it was simply sheer craziness—part of what led them to this journey was something that had happened two years earlier. A train struck Daggett's family car, killing his wife, who was pregnant, and his two young daughters. Daggett ended up moving in with Beer. And they ended up hatching the plan to swim the river.

Beer wrote a book about the experience. A very funny book. But one of the parts that stays with you is the description of when they're floating through a peaceful stretch of the river, surrounded by towering rock walls. They start yelling, listening to their voices bounce of the walls. And Daggett starts calling out a name—of one of his little girls.

They kept swimming and floating for twenty-six days. Daggett nearly drowned when he got trapped next to a boulder at President Harding Rapid. And that, Beer recalled one year at the river guides gathering, is when his buddy was certain he wanted to live.

When I got to the bottom of the canyon, I went to the little beach, took off my shoes, and dipped my feet in the Colorado. After a slight detour to Phantom Ranch for lemonade and M&M's and a refill of the hydration pack, I crossed the river on the Silver Bridge and began hiking out the Bright Angel Trail.

This is the superhighway of the canyon, undoubtedly the most heavily traveled trail beneath the rim. And yet after I crossed the river and made the turn at Pipe Creek—into a wind that was whipping down the side canyon—I went more than two hours without seeing another person.

Not that the canyon was quiet. I heard canyon wrens, frogs, waterfalls, and wind. I saw and smelled a skunk. As I moved up the trail, its scent faded and was replaced by the smell of the trees lining the creek.

At about Indian Garden the vibe started to change. And by the time I made it to near the top of the seemingly endless switchbacks up the final stretch of the trail, cell phones were ringing and people were walking and talking.

"Yeah, we're in the freaking Grand Canyon!" said one twenty-something guy wearing flip-flops.

It reminded me of when we hiked out of the canyon after our 1998 family rafting trip. We had a room booked on the rim. Two nights. But after just one week in the canyon, the South Rim felt like Times Square. It made me edgy and antsy. I wanted to get away from all these people. And we did. We canceled the second night of the hotel reservation. On the way out, I picked up a newspaper. The big story in the Arizona papers was that Barry Goldwater had died at age eighty-nine.

I was only three years old when Goldwater ran for president in 1964. My knowledge of him was fairly simplistic—conservative icon, made the speech at the Republican convention where he said, "extremism in the defense of liberty is no vice," got hammered by LBJ after a campaign that included the mushroom cloud ad.

One thing that jumped out at me in his obits was his history with the Grand Canyon—he rafted through it in 1940, the beginning of a lifelong love of the place—and his about-face on dams. In the 1950s, as a senator, he was one of the leading proponents of building dams all across the West. By the 1990s, he and environmentalist David Brower, fierce advocates for decades, were in agreement: They shouldn't have allowed Glen Canyon Dam to be built.

In the 1997 documentary *Cadillac Desert*, Goldwater said: "What have we done to this beautiful desert, to our wild rivers? All that dam building on the Colorado, across the West, was a big mistake. What in the world were we thinking?"

Brower told author Paul VanDevelder that he called Goldwater after that and suggested he help him take out the dam. Goldwater said that was "a grand idea." Then he died a few months later. And Brower died. The dam continues to live. Although it does have a life expectancy.

THE DAY AFTER I hiked to the river, I decided to do something really hard—something I wasn't sure many Americans, including myself, could do for more than a few minutes.

Sit still. Say nothing. Do nothing other than soak up what's around you.

It was something Mom always was good at. Better than anyone I know. I think Dad struggled a little more with it. And in this, and many other ways, I'm more like Dad.

After going to the main visitor center, I wandered a few hundred yards east on the rim trail, enough to get away from most of the crowd. I sat down a few feet from the rim, underneath a tree. I set down my backpack and got comfortable. I told myself I was going to just sit there for one hour. No checking my cell phone. No taking pictures. No moving to someplace else. Just sit in that spot and take in the canyon.

I took a deep breath. I made it maybe thirty seconds before I felt the gravitational pull of the phone in my pocket. I resisted the urge to pull it out. I squirmed. I refocused on the canyon. I reached for a notepad to scribble down something. I stopped myself. My mind wandered to a checklist of things I needed to do tomorrow and the next day. I told myself to stop thinking about those things and to look at what was in front of me—a view that I had spent many an hour daydreaming about while sitting at home or staring at a computer.

I thought about the story about Buzz Holmstrom. How he couldn't even be a human being. He had to be a human doing. I tried to do nothing. I watched the shadows of the clouds gliding over the topography. I noticed what the air smelled like, how the scent changed along with the wind. Eventually my body relaxed and my mind did something that came naturally when we were children. I daydreamed. I watched the clouds and listened to the vast stillness. The great loneliness.

That's what Teddy Roosevelt called it when he first saw the Grand Canyon in 1903. Roosevelt knew loneliness. In 1884, his wife and his mother had died within hours of each other. He sought solace in the Dakota territories, where a national park now bears his name. When he made it to the Grand Canyon a couple of decades later, he delivered the speech in which he made it clear what he thought we should do with a place like this. Nothing. Leave it as it is, he said. Allow future generations to experience "the wonderful grandeur, the sublimity and great loneliness."

We don't typically use those last two words together. But what I felt at this moment in this spot on the edge of the Grand Canyon was indeed a great, comforting loneliness.

5

*

MAY: THE DRY TORTUGAS

It was five A.M., a nearly deserted State Road A1A in front of me, a giant moon reflecting on the water next to it. Every other time I had driven the one road running through the Florida Keys, it was in the daylight. That seemed like the natural way to roll down a road so vintage Florida that Jimmy Buffett named an album after it—in the bright sunlight, feeling like you're passing through a pastel painting.

When Toni and I went to Key West for our honeymoon, we rented a convertible in Orlando, spent a night in Key Largo, then drove A1A with the roof down, feeling the sun and wind and salt air.

Not that I would ever say any drive through the Keys tops that one—I wanted to be celebrating my twenty-fifth wedding anniversary in 2016—but when I left the Siesta Motel in Marathon before dawn, the road was empty and the moon I had been reading about filled the sky. It was a sphere so big that it was living up to its billing as a supermoon, its light silhouetting the bridges and dancing across the water. The calm water.

For weeks, the seventy miles of sea between Key West and the Dry Tortugas had been swirling like a washing machine, leaving quite a few passengers on the two-and-a-half-hour ferry ride feeling sick. And when I talked to Marty, the owner of a Key West company about renting one of his kayaks and taking it to the Dry Tortugas, he said that as much as he wanted my business, if the water was like it had been lately, it wasn't even worth going out there. Period.

If it's like that, he said, you'll be begging to get off the island.

This was hardly just a modern sentiment. Samuel Arnold, one of four co-conspirators in the Lincoln assassination shipped to the Dry Tortugas, later wrote: "Without exception, it was the most horrible place the eye of man ever rested upon."

But assuming you're not a nineteenth-century prisoner and the weather is good, it can be paradise. And when I headed there in early May, the weather had turned better than good, the water was smooth, and the moon was super.

WHY DRY TORTUGAS National Park?

Partly because I liked the jarring juxtaposition of going from April on the arid Colorado Plateau, where layers of land go a mile deep and a river constantly quenches the thirst of millions of Americans, to May in this place: a national park that includes a hundred square miles of water, none of it drinkable, and less than a hundred acres of dry land.

When Ponce de León and his crew found the cluster of small islands teeming with wildlife in 1513, the Spanish explorer named them Las Islas de Tortugas (the islands of turtles). On mariners' charts, they eventually were labeled as "Dry" to alert those sailing the Gulf of Mexico that there wasn't any freshwater there.

Five hundred years later there still were all kinds of wildlife. And no fresh water.

It was a real place that seemed ripped from the pages of *Treasure Island* (Long John Silver told stories of the Dry Tortugas) or a Hemingway novel (the author and some buddies once were stranded there for seventeen days). And while many national parks feature natural treasures or cultural ones, this park had it all, above and below the water: coral, fish, rare birds, shipwrecks, and all the stories behind one of the largest forts America ever built (but never finished), Fort Jefferson.

But mainly I was headed there because by the time the park service celebrates its two hundredth anniversary, this park almost certainly will have changed dramatically. Much of what led to this becoming a part of the park system in 1935 and a national park in 1992 might even be gone, wiped out or washed away by the effects of climate change.

Within the park service, climate change isn't a controversial issue. Or at least not in the way it is on the campaign trail and cable news. The question isn't whether it's occurring, but how it is altering parks and—perhaps an even tougher question—how the park service should react to these changes.

In some way, all of the NPS sites—everywhere from Alaska to the Virgin Islands—were being affected. I thought about going to Glacier, where the glaciers are disappearing. Or to the Everglades, where it doesn't take a scientist to figure out that even the slightest rise in sea level could have dramatic implications not only for the park but for millions of people living near it in South Florida.

But when it comes to climate change, the Dry Tortugas might be the canary in the coal mine. Or, to be more accurate, the thousands of sooty terns on a coral island.

I FOUND A seat on the upper deck of the ferry, next to two men from Montreal, Ken and Lance. They and several others on board clearly were birders. They didn't just have large binoculars around their necks. They were carrying sturdy tripods and even larger viewing scopes.

We started chatting as we pulled away from the dock and Key West faded into the distance. In the two previous days, Ken saw three birds he had never seen before. The cave swallow, the spot-breasted oriole, and the Antillean nighthawk. This brought his personal lifetime North American total to 605.

He downplayed this, saying some hard-core birders top that in a single year.

"Did you see *The Big Year*?" he said, referring to the book that was turned into a movie featuring Steve Martin, Jack Black, and Owen Wilson.

"I did," I said.

They quickly insisted they weren't as obsessive as that trio. And while I didn't doubt that to be true, they weren't going to the Dry Tortugas because of the snorkeling or the fort. They were going in hopes of spotting a bird. Not one species. One bird.

A black noddy had been seen there.

"What does it look like?" I asked.

He pulled out his iPhone, tapped it, and showed me a picture.

He tapped it again and a birdcall played.

It was one more way technology was changing the world. Avid birders weren't carrying bird books. Not that any app can compare to actually seeing—and hearing—the birds in the Dry Tortugas. When John James Audubon visited in 1832, he said, "I felt for a moment as if the birds would raise me from the ground, so thick were they all around, and so quick the motion of their wings."

More than a century later, Roger Tory Peterson declared the sight and sound of the sooty tern colony on Bush Key to be the "number one ornithological spectacle of the continent."

The birds still were coming—three hundred species had been spotted on the Dry Tortugas—and so were the birders. But with temperatures inching up, both were arriving earlier and earlier.

FOR MOST OF the ferry ride, you see nothing but water in every direction.

Then it appears, rising out of the water in the distance. The red bricks—16 million of them—of a fort that nearly covers an island.

This often is described as a remote, hardly visited national park. And in some ways, I suppose that's true. Just seeing the words "no service" on your cell phone and knowing there isn't any service for many miles make it feel remote. But it's not nearly as remote as most of the Alaska parks or Isle Royale in Lake Superior or quite a few other parks. And while the Grand Canyon has more visitors in a year than the Dry Tortugas has had in its history, it's not as if people don't make it here.

More than a million people have experienced what it's like to see the fort appear in the distance. And when I stepped onto Garden Key, I was one of more than a hundred visitors on its twenty-two acres.

It used to be much more crowded, though. One hundred and fifty years earlier, in the spring of 1862, more than a thousand soldiers arrived. And by 1865, there were nearly two thousand people—soldiers, prisoners, and some civilians—not just visiting, but living in a fort with a sixteen-acre footprint. It was more densely populated than Manhattan at the time.

These days the vast majority of people come just for a few hours, arriving by ferry or seaplane in the morning and heading back to Key West in time for happy hour.

I wanted to be there after the sun set.

There are eight first-come, first-served campsites located on the small patch of land outside the fort. Although I started the year planning to go to the Dry Tortugas in February or March, going in early May turned out to be fortuitous timing. And not just because of calm seas and a supermoon. When I went to Garden Key, Mike Jester was there.

FEW PEOPLE ALIVE have spent more time in the Dry Tortugas than Jester.

He grew up in Wyoming, and even after his family moved to Ohio, they vacationed in the West. From a young age, he knew he wanted to work in the outdoors. He studied forestry in college. But when it came time to find a job, his first job opportunity was in maintenance.

He had risen in the NPS ranks, becoming facility manager for Everglades and Dry Tortugas, but his specialty remained maintenance and logistics, which made him ideally suited for a place with overwhelming maintenance and logistical challenges.

It was one thing to build a fort in the middle of all this water in the nineteenth century. It's another to keep that fort standing in the twenty-first century as the water slowly rises.

After unloading my gear from the ferry, I found the park service office, tucked inside the fort. The small office was air-conditioned and had several cubicles with computers; on the wall was a sign reminding everyone that everything inside the fort quickly becomes covered with dust and debris: "Please cover everything when you are through."

Jester started by giving me a tour inside the fort, explaining some of the history and the inner workings of the structure today. We climbed one of the sets of stairs to the top of the fort. Standing there, gazing out at water as far as the eye could see, I asked about the future of this place. Jester recalled the park service director describing South Florida, specifically the Everglades, as ground zero for climate change.

"That's probably more like ground zero plus," he said. "*This* is ground zero."

There were places in the Everglades that soared to fourteen feet above sea level. The highest natural point in the Dry Tortugas was on Loggerhead Key. Ten feet.

Jester first came to these islands in 1984. He recalls his wife's reaction when she saw the fort rising out of the distance and realized that this was going to be their home.

"She doesn't usually swear, but . . ." he said, laughing.

Four years later, he said, she had to be dragged off the island.

In several decades, he has seen keys morph, connecting and disconnecting, sometimes growing and more times shrinking. When Ponce de León arrived here, there were eleven islands. Now there are seven—or four, if you count the three that are now connected as one.

"These are all islands that move and shift," he said. "They're sandbars. Some of them have some rock base down ninety feet that allows them to stay here, but . . ."

He pointed to one edge of Garden Key.

"The key extended off that point and around the corner. It's hard to say whether that's sea level rise or we hardened these shorelines and it changed the drift pattern. I'm sure that's part of it. But we do have other keys that are shrinking. I went to East Key a couple weeks ago and it was half the size it was twenty-five years ago."

We continued to walk around the top of the walls.

Forty feet below, visitors strolled atop the wall of a moat that circles the fort. It's a walkway featured in thousands of vacation and travel photos, its red brick standing out against the aqua water. When we wandered down to the moat wall, the water was gently lapping against the bricks.

Jester said I should talk to Christopher Ziegler, a Tennessee native who had been the lead interpretative ranger and historian for four years. Most young rangers don't stay here long, but Ziegler clearly loves the fort and its history.

The fort isn't as iconic as many in America, partly because it was never a part of any battles. And yet it isn't just the third largest fort this country ever built and the largest brick fort in the world, it is the most sophisticated and, some would say, most beautiful of a chain of coastal forts.

In a way, it's a nineteenth-century version of Microsoft, Google, and Facebook. It was built by America's best and brightest engineers and architects, filled with innovations in materials and design—many of which still can't be trumped today.

"To lose that, we lose part of the American history and American culture that people today do not recognize—that era when we were not the predominant military in the planet and we had to build forts to protect our harbors," Ziegler said.

To this day, he said, those who study the fort are amazed by it. There isn't a construction joint in it. On a hot day, it can grow in width by two feet without breaking a bond. There are small details throughout, meticulously designed and implemented.

"People have this misconception that we do things better now, that we know how people used to do things and we choose not to do that because things are better," Ziegler said. "No. . . . The ability to make things like this, in this style of architecture and craftsmanship cannot be duplicated."

He can point to places in the fort where the wood is still original, where there are pencil lines going back to 1862.

"You might say these things are not important," he said. "But the National Park Service has been charged with saying, yes, these are important and we're going to take care of these for future generations."

And yet he realizes that might not be possible.

In the last fifteen years, the fort has undergone some major restoration. Five of the six sides have had work done. But the untouched side is the one in the worst condition. To restore it would cost $13 million. And to completely repair the fort?

"The conservative price tag is $100 million," Jester said. "Our annual budget for the line item construction in the entire National Park Service this year is something like $52 million. . . . So what is our strategy for this park?"

Previous repairs had already been questioned and criticized. When $13.3 million of stimulus money was used to do restoration work, two senators put it on a list of the top 100 wasteful projects (No. 16 on the list), writing in a report: "Those willing to take the 4½-hour round-trip ferry ride aboard the *Yankee Freedom II* have to pay as much as $165 per person, but will discover that only 40 of the park's 65,000 acres are dry land."

Some park advocates argued that the stimulus money wouldn't have been necessary if restoration of the fort had been funded in the past—and that doing it now saves money in the future.

This may be true, but even those within the park service wonder about that future. When I met with the park service director, he specifically brought up Fort Jefferson. He had visited the fort. He called the living conditions for the rangers—inside the fort, with sheets covering tables and beds because of falling mortar—the worst he had seen in the park system. And when he looked at the bigger picture, he couldn't help but raise the ultimate question.

"When do you let it go?" he said.

It's not just that the water is rising. The fort is sinking.

As I walked around it with Mike Jester, I mentioned that at some point the park service is going to be faced with some tough questions.

That point, he said, is now.

"We feel like we should be developing an exit strategy for this park twenty-five years out," he said. "By exit strategy, I mean a significantly different way of approaching our mission. Not abandonment. But do we need all this infrastructure out here? Do we need all these people working out here?"

The fort will be here when the park service celebrates its centennial. People still will be visiting it every day. But in another hundred years, Jester expects it to be a vastly different place. An abandoned one.

That has happened before. One hundred years ago, after a hurricane in 1910 and a fire in 1912, the place was deserted except for the wildlife and occasional boaters passing through. But when abandonment happens again, it likely will be different. It likely will be permanent.

ON MY SECOND night on Garden Key, I did a head count. There were eleven people camping. The other ten came in pairs—four couples and a father and son.

I had tried to convince a few friends to join me for this trip. Several were interested but the timing didn't work out. So I was by myself, the lone solo camper.

I was a little nervous. Partly because of the lack of potable water. Partly because of the uncertainty of whether this was the right place to be for this part of the year. And partly because of something brought up by one of the people who couldn't make the trip.

"What do you think about the rats?" he asked.

Up until that point, I hadn't thought about them at all. I didn't know there were rats on the island. But then, while reading about camping on Garden Key, I saw that the park service site said: "Rats have inhabited the Tortugas probably since the arrival of humans. Though the size of the rat population is controlled, rats may be encountered as they forage through campsites looking for food. The only way to protect your food and prevent damage to your gear (rats will chew through tents and backpacks if they smell food) is to store your food in hard-sided containers or hang it from the posts provided."

Another friend who had wanted to make the trip shrugged this off. "I'll take rats over bears any day," Mathew Rini said.

When I got to this island, I grabbed one of the carts available on the dock and loaded my stuff onto it. I had a large duffel with my tent, a few pieces of clothing, and a book; and a cooler full of ice, bread, peanut butter, jelly, tuna, Clif bars, cereal, milk, a couple of beers, and several gallons of water.

It turned out I didn't need to worry about water. Everyone, it seemed, brought more than enough. As we arrived, the campers who were leaving that day offered what they had left over. Plus, I realized that the ferry would be docking there each day, bringing a chance to get not only water, but soda and snacks. This was hardly the backcountry of Alaska.

As I wheeled the cart toward the campsites, clustered in a corner of the island outside the fort, it already was steamy, Florida hot. All of the prime shaded spots, near a clump of trees, were claimed. So I took one next to the fort, in the bright sunlight and blistering sand, figuring it would cool off when the sun set.

I set up my tent. With the fort and sand and water, it was a visually stunning campsite. But I quickly realized that not only was it hot at the moment, but it was noisy. A generator on that side of the fort was roaring like a freight train.

There was no way to get completely away from this, but I

checked out a few of the open spots slightly farther away from the fort. At one, the ground was covered with peanut shells and cigarette butts. I'm not sure if the previous camper thought a national park was like a theme park, where someone shows up within seconds to sweep up any litter. But I looked at this spot, thought about the rats, and moved on to a cleaner spot, a little farther away from the generator.

About midafternoon, people started heading back to the dock. I saw the two birders I met on the ferry ride to the island.

"Did you find your bird?" I asked.

They shook their heads. They had seen many birds, but not the one they were hoping to add to their lists. They boarded along with the rest of the day visitors. And when the ferry pulled away, the island instantly changed.

It was just the campers, park service staff and volunteers, and the boaters who were docked in the harbor. There were more than a dozen sailboats, part of a sailing club from Florida's West Coast, and one massive yacht. But by early evening, most of the boaters were on their boats and the employees were in their accommodations within the casemates of the fort.

It felt like we, the campers, had the place to ourselves.

Sunset was still a couple of hours away. I decided to go for a swim.

With the campground and marina out of view, it felt as if I was alone. As a brilliant blue fish swam a few feet beneath me, I thought about how there are few things more relaxing than snorkeling in the Keys—once I get past the initial panic.

It happens every time. I put my face in the water and feel as if I can't breathe. I have to force the first few breaths in and out, in and out. After maybe thirty seconds of this, it's like my body flips a switch. My lungs relax. My breathing becomes normal. I'm in heaven.

Maybe it goes back to when I was fifteen years old, doing a summer job at the city pool, vacuuming out the deep end, wearing a weight belt and an old mask hooked up to a thin hose that led to an air compressor on the deck. The hose kinked. The flow of air stopped. I yanked on the hose to unkink it. Nothing. I yanked again. Nothing. I frantically took off the weight belt and shot to the surface, yanking at the rusty buckles on the mask, eventually popping it off and flopping onto the deck, gasping for air.

That was one of the first times I felt vincible. That feeling, of course, passed quickly. I was a teenager. Thirty-five years later, though, it came back. If you prepared a checklist of how to live a healthful life, Mom would have put a check in every box and added some extra credit checks. If she was vincible, so was I.

I stopped swimming and treaded water, looking at the miles and miles of open water, before turning around and heading back to the small beach next to the campsite.

I had dinner under a tree near the edge of the beach. A peanut butter and jelly sandwich and a can of cold Yuengling.

The sandwich was my meal of choice because I didn't feel like bringing charcoal and cooking for one. (The fuel canisters I used with my Snow Peak stove were among the list of items banned from the ferry.) As I ate and then enjoyed my dessert, a bag of Peanut M&M's, a young couple sat on one side of a picnic table, facing the water. I watched them break out some wineglasses, open a bottle of red, and eat the steak he had just grilled. Not that I was complaining.

After dinner, I wandered through the empty fort, starting with the parade grounds in the middle of it. Next to one of the remaining freestanding buildings inside the fort—one of the original powder magazines—was a cactus. Night-blooming cereus, reminiscent of something I'd see in Tucson.

I climbed to the top of the fort. The only people I could see were a young couple sitting on the moat below, looking to the west, the woman resting her head on the man's shoulder.

It looked like it was going to be a rarity for the Keys, a dud of a sunset. It was hazy, and as the sun dipped below the clouds on the horizon, all the colors were muted, almost gray. Then the lower left corner of the sun peeked out from below the cloud. It was bright red and illuminated the water below it.

When it disappeared, I was reminded I wasn't the only one watching it. From one side of the fort came the sound of honking boat horns.

Behind me, the birds on Bush Key chirped frantically. And in front of me, the lighthouse on Loggerhead Key, three miles away and seemingly right next to where the sun had dropped into the water, began to blink.

Then came the main act. The moon.

I ended up sitting on a picnic table near the fort with Mark Freund and his son, Kevin, waiting to see it.

Freund is a deeply tanned, sixty-two-year-old basket weaver. He has been living in the Keys for about thirty years. His home is a sailboat near Big Pine Key. But this was his first visit to the Dry Tortugas, a camping trip with his twentysomething son, timed to coincide with the supermoon.

They came over on the ferry the same day I did. I ended up chatting with them more than anyone else, partly just because I didn't feel like breaking up some romantic getaway but also because they were so excited about everything. I'd see them in the morning and they'd smile and say, "Another day in paradise." And even if there were things that others (including me) might have grumbled about— the heat, the generator noise, the thoughtlessness of fellow visitors— they never seemed to waver from that another-day-in-paradise attitude.

"This is amazing," said Kevin as we sat on the picnic table and waited for the moon to rise. "Just three of us out here. I mean, I know there are more people out here. But this is awesome."

Before the moon rose, the sky started to get dark—dark enough for some stars to start appearing.

"There's the North Star," the father said, pointing to the sky above the fort.

I knew that for centuries man had been using Polaris to find his way. Sailing seas, crossing deserts. Slaves even used it to show them the way to freedom. And I used to know how to find it, but I had forgotten. I couldn't help but think there was some sort of metaphor about being lost.

"See the Big Dipper?" the father said. "See those two stars that make the outer edge of the pan? If you carry those down, they'll point right to the North Star."

Such a simple lesson. It felt good to remember it. I might not know where I was going. But at least I knew how to find the North Star again.

The stars kept appearing. We talked about how you forget just how many there are up there. And then you come to a place like this and . . .

"What's that?" the father yelled.

He pointed to a row of three red dots in the sky. They sat there, seemingly stationary, for a few seconds, and then they were gone.

"Meteors?" I said.

"No," the son said. "I've seen meteors. Those were something else."

We debated what the dots might have been. They were convinced it was something suspicious, maybe UFOs, maybe some sort of secret military exercise.

The conversation stopped. It was still warm and humid. But with a slight breeze, the air felt comfortable, almost cool on the skin.

"Look!" the son said.

This time he wasn't pointing to the sky over the fort. He was pointing to the horizon in front of us. The top of a big orange moon.

The only sound was the sooty terns chirping on the nearby key. We sat and watched, not saying anything as the rest of the moon appeared and it got brighter and brighter. By the time the moon was high in the sky, the island was covered in moonshadows.

I walked back to my tent, not even bothering to use my headlamp. When I crawled inside, the air still was steamy. I had brought a sleeping bag with almost no insulation, but even it was too warm. So I just lay on top of it and listened. I could hear the birds on Bush Key, some people partying on sailboats in the harbor, and something scurrying on the ground right outside the tent.

The previous night, when I heard a similar noise, I got up to pee and saw it was being made by a small crab. I never did see a rat.

I lay there and thought that the island at night would be the memory that would stick with me most. Then I woke up to the first rays of sunlight on my final morning there. When I crawled out of my tent and looked at the harbor, I saw something Mike Jester had described.

Sometimes, he said, it looks like the horizon has disappeared.

This was one of those times. The water was so mirror smooth that it was hard to tell where light blue fluid ended and light blue air began. The boats in the harbor appeared to be floating in midair.

I grabbed the yellow kayak and began paddling away from Garden Key, feeling like I was gliding through an M. C. Escher drawing. I kept waiting for the birds and fish to blend into one another, the fort's staircases and two thousand brick arches to connect in displays of impossible reality.

The first seaplane of the day would be arriving soon, the roar of its engine signaling the arrival of the first wave of another day's visitors. But for now, everything was quiet and calm.

Magnificent frigate birds glided overhead. With a wingspan of eight feet and an average body weight of three pounds, they have the largest wing-to-weight ratio of any bird, explaining how they glide so effortlessly, so slowly. I had read that they could fly for a week without landing. I watched one land on a buoy and thought, *Slacker.*

The frigate birds and sooty terns have selected the Tortugas as their only significant nesting areas in the continental United States. And if the land is gone? That's one of the many unknowns about the future of this place and its inhabitants.

As I paddled, every so often small fish jumped out of the water, temporarily breaking both the surface and the silence. A few dolphins passed through the harbor. And then a half-dozen large fish surfaced about fifty yards away. At first I assumed they were more dolphins. But as they rolled gently yet powerfully out of the water, the early-morning light making their silvery backs seem even shinier, I realized these were tarpon.

I paddled toward their path and they disappeared below the surface. I stopped, expecting to see them emerge again in the distance. Then I heard a splash about twenty yards behind me. They were headed the other direction, rolling into the sunrise.

I looked around—at the red fort, at the blue water/sky, at the silvery fish—and thought about what one of the visitors to this place had written in the register on the dock. Clement S. Barilett of Bordeaux, France. Or at least I think that was the name. I couldn't quite make out the handwriting. And the first part of his message I had to translate.

Le Paradis sur terre! GOD BLESS AMERICA.

Here was a visitor from a place in France renowned for wine and history, declaring this—a place that still doesn't even have freshwater—to be "heaven on earth." And adding "GOD BLESS AMERICA."

A few hours later, it was time to board the ferry.

Mark and Kevin Freund waited until the last minute. As the boat pulled away, the fort fading back into the distance, the father leaned on the railing of the second deck.

"This is the kind of trip where you wake up the next day and say, 'Did this really happen?' " he said.

I agreed.

This is the kind of place that if it is gone in another hundred years—if the fort crumbles, the islands disappear, and the seas turn lifeless—people will be asking, "Did it really exist?"

I'll vouch for it. It did exist. And when the skies were clear and the waters were calm, it was *le paradis sur terre.*

———

I TURNED MY cell phone back on as we approached the dock in Key West.

It got a signal and started vibrating, a couple of days worth of text messages pouring in all at once. I wished I could go back to Garden Key.

There wasn't anything urgent in the messages or e-mails. So I got everything off the ferry, took it to my car in a nearby parking garage, and called home, then to Tucson.

I told Mom about the trip. Camping under the supermoon, snorkeling and kayaking, watching the sun set from atop the fort.

"I'd like to get there someday," she said.

"Mom, you've been there," I said. "You went there with Dad and then you went back with Abe."

"Oh, that's right," she said.

I sat in the car in the parking garage, talking to her about the parks and other things for quite a while.

It wasn't always like this. When I went off to college, we'd go months without talking on the phone. And even when we did, there always was that sense of the long-distance meter running. The conversations were quick and to the point. And I know this wasn't just our family. One of my college friends had a system that he and his parents had worked out to let them know he had made it back to school safely. He would call home collect, using a predetermined made-up name. His parents would decline the call, saving the long-distance charges.

At some point, I started talking to my mom more regularly. Maybe after Dad died. The calls gradually became longer and longer, although I'm not sure any more was said. Talking to my mom on the phone was unlike talking to anyone else. There were these long pauses that I instinctively tried to fill by chattering. But sometimes I just ran out of things to say. And there would be this silence, dead air that drove me crazy.

Mom's diagnosis had changed the way I thought of our calls.

I thought about this while heading north on A1A, in broad day-light this time. And when I got back to Jacksonville, I wrote a column about it for Mother's Day.

We know that next Sunday won't be just another Mother's Day. A phone call and a scribbled note on a Hall-mark card won't do. So what do I say to Mom?

This is hardly a new question, just one with new wrinkles.

I've watched friends go through this. And I've tried to convince myself that now that I'm allegedly grown-up and independent, I should be ready for this. We haven't lived in the same state since I left home for college 30-some years ago. So I'm used to not seeing or talking to Mom.

We get together a few times a year and try to catch up on the phone a few times a month. And, until recently, these conversations were rarely deep. In fact, they'd often include awkward silences. Or at least that's how I'd describe the gaps.

"Should I let you go, Mom?" I'd say when a pause came.

"Maybe," she'd say in a way that seemed to mean not yet. So we'd talk about the weather, the news, the grandkids. But sometimes there would be another lull and maybe another. And Mom still seemed to want to talk. Or not talk. So one time I was determined not to say anything, to make Mom continue the conversation.

I looked at my watch. For two minutes, neither of us said a word.

It's one thing to be sitting in a restaurant and not say anything to someone for two minutes. It's another on the phone. Two minutes feels like forever. During that time, I started pacing impatiently, a voice in my head screaming, "Say something."

Silence never has bothered my mom. To the contrary, she embraces it. When she was first diagnosed with cancer, she

spent a week in the hospital and turned on the television only
once for an hour. I'd walk through the halls and pretty much
every other television was on, some twenty-four hours a day.

I realized recently that when she describes her favorite
places, she talks as much about how they sound as how they
look. They're peaceful, serene, quiet. . . .

There is something to be said for moments of silence, especially in today's cacophonous world. Still, until recently, when
the lulls in the phone conversations with Mom came, the silence inevitably would make me uncomfortable and antsy.

"Should I let you go?"

Now I hear myself saying this and think about how I'm
not ready to let her go. Now I'm grateful for the sound of
her voice and the sound of silence. Now I'm realizing this is
another gift she gave me.

There will come a time when I won't have her for
Mother's Day. And while I'm sure I will miss being able to
hear her voice, it struck me recently that I'll always be able
to hear some of our best conversations.

> In the roar of the Colorado River.
> In the rustling of redwoods.
> In the rhythm of the surf.
> In the squawking of cactus wrens.
> In the stillness of a starry night.

What do you say to Mom on Mother's Day?

In the last few months, we've said plenty. So next Sunday when I see her, I'm hoping to sit with her on the patio,
look at the desert, and do my best to say nothing.

I FLEW TO Tucson on Mother's Day, arriving in time for brunch.

Abe, Mom, and my sister Lisa picked me up at the airport and
we went downtown to the arts district. Beth was on her way from

Mom hiking the Boy Scout Tree Trail in Redwood National and State Parks, California, in the summer of 2011.

Mom and Dad backpacking.

Mom and me—with, as often was the case, a camera around my neck and a Band-Aid on my chin.

Cooking s'mores on one of my many camping trips as a child.

When I wanted to grow up to be Ansel Adams, an astronaut, and a Detroit Tigers baseball player.

The fiftieth birthday trip and a hike to the Boy Scout Tree with my family, Redwood National and State Parks, California.

One of the photos Mia took of Mama, the gray whale, swimming in the Klamath River. *Courtesy of Mia Woods*

Mom and Mia explore the tide pools of Redwood National and State Parks, California.

Mia writes a haiku on the beach at Redwood National and State Parks, California: Fun and family / Camping at the Redwoods Park / Being together

New Year's Day sunrise atop Cadillac Mountain in Maine's Acadia National Park.

Carol Bult and Lili Pew wait for sunrise, staying warm in bivy sacks on top of Cadillac Mountain, Acadia National Park, Maine.

Lili and Carol ride down Cadillac Mountain, passing the icefall, Acadia National Park, Maine.

Getting a tour of the carriage roads from Lili, Acadia National Park, Maine. *Courtesy of Lili Pew*

Saguaros on the King Canyon Trail at Saguaro National Park, Arizona.

Two saguaros, one dying and one healthy, give a reminder of what Edward Abbey noted: In the desert "death and life usually appear close together, sometimes side by side." Saguaro National Park, Arizona.

Standing atop Wasson Peak: Ross Zimmerman, Pam Golden, and Tom Alston. Saguaro National Park, Arizona.

For years, how Mom started nearly every morning: with a walk in the desert. Saguaro National Park, Arizona.

A morning hike from the Grand Canyon's South Rim down the South Kaibab Trail, Grand Canyon National Park, Arizona.

Among the memories brought back by the Colorado River: a rafting trip with Mom through Utah's Canyonlands National Park in 2007.

Taking a leap into the Colorado River in Canyonlands National Park, Utah, 2007.

Mom hangs on through one of the rapids in Cataract Canyon, Canyonlands National Park, Utah, 2007.

Snowfall on the South Rim of the Grand Canyon in Grand Canyon National Park, Arizona.

The view of Lake Powell from the visitor center at the Glen Canyon Dam in Glen Canyon National Recreation Area, Arizona.

The night skies over the historic Navajo Bridge and the new Navajo Bridge, not far from where the Grand Canyon River Guides hold their annual gathering. Glen Canyon National Recreation Area, Arizona.

Park ranger Mike Jester first came to live on Garden Key in 1984. Dry Tortugas National Park, Florida.

Seventy miles from Key West, Fort Jefferson in Dry Tortugas National Park, Florida.

Sunset at Mammoth Hot Springs in Yellowstone National Park, Wyoming.

Steam and storm in Yellowstone National Park, Wyoming.

With my wife and daughter on the boardwalks leading to geysers near Old Faithful, Yellowstone National Park, Wyoming.

A bison wanders through Madison Junction campground in Yellowstone National Park, Wyoming.

Where the bison roam—and have roamed since prehistoric times. Yellowstone National Park, Wyoming.

From Yellowstone, I headed back to Tucson. Mom died June 30. We held a memorial service at the Saguaro National Park visitor center where she volunteered.

Sunrise in Mom's backyard.

Detroit. It was brutally hot. But Mom insisted she wanted to eat outside in a courtyard.

She wore a sweater that kept slipping off her shrinking shoulders. She was noticeably weaker than when I had seen her several weeks earlier. She needed help walking the short distance from the car to the courtyard. And even with help, she shuffled along.

She ordered a salad and then just picked at it.

Her appetite was gone and, Abe said, it was a constant battle to try to get her to keep eating.

Some things hadn't changed, though. As we finished up, she started piling up the dishes and silverware.

"Mom," I said. "You don't have to do that. They have people who are paid to clear the table."

She smiled, continuing to pile up dishes. I shook my head and let her do it.

I was there for a week. And every morning she asked, "So you're leaving today?"

"No, Mom, I'll be here until Saturday," I said, getting frustrated— and then hating myself for getting frustrated.

"Oh, good," she said.

She no longer could take Wally, a wheaten terrier mix, for a morning walk down the hill to a fifty-acre county park. But when she felt up to it, we took the dog, her wheelchair, and her to Feliz Paseos Park. She said she had thought she would hate being stuck in a wheelchair for these walks, but she was learning to enjoy it. She was in the desert, with her dog and family.

While we pushed her around the park's mix of paved and dirt paths, she kept pointing out things along the path, just as she had done on hundreds of hikes through the decades.

One night we decided to rent a movie, *The Descendants,* a George Clooney film set in Hawaii. Mom made it about halfway through before falling asleep. And when we started to watch the second half the next night, she didn't remember much of what we had already seen.

We tried to catch her up. George Clooney's character, Matt King, is an attorney who, as the sole trustee of a family trust, is faced with the decision of whether to sell 25,000 acres of Kauai land, rich in beauty and history, to a developer. His wife is in a coma after a boating accident. He learned she had been having an affair. He is trying to figure out how to be a father to his two daughters. The movie ended with King forgiving his wife before saying good-bye, connecting with his daughters, and—the part I think Mom liked most—deciding not to sell the land to the developer.

It reminded me of a Native American proverb that appeared in Friends of Saguaro material. Mom had cut out: "We do not inherit the earth from our ancestors, we borrow it from our children."

My sisters and I decided to get up early one morning and take Mom to the eastern section of Saguaro National Park. Mom was too weak to get out, but as we drove the Loop Road, she pointed out birds and blooms.

Across the landscape, saguaros were topped with what looked like bouquets—clusters of fist-sized creamy white flowers with yellow centers.

I couldn't recall ever seeing this. I realized that most of my visits to Tucson through the years had been during optimal weather months—basically October through March. The saguaros typically bloom in late April through early June.

It also was a reminder that, in the desert, beauty isn't about youth. A saguaro doesn't produce its first flower until it's about seventy years old. And as it ages, it often becomes more stunning.

We passed one old saguaro—more than a dozen long arms, some of them pointing skyward, others drooping toward the ground—that was decorated with hundreds of flowers. All of which, Mom reminded us, would soon be gone.

Before we finished the drive around the loop, she was lying down in the backseat, asleep. That evening she was sitting on her deck, looking at the desert, watching as the mountain changed colors. I sat down by her and she just smiled and patted my arm.

I thought about what I had pondered while writing the column before coming to Tucson for this trip. What do you say to your mother on your last Mother's Day together?

I cleared my throat and stumbled through trying to say something about not wanting there to be things we wished we had said to each other.

She shook her head. "I don't think we have to worry about that," she said.

And that was it.

We sat there, not saying a thing.

The chatter of birds faded along with the sun. The insects chirped. The brush rustled in the slight breeze. In the distance, a coyote howled.

6

*

JUNE: YELLOWSTONE

$\mathcal{M}$ia lagged behind as two of her cousins raced ahead on the path, excited to be out of the car and exploring our home for the next week: Madison Campground in Yellowstone National Park.

My daughter, now ten and a half—she made a point to remind us when it was her half birthday—was moping, upset that on the drive from the West Yellowstone entrance along the Madison River, one of her cousins had been the first to spot a wild animal.

The three girls had been in the backseat, playing elaborate clapping games and singing along to the tinny music coming from a cell phone—'cause, baby, you're a firework—when Marin or Jadyn spotted elk galloping across the field in the distance. This prompted us to do what every tourist in Yellowstone does the first few hundred times they spot wildlife. Pull over.

We got out binoculars and watched the elk bound through the meadow, then splash through a river.

When we got back in the car, Mia was quiet. She stayed that way as we were checking in at the campground, buying some firewood, and walking down a path to the nearest bathroom.

I caught up with her and prepared to say something that I hoped would defuse whatever was going on. Before I got a chance, she held out her hand, opened it up, and showed me something.

A small rock.

"Remember that book Nana read to us?" she said.

In the months since the trip to the redwoods, I had forgotten about Mom's buying a copy of Byrd Baylor's *Everybody Needs a Rock* in the gift shop at the campground, reading it to her grandchildren, and then watching them each search for their own special rock. One that fits just right in your hand, not too small and not too big. A rock that you find yourself and keep as long as you can, maybe forever.

Mia clearly had not forgotten. The story or Nana's reading it to her.

I knew that this was where I was supposed to tell her that we don't remove anything from the national parks, that if everyone took a souvenir—even a little one—the place wouldn't be the same for the kids who come in the future.

But I didn't say that.

"That's a very nice rock," I said. "I'm sure that Nana would be very happy that you remembered the story."

And that was it. Whatever storm was brewing inside her had passed. She sprinted ahead to catch up with her cousins, her right hand fisted, holding her rock.

I stood there for a minute. When Toni caught up, I tried to tell her what had just happened. Before I even got out a word, my voice cracked.

We had been in the park for less than an hour. And I already knew that I was wrong about Yellowstone. Wrong to wonder if it was just some overhyped piece to the national park puzzle. Wrong to be having traveler's remorse, thinking if I was going to be able to take my wife and daughter on only one of these trips, maybe it should have been to Zion or Yosemite or Glacier.

I was in the right place. And not just the right park. The right part of the park. Madison Junction.

This would become my favorite place in Yellowstone National Park. Not one of the geyser basins or the Grand Canyon of the Yellowstone or Mammoth Hot Springs or the top of Mount Washburn or any of the other places that far exceeded my expectations.

It would become my favorite spot because—and I had no idea

of this when I made the campsite reservation months earlier—it was the perfect spot to symbolize the future of the national parks. Because it was a spot that, in unplanned ways, had come to represent the messy, complicated past and present of Yellowstone and the National Park Service.

This was where it all began with a campfire in 1870.

Or so the story of Yellowstone and the national parks—promoted and perpetuated by the park and the park service—went for seventy-five years.

The truth was like history itself. Complicated.

The past wasn't simple. The present wasn't simple. And if one thing seemed certain about the future of this place and that of every other national park, it was that it wouldn't be simple.

That's why this became my favorite place. Well, that and because it was stunningly beautiful in the early morning light, with steam rising off the winding water.

And because this is where Mia found her rock.

And where she eventually left it.

I INITIALLY WASN'T as excited about going to Yellowstone as I was about some other parks. It seemed more like a mandatory stop. If I was trying to look into the future of the national parks, at some point I had to go to where it all started, to the first national park in the world, established on March 1, 1872.

I had gone to Yellowstone once before, as a child, near the end of a cross-country road trip. While I have vivid memories of other national parks on that trip, I don't remember anything about Yellowstone beyond Old Faithful, heat, and crowds.

I asked my mom about that back in February, when she first was in the hospital after being diagnosed, her memory still clear.

"We only spent one full day there," she said. "We couldn't get into any of the campgrounds in the park. So we stayed at a KOA. And the bugs were horrible."

It reminded me that if you spend a few hours in a national park, you check it off a list. If you spend a few days, you develop an attachment that lasts a long time, maybe even a lifetime. If you spend more than that, you become an advocate, a defender, an evangelist.

I was going to spend two weeks here this time—one with my family, one meeting with people inside and outside the park.

On that first day, Toni and I were setting up the tent. We had crawled inside it when Mia came running up.

"There's a bison!" she said.

Mia was at a stage where she loved to play games that involved tricking her parents. When one of us came home from work, she would pretend to be asleep, waiting for us to comment on her falling asleep very early, before popping up and chattering away about something. She would say that they got their test results at school and, with a mock frown, say she didn't do very well, then grin and tell us that she got a 100.

So I assumed that this was just the Yellowstone version of that. She was the girl who cried bison.

"Oh, yeah," I said, not even bothering to look.

"No, really," she said. "There's a bison right there, in the campground."

I eventually crawled out of the tent. And sure enough, there was a bison, about five campsites away. He was grazing on some grass, right next to an RV. The hump on his back came up to the driver's side window. He was huge. And by adult bison standards, he was just an average Joe. It's one thing to read that a bison is the largest land mammal in North America—that males weigh up to two thousand pounds and females up to a thousand. It's another to see one.

We would see hundreds of bison, grazing in fields, crossing roads, lying by streams. But this was the first we saw. And Mia had proudly spotted him.

The next day we got the obligatory trip to Old Faithful out of the way. We pulled into the huge parking lot and made our way toward the geyser with hundreds of other people. After watching

Old Faithful erupt, drawing the kinds of oohs and aahs that brought to mind Fourth of July fireworks, we took a walk along the nearby boardwalks, passing by a variety of Yellowstone's geothermal features, including one geyser named Old Tardy.

At one point, we came across evidence that bison had been here too.

"Is that poop?" Mia asked.

"Yes," I said.

"*All* of that?" she said.

"Yes," I said.

"Awesome," she said.

She pulled out her camera, framed the poop on the screen, and pressed the button. It beeped. She looked at the image and grinned. A few minutes later, she realized her camera's memory card was almost full. She had to decide whether to take pictures of geysers or poop. And although she was enjoying the geysers more than she expected, it wasn't really much of a choice.

"Wait till I show my friends this," she said, snapping another picture of bison poop.

IN THE EVENING, after cooking dinner at the campsite, we walked down a hill to an amphitheater for a ranger talk.

The sun was setting in the background. The ranger gave the weather forecast for the next day—cloudy and breezy, a high of 62, a 50 percent chance of precipitation—followed by a reminder about food storage in the campground.

Then she started to sing.

"Oh, give me a home, where the buffalo roam . . ."

She gave some statistics about the wild bison—scientifically called *Bison bison,* commonly called the American bison, and often referred to simply as buffalo. They stand about six feet tall and can leap as high. They can run thirty miles per hour. They have horns, both males and females, and unlike the elk and moose, they don't shed them each year. Their mating season is July and August. The gestation period is nine to nine and a half months. The babies are born in the spring. And once upon a time, tens of millions of them roamed from the Pacific Ocean to Appalachia.

In the late 1800s, bison were hunted almost to extinction. Indian tribes had been hunting the bison for centuries, but in a way that the bison population continued to thrive and provide for future generations. Which is exactly why the U.S. Army launched a campaign to eliminate bison. It saw it as a way to control the Indians. And what bison the U.S. government didn't kill, poachers took care of.

There is only one place in America where the bison have lived continuously since prehistoric times: the land that is now Yellowstone National Park.

When the park was created in 1872, there were about a thousand bison there. But despite efforts by the Army, which fought to protect bison from poachers when it took over management of the park in 1886, those numbers continued to dwindle rapidly.

A turning point came in 1894, when the Army caught poacher Ed Howell removing the head of one of five bison carcasses.

At the campfire program, when the ranger told the story of Howell's capture and the coverage in *Field & Stream* magazine, she put a photo on the screen that prompted Mia and her cousins to start whispering.

"Scary," one of them said.

In the photo, four members of the U.S. Army's 6th Cavalry are posing with what they seized from Howell: seven bison heads.

This moment sparked action in Washington. Still, by 1902, the population of bison in Yellowstone was down to about two dozen, most of which were found in a remote part of the park known as Pelican Valley.

Few people had ever seen a wild bison. Think about that, the ranger said, when you get stuck in a bison jam.

When the ranger talk ended, it was pitch-black. We turned on our flashlights and found our way on the path leading up the hill and back to the campground. The temperature dropped quickly. Even though summer was officially right around the corner, it was getting into the low thirties at night.

Mia's sleeping bag was in the middle of our four-person tent, sandwiched between mine and Toni's. When she crawled into it at night, she put on a stocking cap and zipped it up completely, leaving just a small circle exposing her eyes, nose and mouth. We told her she could go sleep with her cousins in the pop-up trailer, which not only had beds up off the ground but had a heater Uncle Keith turned on at night.

"No," she said. "I want to be a real camper."

We told her that sleeping in the trailer *was* camping, and that we'd still consider her a real camper if she spent a night or two with her cousins, the daughters of Toni's sister, Jan. Still, I was kind of happy that she was determined to spend every night in the tent, sleeping on the ground between her parents, in temperatures that to a born-in-Florida girl were downright frigid.

At some point in the middle of this night, Mia woke up crying. Not because she was cold. Because she was having nightmares about the photo in the ranger talk, the one of the row of bison heads.

"Hold my hand, Daddy," she said.

She had unzipped her sleeping bag enough to stick out her right hand.

I unzipped mine enough to stick out my left hand.

We lay there, holding hands.

Hers felt small.

I thought about when she was a baby and wrapped all of her tiny fingers around one of my index fingers. Which made me think about taking her to preschool and how, every morning for weeks, I had to pry her little hand off my wrist. I'd successfully get one of her hands off and she'd latch on with the other. There were times when this went on for ten minutes, and it felt like an eternity.

When she went to elementary school, she didn't want to carpool. She wanted me to walk her in, holding her hand. At first I had to walk her all the way to her classroom. Slowly but surely that changed, with her letting go of my hand and giving me a kiss about twenty yards from her classroom, then at the end of the sidewalk, then agreeing that carpooling was fine.

My friends with teenagers said to enjoy it while it lasts, that it was only a matter of time before she'd be asking me to drop her off blocks away from school.

So when she fell asleep, still holding my hand, I didn't let go.

SHORTLY BEFORE TWO A.M., a sound jolted me awake. In my grogginess, I tried to process what it was. The wail of a siren? No. This sound was being made by something living. Or maybe dying. I thought it was a woman screaming. As I wondered if I should do something, I realized this sound wasn't human. It was coming from an animal. It was farther away than I had originally imagined. Maybe down by the rivers, perhaps even farther. It was hard to tell. Even so, it still sounded remarkably nearby.

Toni woke up too. But somehow Mia slept right through it.

The next morning I stopped in the ranger station and tried to describe the sound. Without hesitation, one of the rangers said it was a coyote. I trusted his expertise, but it sounded unlike any coyote I had ever heard in Tucson. I was used to an almost doglike yip-yip howl. I wouldn't have described this as a howl. It was more of a scream, wild and primal. And it was one piece of everyday sensory experience that made me quickly fall in love with Yellowstone.

It was June 15, Mom's seventy-fourth birthday. After breakfast, I drove out of the park, back to West Yellowstone, to get a cell signal so I could call Tucson. As the phone rang, I braced myself.

It seemed like whenever I called from one of my stops on the road—going back to that one at Glen Canyon Dam—there was bad news.

"Hello," said my sister Lisa.

Lisa had taken leave from her job with the VA in Reno. She and her daughter, Sophie, were spending the summer in Tucson with Mom. Sophie was fifteen years old. I wondered how this was affecting her. It was hard enough for an adult to deal with. And I often felt like I wasn't even dealing with it: I was off with my family, roaming with the buffalo, while my sisters and Sophie were taking care of Mom.

"Things are pretty rough," Lisa said in a weary voice. "Mom is really, really confused."

I wondered if I should cut the trip short and head to Tucson. A hospice nurse had told Lisa that Mom didn't have much time left. I was a bit skeptical. And not necessarily because I was in denial. A couple of months earlier, a different hospice nurse had told us it was only a matter of weeks. I had flown to Tucson, wondering if it would be the last time I would see her alive. I had been there several times since. And while Mom's body certainly continued to deteriorate, she also continued to defy everyone's predictions.

I was quite aware that I wasn't the only one losing parents, that a wave of baby boomers were also reaching a similar point in life.

When I had headed to Yellowstone, the cover of the *Time* magazine issue on newsstands read "How to Die: What I Learned from the Last Days of My Mom and Dad." This came on the heels of the March issue of *New York* magazine and a cover that read, "Mom, I Love You. I Also Wish You Were Dead. And I Expect You Do, Too." And while I was in Yellowstone, *The New York Times* ran a story that tied together these two covers and other essays and books about baby boomers dealing with caring for and losing parents.

In his *Time* piece, Joe Klein had quite a few thought-provoking observations about the way our medical system handles death and dying. But the line that stuck with me was about how we, the children, handle it. Klein described the process as "this passage toward my own maturity."

I realized that in many ways, that's what I was already mourning. It wasn't just the impending loss of a parent. It was a more selfish loss, of my own childhood and youth. Yes, I was fifty and now grudgingly had an AARP card in my wallet (although I couldn't bring myself to use it to get any of the "senior" discounts). But in many ways, I still felt like I was closer to childhood than adulthood. Not having any living parents changes that. It instantly tips the teeter-totter of your own life-span.

I read some of these stories and essays about losing parents, taking some comfort in the reminder of the ubiquitousness of this experience and trying to learn from how others navigated through it. Klein wrote, "We grieve in different ways, and my way, I guess, is to write about it."

At the time I didn't write much about it or anything. I've always envied people who say writing comes easily. For me, it always was more than hard. It was painful. So I didn't grieve by writing. At least not initially. I grieved by going to a place like Yellowstone and experiencing, exploring, thinking.

In Yellowstone, I tried to think about the most basic question for this place and the hundreds that followed: What is a national park?

THIS IS A question the National Park Service has been grappling with since August 25, 1916, the day President Woodrow Wilson signed into law the Organic Act, creating a new Department of the Interior agency to oversee 5.5 million acres of America.

Before this, there was a loose collection of national parks, each managed individually, some by the United States Army. Repeated efforts to pull the parks together under one agency had died in Congress, typically after intense lobbying by those who saw the potential to make money off that land. Stephen Mather, the wealthy industrialist and conservationist who became the first NPS director, took the same argument—there are dollars in these hills and forests and rivers—and used it to push for a national park system. He said that by *not* creating one, America was missing an economic opportunity.

"This Nation is richer in natural scenery of the first order than any other nation, but it does not know it," he wrote. "It possesses an empire of grandeur and beauty which it scarcely has heard of. It owns the most inspiring playgrounds and the best equipped nature schools in the world and is serenely ignorant of the fact. In its national parks it has neglected, because it has quite overlooked, an economic asset of incalculable value."

The public—from schoolchildren to chambers of commerce to newspaper editorial writers—rallied around the idea. And Congress finally agreed, partly because of the way the mission of the National Park Service was framed: with an inherent paradox, the beginning of an ongoing tug-of-war between the present and the future and two words: "enjoyment" and "unimpaired."

The Organic Act created the National Park Service, saying its purpose was "to conserve the scenery and the natural and historic objects and the wild life therein and to provide for the enjoyment of the same in such manner and by such means as will leave them unimpaired for the enjoyment of future generations."

When I met with NPS director Jonathan Jarvis, he said, "Try to find anybody else who has been given the legal mandate to provide enjoyment. And for future generations."

If either of these mandates—providing enjoyment now or preserving for the future—is carried to its extreme, it harms the other. So this leads to a never-ending balancing act, one I believe works. But some whose opinions I certainly value, including some retired park service employees who have spent decades walking this tightrope, say it's time to rethink the Organic Act.

One of the books I read before beginning the year was *Uncertain Path: A Search for the Future of National Parks,* by William Tweed. After finishing a thirty-year career as the chief park naturalist at Sequoia and Kings Canyon National Parks, Tweed hiked the John Muir and High Sierra trails in California, contemplating the future of the parks. One of his conclusions: The park service must abandon something that has been at its core.

For much of the last hundred years, national parks were created and managed with the goal of taking what was within their boundaries and freezing it in time. And not just any time. A time before European settlers. Tweed and others argue that this idea of a Virgin Continent is a myth, one that is much larger and more dangerous than a story about a bunch of explorers gathering around a campfire in Wyoming and hatching plans for a national park. It not only ignores the history and impact of large populations of Native Americans but discounts centuries of perpetual change.

At the end of his hike and book, Tweed asks: "Can national parks evolve successfully in a world where nearly all of their founding assumptions have been proven wrong?"

OUR NATIONAL PARKS—and the way we manage and experience them—certainly are capable of evolving. Perhaps nowhere is that more evident than Yellowstone.

It's a place where tourists used to gather nightly to watch bears feed at garbage dumps; where predators were treated like large pests and exterminated upon sight; where the instinctive reaction to a wildfire was to extinguish it as quickly as possible.

When I was there, smoke was visible in several parts of the park. Signs let visitors know that officials were aware of these fires and, at least for now, were letting them burn. Partly because of what has happened in Yellowstone—the devastating fires of 1988 were partially the result of a century of fire suppression—we have drastically changed the way we manage fires.

The bear shows long ago went the way of other traditions that, while often quite popular, now feel more befitting for a roadside attraction in Florida than for a national park. And as the park service approached its centennial, perhaps no animal symbolized the challenges of the future quite like the one that symbolized its past. The animal on the patch. The bison.

It's tempting to say that imagining Yellowstone without the

bison would be like imagining it without Old Faithful. But that doesn't do justice to the bison. There are other geysers. There are no other bison quite like the ones that roam Yellowstone.

Early park leaders wanted to save the nearly extinct bison. But their methods and motives weren't always built on conservation. Philetus Norris, who served as Yellowstone's second superintendent from 1877 to 1882, envisioned a future where domesticated bison herds became perpetual cash cows for the park.

In 1919, three years after the National Park Service was created, management of Yellowstone was turned over to Horace Albright, a man whose name is all over the national parks, but whose legacy is as complex as the parks' history. Albright was among those who embraced and nourished the story that the national parks were born around a campfire at Madison Junction. And when it came to wildlife management, his approach might be summed up by a famous picture of him sitting at a wooden table, having dinner with three bears. In *To Save the Wild Bison,* Mary Ann Franke wrote: "Albright regarded wildlife largely as a tourist attraction and never embraced the goal of protecting an untouched nature. Rather like the man who puts a woman on a pedestal so he can look up her skirt, Albright protected wildlife so that visitors could enjoy seeing it at close range, even if it meant sacrificing the animals' dignity and autonomy."

At Mammoth Hot Springs, near the north entrance of the park, you still can find remnants of concrete pens where bison were kept on display for tourists, more like zoo animals than wildlife. Today the pens are gone but the bison more than remain.

The park service estimated the park's bison population—once down to a couple of dozen—to be up to 4,230, including 600 calves born that spring.

All of these bison were wild, free to roam wherever they pleased. Inside the park. It's when Yellowstone bison step across a park boundary—as they often do during the winter—that things get complicated and contentious.

To understand why, you have to go back to 1916. The same year the National Park Service was born, the United States Livestock Sanitary Association was creating the Committee on Contagious Abortion in Cattle. The concern was a disease called brucellosis, which causes spontaneous abortion in cattle.

In the spring of 1917, two bison in one of Yellowstone's herds miscarried. Testing revealed *Brucella abortus,* the bacterial organism that produces brucellosis. Today about half of the Yellowstone bison test positive for *Brucella.* And while there hadn't been a single case of brucellosis being transmitted from bison to cattle in the wild, there had been nonstop dilemmas and border battles.

For decades, the border between Yellowstone National Park and the state of Montana, while invisible to the bison, represented a clear line in the snow for humans. Bison that followed their natural migratory instinct, heading to lower ground in the north and to the west in the winter, were protected—until they left the park.

In 2000, the federal government and the state of Montana agreed to the Interagency Bison Management Plan, allowing some bison to occupy winter ranges on public land in Montana. When I arrived in Yellowstone more than a decade later, the IBMP was still in place, with some adjustments, and still managing to anger people on both sides of the battle—from ranchers who didn't want bison to be protected when they left the park, to bison advocates who said they should be able to roam everywhere.

I spent one day west of the park, at the Buffalo Field Campaign headquarters, and the next to the north, at the Kinkie family ranch. The two places offered wildly different settings and viewpoints. Even when nearly empty, the BFC headquarters had a frenetic, Greenpeace-on-the-plains vibe, with an old bus, a Chevy Suburban named Jackson Browne (it was donated by the singer), tepees, and log cabins where walls were adorned with bumper stickers that said things like "Buffalo poop, Buffalo poop . . . all over this land!" In sharp contrast, the Kinkie ranch house was spotless and uncluttered, with animal heads on the walls.

The two places did have a couple of things in common. Stunningly beautiful views and contempt for the park service.

It illustrated what Dave Hallac, chief of the Yellowstone Center for Resources, had told me a couple of days earlier when I met him in one of the dozens of buildings at Mammoth Hot Springs that date back to the days of Fort Yellowstone and the U.S. military's running the park. When I asked Hallac the same questions I asked at every park—What do you think this place will look like in the future?—I expected him to talk about the seemingly never-ending debates about how to manage what happens in Yellowstone's 2.2 million acres. Snowmobiles and kayaks, grizzly bears and wolves, cell towers and personal drones.

But he started by talking about how the challenges will come on the boundaries and beyond.

"I can show you a map," he said, pointing to one on the wall.

We can see the boundaries, he said. But a butterfly or a bison can't. And while it doesn't create much of a fuss when a butterfly crosses that line, the bison are another story.

I mentioned to Hallac that I was trying to write about the bison, because it's such an iconic animal in American history, and it's on the patch on his uniform . . .

"And I spend all my time on it?" he said with a laugh. "I talk a lot with my staff about managing bison, and it is incredibly easy to get depressed over it, because it is a challenge, and it's political and it's contentious and it requires a lot of resources and a lot of hard work. And some days staff feel as if they're banging their heads against the wall. But what I constantly remind them is bison management in Yellowstone National Park is one of the great conservation successes of America—and of the world."

ON ONE OF their final mornings in the park, Mia and her cousins walked down to the hill from the Madison Junction campground to the small, rustic building on the edge of the meadow.

When the stone and log structure was built in 1929, it was supposed to be a shrine to the birthplace of the national parks. But once the story behind that birth was debunked by Yellowstone historian Aubrey Haines, the building lost its lofty status and eventually was relegated to being a place where Junior Ranger badges were handed out. Or at least that's how another historian described its evolution, upsetting one of the rangers who now handed out badges there.

Bob Hamilton, a retired teacher who spends part of the year at Big Bend and part at Yellowstone, figured that what happens at the Madison Information Station these days—educating and exciting a future generation of park visitors—is at the heart of the park's mission and survival.

On this sunny morning, Hamilton told Mia and about a dozen other kids the story of the wolves. How by 1926 they were wiped out in the park. How they were reintroduced in 1995. How when they were brought back, there was controversy and conflict, especially when they left the park and killed cattle. He didn't vilify the ranchers. If anything, as a kid who grew up on a farm, he hinted at empathy. But he wanted the kids to think about what happened in Yellowstone when wolves returned.

He held out his hand, his thumb pointed sideways, asking the children to guess what happened to populations of other animals.

Elk, up or down? . . . Way down, but the ones left are healthier.

Coyotes, up or down? . . . Down because of wolves.

Ground squirrels? . . . Up because of fewer coyotes.

Hawks and eagles? . . . Up because there are more ground squirrels.

Pronghorn? . . . Up, because wolves can't catch them and there are fewer coyotes.

Beavers? . . . Way up because with fewer elk, the willows return along the rivers.

Ducks, ospreys, songbirds . . . up, up, up.

He went on, detailing the ripple effect made by the return of one animal known for killing other animals.

He said a visitor came in one day and said she had the solution to the problems when wolves left the park. Just build a fifteen-foot fence around the whole park.

"If you did that, what happens?" he said, describing winter at Madison Junction with eight feet of snow and 40-below temperatures. "Those that are trapped inside perish, and that are outside can't get in to feed. Then you haven't got a park anymore. You have Disneyland Wyoming. You might as well put water slides at Old Faithful because you're going to turn it into something it's not."

What it is, he said, is a pretty special place.

A place where life leads to death and death leads to life.

I LEFT YELLOWSTONE, passing through the Roosevelt Arch at the north entrance, and instead of flying from Bozeman to Florida as planned, went to Arizona.

Abe picked me up at the airport. We parked in the garage and I entered the house through the laundry room.

"Hello?" I said.

Lisa came from another part of the house. She looked exhausted. But she managed a smile when she saw me—and said that when Mom had heard my voice, she had a big smile.

I went into the small room at the back of the house that had been Mom's office. Now it was basically her bedroom, living room, and dining room. A hospital bed had been set up next to a couch.

Mom wasn't in the bed. She was sitting on the couch. And at first I thought that this wasn't as bad as I had feared. She looked frail. But she was sitting there. She was smiling.

But then I went over to her. I sat down next to her and gave her a hug. She looked at me. Intensely. Her eyes staring at mine. And she started to cry. A quiet, rasping cry. The tears started to roll down her face.

She looked like she wanted to say something. But no words came out.

Lisa said they were just about to use the bathroom. My sister put her hands under my mom's arms and lifted her to her feet and helped her slowly shuffle to a bathroom that was attached to the office.

I offered to help but mostly just stood there, watching, shocked, realizing Lisa had been doing this for a while.

How did this happen? Last fall I was hiking through the redwoods with Mom. Six miles. Now she can't make it six feet without help? My birthday was the next day. I was going to turn fifty-one. A year earlier, as I prepared to turn fifty, I felt much younger than my age. At fifty-one, I suddenly felt much older.

My youngest sister, Beth, arrived. Paul and Dolores Ghodes, friends of my parents going back to when they all lived in Wisconsin, brought her. They also brought photos of trips to national parks they had done with my mom. Acadia, Rainier, Big Bend, Olympic, and, just last fall, Yellowstone.

When I saw those pictures, it hit me that her last national park was going to be America's first, the one I had just left.

We went for a walk through the neighborhood in the late afternoon. Mom, slumped over in her wheelchair, didn't speak. But she seemed to be happy looking at and smelling the desert. And she smiled when I said she had found a good dog in Wally.

A hospice nurse that stopped by the house told us that she was surprised Mom was still hanging on. She said she had seen this before, and the person usually is waiting for something or someone. Had we all said our good-byes? Had we given her permission to go?

This bothered me a bit. I knew the nurse meant well, but we had said our good-byes. We had given her permission to go. We had assured her that, while we'd miss her terribly, we'd be okay.

I didn't think she was waiting for anything.

I thought she didn't want to die. Plain and simple.

When her body began to deteriorate, she certainly didn't have the heart and lungs of an average seventysomething. Until the past few months, she hadn't had a sedentary day in her life. Those lungs, that heart, were keeping her going longer than expected.

We decided to take turns sleeping on the couch next to Mom in her office. Once she no longer could get out of bed, we moved the bed into the middle of the living room—where the big windows gave her a view of the desert and the mountains.

Wally often hopped into the bed with her, curling up in the space behind her bent knees.

She was in and out of being aware of those around her. We gave her water with an eyedropper. At one point, when Beth asked her if she wanted anything, she tried to say something.

"I . . . want to . . . ," she said.

She paused and tried again.

"I want to . . . go . . . home."

"Home?" Beth said. "You are home. Where is home?"

Mom swallowed and began working on getting out a single word, the state where she grew up.

"Illinois," she said.

The next morning, June 27, I got up early and went for a hike in the mountains behind Mom's house. I saw nine deer bounding through a small canyon and two hot-air balloons floating in the distance. The desert seemed greener than usual, as if it had sucked up every drop of rain from the monsoons.

When I got home, I sat down by Mom. After initially not showing any sign of even knowing I was there, she stirred slightly and opened her eyes.

"Can I get you something?" I asked.

She nodded her head emphatically. Well, as emphatically as was physically possible at this point.

She swallowed and worked to get the words out. "Ice . . . cream."

I went into the kitchen and scooped a dish of homemade ice cream.

We had made it on my birthday, continuing a family tradition. While I was growing up, we made homemade ice cream for every birthday. And all five of our birthdays, starting with my mom's and ending with my dad's, fell in a six-week span in June and July. Summers meant ice cream, churned with an old-fashioned (even then), hand-cranked ice-cream maker.

The wood exterior was warped and weathered, the result of years of being packed with ice and salt. A latch that was supposed to hold one end of the crank in place was rusty and loose, making the already difficult task of cranking even harder.

We'd take turns at it. At first I'd have to use what little weight and muscle I had to even budge the metal cylinder in the middle of the ice. But as the rock salt started to melt the ice, making it conform to the shape of the container, it would become easier and easier to crank. When it started to become harder again, this was a sign that the ice cream was thickening. Eventually Dad would pull out the metal container, carefully remove the top and—voilà—there it was. This thick, creamy ice cream that tasted better than anything you could buy anywhere. And the birthday boy or girl got first dibs on licking the paddle.

When we made the ice cream at Mom's house, it felt like we were cheating. The churn was electric. No cranking necessary. But the result still tasted like childhood summers.

I sat back down next to Mom with a bowl of it and fed her a small spoonful. She was extremely jaundiced and thin and her teeth and tongue were coated in something. She hadn't been interested in eating much of anything for days. But she clearly appreciated this. She let the ice cream melt on her tongue and then swallowed, ready for another bite.

"It's my birthday ice cream," I said as I put it on her tongue.

I immediately wished I hadn't said this, because she immediately started crying. Her body was so dehydrated I wouldn't have thought it could still produce tears.

She took her left arm, the one closest to me, and slowly moved it toward me, hugging my head with it.

"It's okay," I said. "It's okay."

I thought about this and changed my mind.

"No," I said. "It's not okay. It makes me angry and frustrated and sad."

She nodded again, even more emphatically than when I had asked if I could get her something.

I wondered if maybe this is what she had needed to hear. Not good-byes and assurances that we were all going to be okay. Acknowledgment that this wasn't okay, that it wasn't fair, and that if we had our way we'd turn the clock back. Maybe back to hiking in the redwoods, maybe all the way back to the summer days of cranking homemade ice cream in our garage in Wisconsin.

IT WAS MONSOON season. Every afternoon we could see and feel the storms brewing seemingly all around us. Sometimes, when the winds kicked up, we could even smell the rain. But it kept missing us. Then one afternoon it finally made it to us, a powerful downpour that doused the desert.

Some of Mom's closest friends stopped by to sit with her. One of them brought a friend with a guitar and sang to her. We eventually convinced Abe to sing to Mom too. I did not sing. Mom already was suffering enough.

But eventually I joined my sisters in something they had been doing, something that Mom had done countless times with each of us—reading aloud to her.

I'd walk through the living room and hear my sisters reading everything from *The No. 1 Ladies' Detective Agency* to the Bible.

There were plenty of options to choose from. Mom had books everywhere in her house. I went into the guest bedroom and thought about what you can learn about someone by looking at her bookshelves. Or what you could learn before the days of Kindles and Nooks.

On the left end of one shelf there was a worn paperback copy of John Irving's *A Prayer for Owen Meany* right next to a hardcover copy of the same book. Dad loved that book. And after he gave me a copy of it when I was in college, so did I.

Next to these were *The Jim Chee Mysteries,* by Tony Hillerman; *The Deputy,* by Rolf Hochhuth; *Les Misérables,* by Victor Hugo; *Zorba the Greek* and *The Last Temptation of Christ,* by Nikos Kazantzakis; *To Dance with the White Dog,* by Terry Kay; *Lake Wobegon Days,* by Garrison Keillor; *The Mermaid Chair,* by Sue Monk Kidd; *Bag of Bones,* by Stephen King; *Animal Dreams,* by Barbara Kingsolver; *Mexico,* by James Michener; *To Kill a Mockingbird,* by Harper Lee; *Davita's Harp* and five other books by Chaim Potok; *Blessings,* by Anna Quindlen; *Ashana,* by E. P. Roesch; *Empire Falls,* by Richard Russo; *The Grapes of Wrath,* by John Steinbeck; several hardcover copies of *The No. 1 Ladies' Detective Agency* series by Alexander McCall Smith; and more—all leading to the far right end of the shelf and a fat paperback copy of *Anna Karenina,* by Leo Tolstoy.

I scanned that shelf and the ones above and below it. I considered pulling down *You're Only Old Once!: A Book for Obsolete Children,* by Dr. Seuss. But when I went into Mom's office and looked at the bookshelves there—mostly related to travel, nature, and the national parks—one book jumped out at me.

I took it off the shelf, went out in the living room and started reading to Mom.

"Everybody needs a rock . . ."

I told her about how, while in Yellowstone, Mia had recalled being in the redwoods and having her read that book to her. And how Mia had found her rock in Yellowstone. And how after a ranger gave a Junior Ranger talk about how we don't leave our garbage in the park and we don't take things from it, she had left her rock.

At some point, I decided Byrd Baylor was right. Everybody does need a rock. Even adults. And maybe not just a metaphorical rock, like faith or family. Those certainly are useful. But there's something to be said for having a real rock, one you stand on and touch and call your own. Like the granite atop Cadillac Mountain.

Or the layers of the Grand Canyon. Or a piece of sand in the Dry Tortugas. And thanks to Mom and Dad, I knew where to find these rocks. And where to leave them.

THERE WAS ANOTHER book. It wasn't on a bookshelf. Mom took it with her whenever she traveled. It was by her bed now.

It was pocket-size, its soft black leather cover worn and tattered, a page marker dangling beneath it. On the front, in gold letters, it simply said, *New Testament Psalms.*

"Look inside," my sister said.

I flipped open the cover and instantly recognized the handwriting, the letters neatly drawn with black ink. Dad always loved fountain pens. It was one of his very few indulgences. He did calligraphy for fun. But even when he was just penning basic notes, his writing was impeccable, an attribute I did not inherit from him.

I started to read what he had written, realizing it was a Valentine's Day gift, from a time before my sisters and I were born, before they were married. They had grown up several blocks from each other in Rock Island, Illinois. But they didn't start dating until after high school. Their first kiss was atop a tower at an American Baptist retreat in Green Lake, Wisconsin. I knew this because, after Dad died, Mom and I went for a trip that included a stop at Green Lake.

> *Feb. 14, 1957*
> *Nancy,*
> *This Bible is a symbol of two loves. First it is a symbol of God's love for all men as shown through His Son. And secondly, this Bible is a symbol of my love for you. All that I have, imperfect as it may be, is yours.*
> *Rex*

Six months later, after a boat ride on the Mississippi River, Vernon Rex Woods took Nancy Kay Hackett to a park and proposed.

When I was an adult, and old enough to learn that life was more complicated than it appears, my mother told me that her mother wasn't thrilled by the engagement. She thought that at nineteen, the oldest of her five daughters was too young. And she didn't know about her tying her future to a minister and his limited earning potential. But they went ahead and got married the following summer. June 28. This very date.

I realized that while sitting next to Mom's bed in the living room, rereading what Dad had written. They would have been celebrating their fifty-fourth anniversary, and since it also was my sister's birthday, we all would have been eating homemade ice cream.

WHEN IT WAS my turn to sleep on the couch in the living room, I couldn't sleep.

Mom's breathing was so labored, so loud. It was that way during the day too, but then it was part of the sounds of the house. People talking, dishes clanking, coffee brewing, the television playing, the phone ringing, Mom breathing.

But at night, it was the only noise. Raspy breath sucked in. Pause. Raspy breath forced out. Pause.

I started pacing, crying. This wasn't what I had imagined when she opted to forgo chemo and start palliative care. I pictured a peaceful ending. This seemed so hard, so cruel. I had reached the point I had heard others describe when talking about losing parents.

I wanted Mom to die.

ON JUNE 29, a Friday night, it was Lisa's turn to sleep on the couch in the living room with Mom. I slept on the foldout couch in Mom's office. At 3:30 A.M., Lisa woke me up.

She said Mom's breathing had really slowed.

She went in the guest room and got Beth.

We gathered around the bed with Abe. After days of hearing

Mom forcing every breath in and out, it appeared she wasn't breathing at all.

I wondered if that was it, if we had barely missed being at her side when she took her last breath.

Then her chest rose and she took another deep breath.

And that was it.

I kissed her on the forehead, as I had kissed Dad's forehead sixteen years earlier. I was grateful that this time the forehead was warm.

I stepped outside. It was 4:30 A.M. Even at this hour, the air in Tucson was warm. There were still some stars in the sky, but an orangish, pinkish light was starting to appear above the mountains. Birds whistled. Insects chirped.

I remembered how when Dad died, seeing life go on had made me angry. How could people go about their lives like it was just another day? This was different. Seeing the sun rise, hearing the life in the desert. That helped.

At 7:40 A.M., two men from the mortuary came. They asked if we wanted to say anything else. We shook our heads. They covered her body and wheeled it out the front door.

The door had barely closed in front of us when, behind us, there was a sudden and loud THUD.

A bird had flown into one of the big windows facing the desert. It was lying on the concrete, lifeless.

A mourning dove.

7

JULY: GATEWAY NATIONAL RECREATION AREA

 few sunrises later, several dozen people gathered on the observation deck behind the visitor center at Saguaro National Park's western district.

Several rows of concrete benches were full. Some people brought folding chairs. Some stood. The sun was just starting to peek over the mountains, and sunshine was streaming toward the faces of those gathered, casting long shadows from the saguaros dotting the landscape and giving the first taste of another hot July day in Tucson.

"Nancy didn't want a traditional service where lots of people spoke," the Reverend Alison Harrington said. "She knew the limits of language and that at times words fail us and that sometimes it is better to fill the space with silence. And Nancy loved the outdoors. So we have gathered here in this beautiful place to remember our dear Nancy."

We sang a hymn. Lisa and Abe read scripture readings. We sang another hymn. Then Alison explained that we were going to remember Nancy Woods not with words, but with silence. And not your traditional, heads-bowed moment of silence.

We were going to take a walk in the desert.

"Nancy knew the great truth that God is not only revealed through his son Jesus Christ and the scriptures and prophets, but in nature itself," she said. "And so we are going to hear what wisdom the cactus and the birds and the morning sun and the mountains can share with us this morning. So you are encouraged to take a walk along a trail . . . And you are encouraged to hold the silence as we walk the trail.

"So, Abe, would you like to lead us out to the trail?"

Abe stood up, slowly and stiffly. "It's not a very long trail," he said. "If I can do it, so can you."

People laughed, the kind of laughter that feels like a giant exhale. It mixed with the murmur of whispers and soft conversations, grunting as people stood up, keys jangling, chairs shifting.

And then there was only the sound of feet on the trail.

And the desert.

We slowly walked the Cactus Garden Trail, passing the trailside signs identifying plants of the Sonoran Desert. Chain fruit cholla, ocotillo, fishhook barrel cactus, paloverde, pencil cholla, creosote bush, saguaro, saguaro skeleton.

In the distance, there was a shrill birdcall. Then closer there was a sweet, melodic whistle. I couldn't identify the birds. And I couldn't ask Mom. A realization that made the sound bittersweet.

We completed the short trail and returned to the observation deck. It was more than a moment of silence. The walk lasted ten minutes. And it wasn't actually silence, because a baby cried a couple of times, and throughout the ten minutes, the birds and breeze continued to speak.

When it was over, when we returned to the observation deck, Alison invited my youngest sister to do a reading. Beth read a prayer, written by Dad and also read at his memorial service. We sang another song. Then the pastor said, "So we have come to the end of this service, but really we have not come to the end. We will continue to remember and love Nancy. And we will discover and realize the ways she has gifted our lives."

TWO WEEKS LATER, I was on a plane to New York.

As the plane took off, I thought about how Mom's dying at the midpoint of the year, the last day of June, made it feel like my year now was neatly divided into two pieces of loss. Death and life after death.

The previous trips had been welcome respites, doses of natural therapy. When this one started, I had trouble getting excited about heading to the airport. More than anything, I felt tired, almost drained of emotion. It didn't help that the alarm went off at four A.M.

It was a six A.M. JetBlue flight with something that I'm sure in the not-so-distant future will seem quaint but at this point still amazed me. There were televisions in the back of every seat, and while flying somewhere over Georgia, I could watch the New York morning shows.

As the guy next to me bitched about not having some channel, I watched a weatherman talk about how hot it already was in Manhattan. The forecast called for it to reach 100 degrees and maybe even hit the record for this date of 101 degrees. Officials had issued a heat advisory until six P.M.

"Stay inside if you can," one of the morning team said.

Great, I thought. Never mind air-conditioning. I wasn't even going to have electricity. I was going to be camping in Brooklyn.

WHEN I STARTED putting together a plan for the year, I was thinking I'd go to Denali with Mom in July. As Mom was dying, I considered sticking with those plans. But every time I pictured being by myself in the Alaska wilderness it felt horribly lonely, like it would make me just want to find the Christopher McCandless bus and curl up and wait for a grizzly or starvation, whichever came first.

So instead I went the opposite direction—to New York City and Gateway National Recreation Area.

I hadn't even heard of Gateway until the previous fall. When I met with some of the staff from the National Parks Conservation Association, one of them mentioned Gateway and gave an interesting pitch for why I should go there.

Because it's a mess. A mess with amazing potential.

In 1972, the National Park Service added two large urban parks, each designated as a national recreation area, on opposite sides of the country: Gateway in New York and Golden Gate in San Francisco.

Golden Gate became sort of a how-to example for urban parks. It had enormous support from local corporations and leaders. It was a park locals knew and loved. It attracted visitors from all over the world.

Gateway and its three units—Jamaica Bay, Staten Island, and Sandy Hook—also became one of the most used pieces of the National Park System. But too often Gateway was neglected, mismanaged, and overlooked.

When the NPCA had Zogby International poll New York City residents in 2006, the first question was simply: Are you aware that a 26,000-acre national park stretches across the New York–New Jersey harbor?

Less than 50 percent said yes.

What hooked me about Gateway was this: There was a campground at Floyd Bennett Field, less than fifteen miles from Manhattan.

It recently had expanded from four sites to thirty-eight. Some overnight camping also had been added to two other Gateway spots. And park officials had visions of someday having the largest urban campground in America.

I went online and booked a site. Goldenrod, Site 25. The rate was twenty dollars a night. But when I hit the button to pay, because I had an NPS annual pass, it was cut to ten dollars a night.

Seven nights in New York for seventy bucks.

"WHERE ARE YOU headed?" asked the woman working at the Thrifty car rental counter near John F. Kennedy International Airport in Queens.

"Gateway National Recreation Area," I said.

"Where's that?" she said.

I told her that it was a few miles away. I wondered if maybe she was unaware of it because she was from somewhere else.

"No," she said. "Lived here all my life."

On the way to Floyd Bennett Field, I stopped at a Rite Aid in Rockaway Park. I asked an employee if they had any battery-operated fans. He led me to an aisle with fans and began looking at what they had on the shelves.

"It has to be battery operated?" he said.

I told him I was camping.

"Where?" he said.

"Gateway National Recreation Area, Floyd Bennett Field," I said, thinking that being more specific might make a difference.

"Oh, yeah?" he said. "Where's that?"

"On the other side of the bridge, in Brooklyn," I said.

"Really?" he said.

I found a small, battery-operated fan. I bought it, some batteries, and several quarts of Gatorade. When I walked back outside, it felt even hotter.

Crossing over the Marine Parkway–Gil Hodges Memorial Bridge, I could see the Manhattan skyline in the distance. I passed through the tollbooth at the bottom of the bridge and saw a sign for my destination, its lettering faded or missing.

Gat way National

R c ation Ar a

F oy B nn tt Fi

I needed more supplies—a Styrofoam cooler, ice, fuel tank for my stove, groceries—so I continued north on Flatbush Avenue.

Just seeing that street name brought back memories. Not that I had ever been here before. But when I was growing up in the 1970s, the son of a Baptist minister in small-town Wisconsin, I wanted to be a Jewish kid living in a Brooklyn brownstone in the 1950s, playing stickball in the streets with my buddies.

I can explain this fairly easily. In 1972, the same year that Gateway was created, *The Boys of Summer* was published. When I thought of Brooklyn, that's what I pictured. Roger Kahn's childhood.

It turned out that searching for camping supplies on Flatbush Avenue a few decades later wasn't quite as charming as taking the subway to Ebbets Field.

By the time I had a cooler and ice and fuel for my stove, the sky had turned from a brilliant blue to slate gray. Lightning flashed to the east. I entered the park and turned left onto Runway 15-33 Road. In the distance, I could see some of the Manhattan skyline, past a cluster of six signs.

One said "Campgrounds" and had an arrow pointing to the right—the same direction as Hangar B, the Fishing Area, and the NYC Sanitation Training Center.

I turned right onto a long stretch of concrete, nearly as wide as eight lanes on the New Jersey Turnpike, only eerily empty.

Tall grass grew on both sides of Old Runway 6-24, until after about a quarter mile, when this wide stretch of concrete was intersected by an even wider one, this former runway blocked off to traffic and dotted with weeds sprouting from its cracks.

And it all was indeed "relentlessly flat."

When a design competition was held in 2007, inviting landscape architects to imagine what they would do with this place— "Envisioning Gateway," it was called—that was the starting point for the description of the place and its challenges. There weren't any mountains here. There weren't even any hills. A report done by Columbia University said the park's history as an airfield gave it a "relentlessly flat topographic condition, which is disorienting and spatially monotonous."

I continued driving nearly to the end of the road/runway, where a giant *24* still appeared on the concrete. In front of a grove of trees, a sign welcomed me to my home for the week. Camp Goldenrod.

As I got out of the car, a jet roared overhead.

I hadn't even entered the path leading into woods when I heard the buzz. Mosquitoes. Worse than anywhere I had been this year. I walked quickly, swatting at my legs and neck, passing empty campsite after empty campsite before finding mine, tucked in a corner, giving a little more privacy and seclusion. Not that this seemed to be necessary.

I stopped there for a moment, scoping it out. The mosquitoes swarmed.

I drove to the nearby RV campground. It was named the Amelia Earhart Campground, presumably to remind visitors of all the aviation history that had occurred on this little island. The campground didn't feel historic. It felt post-apocalyptic.

The massive square of concrete was empty except for what was on the south edge. Along a tall chain-link fence, there were brown signs that said things like "Amelia Earhart, RV Site, #43."

In front of each sign was a picnic table.

Two lonely RVs were parked there. One was a Cruise America rental RV, its exterior covered with pictures of happy family members riding horses through a western landscape.

Beyond the fence was Hangar B, weeds crawling up its exterior, many of its windows broken or cracked.

I used to think that some of the treeless RV campgrounds in Florida were depressing. Compared to this, they seemed lush and cheery.

On the far side of the concrete square, near Jamaica Bay, sat the remnants of several small boats. Weeds had sprouted through them. One was covered with spray-painted graffiti. Nearby, yellow caution tape wrapped around a tree. On the ground, there were tires, cigarette butts, beer cans, McDonald's wrappers.

People had been here. But I didn't see a single person now. Not in the tent campground. Not in the RV campground. It felt as if I had Floyd Bennett Field, or at least this part of it at this moment, all to myself.

I wasn't sure I wanted it.

At least I had the sunset cruise to look forward to that evening.

When I was trying to figure out exactly when to go to Gateway, I built the trip around the third weekend in July, when the park service was holding an overnight family camping program. I figured that would give me an opportunity to spend time with New Yorkers who were getting their first taste of camping. By arriving earlier in the week, I could also squeeze in a variety of other interviews and programs.

"Enjoy a ranger-led ecology cruise aboard the *American Princess*," it said on the park website. "You'll hear about the nature and history of Jamaica Bay and what the future may hold . . ."

Before heading to Riis Landing, I found out that the cruise was canceled. Lightning.

When the storm passed and the rain stopped, I went back to set up my tent. Remembering the mosquitoes, I first put on pants, a long-sleeve shirt, and bug spray. It didn't seem to make much difference.

I unzipped my tent for about five seconds, threw in my sleeping bag, backpack, and battery-operated fan, then tumbled inside.

I zipped the tent closed. And felt a mosquito bite my neck. And another. There were dozens of mosquitoes inside my tent, perhaps because I was one of only a few targets.

Best as I could tell, there were two other tents in the campground, and the two RVs on the nearby swath of concrete. But I had yet to see another person. So I jumped when I heard a gruff voice outside.

"Is that your car parked on the road?" the person said.

"Yes," I said.

"It's not supposed to be there," he said. "Move it across the road."

I unzipped the tent. In the dark, I couldn't exactly tell what kind of uniform the man had on. It didn't appear to be park service. Maybe security.

I got out of the tent, walked out to the road, and moved my car to the other side of the old runway, where there was indeed a parking lot with a sign that said "Campground Parking." And there was another car parked there now. It had Ontario plates.

When I got back in my tent, I called home. I was having trouble hearing my daughter, not because the signal was weak, but because of the constant roar of jets taking off from JFK, just a few miles away, and seemingly gaining little elevation by the time they passed over my tent.

"I . . ." she said right as another plane roared by, drowning out everything until the final word. "Bye."

"Bye," I said.

The sound of the plane faded and was replaced by the wail of a siren.

Lying in a tent in a city with 8 million people, I felt incredibly alone. And not a good kind of alone, as I had experienced from Acadia to Yellowstone. The kind of alone that comes when it starts to sink in that, for the first time in your life, you don't have either of your parents.

It was still steamy out. In an effort to stay hydrated, I had been drinking fluids all day. Now I needed to pee. I knew I couldn't make it until morning. But I didn't want to leave the tent and deal with the mosquitoes.

I looked at the empty thirty-two-ounce Gatorade bottle in the corner of the tent.

I thought about using it. But then I imagined waking up a few hours later, feeling thirsty, and accidentally drinking my own pee, kind of like in *127 Hours*, albeit with a major difference. My arm wasn't trapped beneath a boulder. So this would be more comedic than heroic.

I decided not to risk it. I unzipped the tent and hopped outside. While I was peeing into the nearby bushes, a jet passed overhead. It wasn't until the noise of it faded somewhat that I could hear the sound of my urine hitting the bush and the buzz of the mosquitoes. They seemed to have pounced on every inch of exposed flesh. My face, my neck, my hands . . .

I finished peeing, quickly zipped up my pants, unzipped the tent, and hopped back into it.

It was too hot and humid to get in the sleeping bag. So I lay on top of it, sweating, swatting mosquitoes, listening to the whining roar of the jets, and asking myself: Why am I here?

In this case, it wasn't some big philosophical question. I could have gone to any national park in America in July. Why was I in this one?

In theory, I came here because urban parks were going to be a part of the future of the national parks. If the last century was about bringing people to the parks, the park service director had said, the next century was about bringing parks to the people.

The previous day there had been a big press conference in Manhattan. Secretary of the Interior Ken Salazar and New York City mayor Michael Bloomberg signed what was called "an unprecedented agreement" between the National Park Service and the New York City Department of Parks and Recreation. The two agencies were going to cooperatively manage ten thousand acres of federal and city parks in and around Jamaica Bay. They had big plans for Floyd Bennett Field. They wanted to take the largest waterfront property in New York City and revitalize it. According to a press release, goals included "improved access" and a "seamless park experience for visitors."

Lying in my tent a day later, I kept thinking that I hoped they would follow through. Because if they didn't, Gateway wouldn't live up to its name and be a gateway to other parks. If you give people this experience, I thought, they will run away from the park, stay home, go to a baseball game, see a Broadway show—anything but go back to that campground at Floyd Bennett Field.

At the risk of attracting the mosquitoes in the tent, I put on my headlamp and read about my home for the week.

I noticed that on this day in 1938, Douglas Corrigan landed in Ireland—twenty-eight hours after taking off from Floyd Bennett Field and presumably heading back to California. He instantly was given a nickname that stuck with him the rest of his life. Wrong Way.

I dozed off briefly, but woke to the sound of a plane that was so loud and so low it felt like it had taken off from the RV campground. The sound of its engine changed from a squeal to a roar and then a hum as it headed west. For a moment, it was quiet. Just the soft hum of my battery-operated fan and the chirping of insects. And then another plane approached from the east. It was 1:30 A.M. and this happened over and over.

IN 1916, IF you had told a New Yorker that someday the newly created National Park System would include this piece of land in Brooklyn—and that there would be a campground here—they would have thought it was one of the craziest things they had ever heard. And not just because national parks were places out west, with mountains and canyons and wild animals.

In 1916, this land was an island. Barren Island. And as bleak as that name makes the place sound, the reality was much worse. Barren Island was a place where the mountains were made out of garbage; where there were smokestacks, not trees; where most of the animals weren't wild, they were dead.

The island was part of New York City's answer to one of the biggest population booms in American history. When New Yorkers wanted to get away, they often vacationed close to home, some going to tent cities that sprang up from Far Rockaway to Rockaway Point. One place they didn't go was Barren Island. They didn't even want to go near it.

And yet for more than sixty years, there were people who called the island home—mostly Polish, Irish, and Italian immigrants who came to America dreaming of a better life and ended up here, sorting through the waste that arrived daily on garbage scows.

At one point, the population of Barren Island topped more than 1,500.

The garbage—or, to be more accurate, the stench that carried for miles—eventually became a political issue. In 1914, a group of real-estate speculators, with property near Jamaica Bay and connections in Manhattan, pushed the city to forbid the disposal of trash "within the confines of Jamaica Bay." And as America transitioned from the horse to the car, another piece of the island's business, horse rendering, faded away. Barren Island became an almost forgotten island. Until 1927.

That's when Charles Lindbergh flew the *Spirit of St. Louis* from New York to Paris. Or at least that's how the flight was billed. Lindbergh actually took off from outside the city limits, Roosevelt Field in Nassau County—a fact that embarrassed some New York City officials and led to a push to build the city's first municipal airport.

A panel searched for a fitting site and eventually settled on one in Brooklyn that was created partly by using landfill to connect the marshy edge of the mainland to several small islands, including Barren Island.

The island that no longer was an island became Floyd Bennett Field, named after a naval aviator and Brooklyn resident who had been the pilot for a 1926 flight to the North Pole. Work began on October 29, 1929—the day the stock market crashed and America plunged into the Great Depression.

This didn't prevent Floyd Bennett Field from being built, though. In an era when grass and dirt runways were the norm, it had long, wide concrete runways. Its hangars could house the largest planes of the day. Its terminal was designed to serve as a welcoming gateway to a city on the rise. And when the airport opened in 1931, it instantly became the center of the aviation world, the place where record-breaking flights started and ended.

As a municipal airport, though, it struggled. It was hard to get to. There wasn't a nearby subway line or highway. In 1939, when New York opened Municipal Airport No. 2—eventually renamed LaGuardia—Floyd Bennett Field was doomed, at least financially.

In 1941, it was sold to the Navy and became Naval Air Station—

New York. During World War II, it was the busiest military airport in the United States. It remained a military site until 1971, when the Navy deactivated the field.

In 1972, when Congress established national recreation areas in New York and San Francisco, one of the pieces at Gateway was Floyd Bennett Field. With 1,358 acres, it was more than 1.5 times the size of Central Park and about 20 percent of all the land in Gateway. And it raised an obvious question, one that forty years later the National Park Service was asking the public as it worked on developing a new plan for the entire park.

What should we do with it?

WHEN I WOKE up, it was starting to get light. It was dramatically cooler and quieter. Birds were chirping. Every few seconds a drop of water fell from a tree and plunked onto the tent. It actually sounded almost peaceful.

Then a plane flew over.

But without even seeing it, I could tell that it was at a different altitude. Much higher and, therefore, much quieter here in Camp Goldenrod. Maybe, I realized, what had happened the previous night was not normal.

Things were looking up.

After breakfast, I went to the parking lot outside Hangar B, the spot where John Warren had suggested we meet. Warren was part of Gateway's public affairs office. And when I prepared for the trip, he and everyone else from the park that I talked to or traded e-mails with had been overwhelmingly welcoming.

Warren suggested we drive to the ranger station near the park entrance and begin with a short walk, across Flatbush Avenue to Dead Horse Bay.

"Before motor vehicles, New York had a lot of horses," he said as we waited for the light to change. "When they die, what do you do with them? You send them to a place where they can be rendered, turned into glue and gelatin and fertilizer. Occasionally we'll still find bits and pieces of hooves. So that's where the name comes from. It's actually better known around here as Bottle Beach. . . . You'll see why."

We walked a short distance on a trail and emerged on a beach. There were bottles everywhere. Thousands of them. Some intact, some broken.

While I was taking this in, Warren pointed out a syringe. He said that if he had told people familiar with the park where he was taking me, they would have said, "Why are you doing that?"

In my head, I already was asking the same question.

"It's about land use and how places change over time," he said.

As a ranger, he's used to parks being amazing, pristine areas. But Gateway isn't that kind of place, he said. New York isn't that kind of place.

"I doubt there's a single piece of New York City soil that hasn't been turned up, flipped over, fed through a filter, spun around, and chemically changed," he said. "But this is a different kind of story. It's a story of resilience of nature. When you do protect nature, when you do enact laws like the Environmental Protection Act and enforce them, nature comes back. Not only does nature come back, but nature and the largest city in the United States can coexist."

A bird squawked nearby.

Warren bent over and picked up a green bottle, poured the water from it, and held it up.

"This was built on a landfill, but the cap busted at one point or another," he said. "So people will come here and see bottles from a hundred years ago. You're going to find bottles for ink. And nobody uses ink in a bottle anymore. You'll find medicine bottles from the last century."

He said that sometimes they bring children here. And before I could ask the next obvious question—Why?—he answered it. When kids come to Ecology Village at Floyd Bennett Field, one of the things they learn about is water. They do some water sample tests. And the nearest place to get to the bay is here.

"But you've got bottles," he said. "So this has to become part of the story. How can you ignore it? . . . It's a way you can tell kids, 'Your garbage doesn't go away. Maybe it gets buried. Maybe it gets burned. Hopefully it gets recycled. But it doesn't disappear.'"

We walked down the beach. There were slight ripples on Dead Horse Bay from a breeze. And when the water lapped against the land, it hit the bottles and tinkled. This mixed with the buzzing of traffic on the bridge and the nearly constant sound of jets passing overhead.

Warren was starting to tell a story about something a student at New York University had said when he stopped midsentence and pointed at the ground.

"Look at this," he said. "A shell. So beautiful."

I hadn't even noticed it. I was still seeing only bottles. When he pointed out this shell, which was indeed beautiful, I started to notice more like it.

He left this shell on the beach and returned to the story about the NYU student. She told him that they really should clean up Bottle Beach, that it sends a bad message about the park.

"I'm, like, 'Yeah, it probably does,'" he said. "But if we had millions of dollars, this is not how we'd spend it. The damage is done."

Gateway had a very long wish list. If the park suddenly had millions of extra dollars, they could save some of the hangars at Floyd Bennett Field. They could put it into salt marsh restoration. They could improve the campground.

We walked back across Flatbush Avenue. I thanked him for showing me Bottle Beach and making me start to think about this place a little differently. Centuries ago, it had been natural. Then it had been unnatural. And now? To say it was coming full circle back to natural makes the process sound too neat, too complete. No, it was becoming a new kind of natural, one that at this point in time included the bottles on the beach and the broken windows at Hangar B. But if you looked around, you might find a beautiful shell. Or a building full of shiny old planes.

AT THE WEST end of Hangar B, just a few hundred yards from the campground, a metal door was propped open with a rock. A round blue sign above the door said:

H.A.R.P.

Historic Aircraft Restoration Project

On Tuesdays, Thursdays, and Saturdays, from nine to three, the hangar was open to the public. Several people had told me I needed to make sure to meet the volunteers, a bunch of old guys who came here to restore planes. But when I walked through the open door shortly after nine, I didn't see any sign of anyone, volunteers or visitors. Unsure of whether I was in the right place, I walked back out.

"Leaving already?" said a man heading toward the door.

I introduced myself and explained what I was doing. Marty Malone introduced himself and led me inside, through some hallways, before reaching a door that led to the hangar. When he opened it, I did something I later saw other first-time visitors do.

I stood there for a second, eyes wide open. This hangar—the same one that from the outside looked like a long-forgotten eyesore—was full of beautiful planes, a mix of types and eras.

Muted light streamed in through the tall windows. Water dripped onto the floor, from leaks somewhere high above. When we started walking, Marty showing me around the place, the sounds—footsteps, voices, dripping water—echoed in the cavernous space.

While many of the volunteers were drawn to the planes because of their time in the military, Marty's career had been in banking. He said he'd been fascinated by planes ever since he was a little boy, building model airplanes.

"And suddenly in my dotage, I get to play with the big ones," he said with a grin.

The volunteers often had their own plane, one that they spent countless hours carefully restoring to "just short of airworthy." Most of the aircraft, from Navy jets to police helicopters, had some sort of tie to Floyd Bennett Field. Some actually flew out of here.

Marty led me over to his plane, a Douglas A-4B Skyhawk attack jet.

"My late brother worked on this type of airplane when he was with the Marine Air Wing down here," he said. "And I always had an affinity for it."

We left the part of the hangar with the planes and headed to a break room, where some other volunteers were having coffee and chatting. Marty was seventy-one years old. And in this group, they only half joked, he was a youngster.

They were chatting about the day's news, especially a story in one of the morning papers. It was about Al Blackman, one of the volunteers. At age eighty-six, he was still working as a mechanic for American Airlines. To celebrate his seventieth anniversary on the job, American took him flying on a fully restored 1937 DC-3. A few minutes after taking off from JFK, the plane rumbled over Floyd Bennett Field.

"He could have come to Hanguh B and hopped in one," someone said.

They were joking. Sort of. They didn't have a 1937 DC-3 in the hangar. But they did have a Douglas C-47 Skytrain. And they had a plane—one that, unlike the others, had never actually flown—that turned the clock back to July 1933. It was a replica of the *Winnie Mae,* the wooden Lockheed Vega that Wiley Post flew in the first solo around-the-world flight, starting and finishing at Floyd Bennett Field.

The actual *Winnie Mae* is in the Smithsonian. And while the old-timers clearly viewed this as a travesty, they also took pride in what they had built with their hands and the tools in the hangar woodshop.

"Some guys retire and play golf," one of them said. "This is what we do."

They said they worried about the future of Hangar B. It wasn't just the broken windows, the leaking roof, and the high cost of repairing it. It also was that they weren't getting any younger.

Before I left, they asked whom else I planned to meet while here. When I mentioned Dave Taft, they said to make sure to tell him I had stopped in Hangar B.

"Tell him that you never saw a better-looking, more intelligent, hard-working, polite group . . . And that they think the world of him . . . Tell him that we have pictures of him all over . . . Maybe we can get ten bucks out of him."

SEVERAL PEOPLE TOLD me I needed to talk to Dave Taft. Not just because he had spent thirty-two years at Gateway National Recreation Area. Or even because he had worked his way up the ranks to become the head ranger for the Jamaica Bay unit, which included Floyd Bennett Field, the Jamaica Bay Wildlife Refuge, Fort Tilden, and more.

He was a local. He grew up in Canarsie, a working-class Brooklyn neighborhood built on the swamps of Jamaica Bay.

We agreed to meet in the parking lot of the William Fitts Ryan Visitor Center. The park service had just finished a three-year renovation of the center, once the air terminal for Floyd Bennett Field, painstakingly restoring it to its 1930s appearance.

"Step back in time to the Golden Age of Aviation . . ." the park's website said.

I had stopped at the building when I arrived at Gateway. And stepping into it did indeed make it possible to picture what it must have been like at Floyd Bennett Field back when flying was glamorous and exciting. But when I stepped back outside, the clock spun back to this time and place.

To the north, two old hangars had been renovated and converted to the Aviator Sports and Events Center. Billed as New York's largest such center, it included ice skating rinks, basketball courts, a rock climbing wall, an arcade, and a food court. But to the south, between a community garden and Flatbush Avenue, two other hangars were surrounded by concrete with tufts of weeds, chain-link fences, padlocks, and signs that said "Danger—Keep Away." And if you looked to the east of the visitor center, toward the middle of Floyd Bennett Field, you saw hundreds of yards of concrete in the foreground and the "Grassland Management Area" beyond it. That's what the maps called it. I saw a field of weeds.

Taft suggested we hop in his car and head a couple of miles up Flatbush to get a cup of coffee.

"I'm glad you decided to come to Gateway," he said.

When I said something about Gateway having so much potential, his response was one I would hear repeatedly. Yes, Gateway has issues. Yes, there are so many things they'd love to change. But it isn't just that this park might be an amazing place someday. It already is.

"Every day I wake up and think, 'Man, I wish this place had existed when I was growing up,'" he said.

He was born in 1960, more than a decade before the creation of a national recreation area in his backyard. At that time, the park service wasn't doing kayak programs in the bay. People were driving their cars into the waterways of Lower Brooklyn and leaving them there to rust. And that fit right in with a landscape that had long been used and abused.

"I think somewhere along the line my brother and I knew it was messed up," he said. "But it was all we knew. We were just inveterate Huck Finns. We'd be, 'Mom, we're going to the ditch.'"

The ditch wasn't some euphemism. Their idea of green space was literally a ditch, a patch of land basically abandoned by Con Edison, overgrown with weeds and full of fascinating creatures. Somebody—not him, he says—would take some wire cutters and cut a hole in the fence. They'd climb through carrying field guides (his mom was a science teacher) and find hairstreak butterflies, box turtles, Fowler's toads. Remnants, he now realizes, of New York's past.

He worries that kids today don't have that kind of experience, even with a place like Gateway.

We talked about our daughters and our efforts to make them comfortable in nature. His daughter, Abby, was three years old. He said one time they were at a place near their house, collecting sticks, when she suddenly jumped into his arms. It wasn't that she heard something. It was that she *didn't* hear anything. It was so quiet, the ground so soft.

And she had already had quite a few doses of nature. They have kids participate in camps at Floyd Bennett Field who have never ventured outside of a few urban blocks.

"Something as simple as a horizon line freaks kids out sometimes," he said.

We pulled back into the park, passing the remote control car racetrack. On the other side of the island, there was an airfield for remote control airplanes. In between, there was an area Taft wanted me to see.

"These are interesting habitats that we're coming into now," he said.

We were driving down the now-familiar runway-turned-road that led to the campgrounds. Taft was pointing to the fields around us. I hadn't thought of this as "interesting habitats." I realized that I hadn't thought about it all. It was just there, stuff on the periphery of what I kept noticing. Concrete, planes, mosquitoes.

"These were all woodlands; they looked very much like what you see in the distance," he said, pointing to the trees surrounding the campground. "They were bayberry and gray birch. When I first got here, they were lining the runways."

With the help of the Audubon Society and volunteers, they spent the better part of four years clearing the trees. The goal was to create a place for grassland-nesting birds. When they created it and endangered species such as the grasshopper sparrow or the up-land sandpiper still didn't come, some saw the grasslands as a failure.

Taft saw it differently. He said that the problem is a lot bigger than this little grassland, or this state or this country. It's a global problem of loss of habitat. And when he looked at the grasslands, he saw a little bit of what New York once was.

It wasn't the Grand Canyon. It wasn't the redwoods. But when he came to the grasslands, he got a thrill.

"And not just from a personal sense, because I remember clearing this," he said. "We cleared the trees, but Mother Nature provided the grass. And you can see it's not just a grassy field. It's filled with things."

He paused and smiled. "I'm sorry if I obsess about these plant things but . . ."

"No, that's good," I said, pointing to the area he had been talking about. "I want you to show me. Because I look out here and see . . ."

I paused, searching for the right word.

"Weeds?" he said with a laugh. "A bunch of weeds, right?"

I nodded.

"There's a plant in here I had been looking for for a trillion years," he continued. "For a long time I wanted to buy it so we could reintroduce it to the refuge."

He slowed down the car, leaned forward as if trying to spot something deep in the grassland.

"I don't know if we can see any from the edge," he said. "And I'm not wearing the right clothing to wander in there."

A few seconds later he apparently decided that he didn't care that he was wearing khaki pants, dress shoes, and a blue dress shirt.

"You want to take a quick look?" he said.

He parked the car and we got out and started walking into the field. As we pushed apart the grass, which was higher than our waists, I heard him say, "Of course, I pulled into the biggest patch of poison ivy here." Poison ivy, he explained, likes to grow into the same kinds of places as the plant he was trying to find.

"Here it is," he said.

He pointed to what to my eye looked like nothing out of the ordinary. *Spiraea tomentosa,* he said, is a shrub, commonly known as steeplebush.

"It's quite rare in New York City," he said.

He slapped his arm.

"Oh, there are mosquitoes too," he said.

The steeplebush, which typically blooms in late summer, hadn't bloomed yet this year. But when it did, the bush would be topped with clusters of deep pink flowers, which would dot the grasslands with color and attract butterflies.

"It's a very attractive plant, very unassuming," he said. "It's just a plant that seemed to be missing here."

And while he had been hoping to buy it, that isn't how it got here. They never did plant it.

"How these seeds got here—how any of these seeds wound up here—is an interesting, maybe a little obsessive question," he said. "Maybe it was by birds. Maybe the seeds were lying fallow all along. But you can see a lot of it growing here now."

We were walking and talking when he stopped. "Look at this," he said, taking in the scene. "I just love this perspective. It's not like a lawn. You're not standing in a managed field. And you're not standing on a hideous runway. It's so beautiful."

He inhaled. "It smells different," he said.

He brushed his hand across the top of the tall grass around him and looked at all the acres of grassland.

While I had been busy comparing it to a place like Lamar Valley in Yellowstone, he was comparing it to what pieces of New York City might have looked like in the 1600s. And to what the ditch near his childhood house looked like in the 1960s.

"It sounds corny, but growing up where I did, I can't think of a more important park for the National Park Service," he said. "I still meet people, even within the park service, who think there is no place for these kinds of parks in the park system. I couldn't disagree more."

THE CAMPGROUND WAS much fuller this night. And while its prior emptiness had made me feel hopelessly lonely, this was a classic example of being careful what you wish for.

A group of teenagers was partying, yelling, blasting music, and generally making me feel like a grumpy old man who wants to yell at the kids to turn down the music and stay off my lawn. Where was the security guard when you needed him?

I almost missed the plane noise. Almost.

The noise of the partyers mixed with the sound of some animals screeching in the woods. And helicopters flying nearby. And sirens. And of course the planes taking off from JFK. But tonight they were higher. And eventually, when the party died out and it started to rain, creating a pitter-patter on top of the tent, I lay there thinking, This isn't bad.

I woke up Friday morning to the BEEP-BEEP-BEEP of sanitation trucks backing up. I could hear the wind whistling through the trees. And before eight A.M., I got a call from the ranger who was going to lead the kayak program.

It had been canceled. Small-craft advisory.

It was hard to believe that a few days earlier there had been heat advisories. Now it was gray and downright chilly.

I spent most of the day driving around the park, grabbing a bite to eat at the Aviator Sports and Events Center. When I returned to the campground, it was dark. The rain had stopped. There were several roaring campfires in the opening behind my campsite. People were hanging out, talking, drinking beer. But the vibe was much different than the previous night, more laid-back.

Four people were gathered around one of the campfires. I introduced myself.

Dana, Patrick, Joe, and Slim (a woman who was indeed slim) were all in their mid-twenties. Dana grew up in Minnesota, but the rest of their group—two more friends showed up a little later—were from the Northeast. They all lived in Brooklyn now, a short drive away.

"This has been an escape," Patrick said.

"What were you saying earlier?" Dana said, pointing to the other side of the clearing. "We were sitting over there, under the pavilion, when it was raining real hard. We were talking about how it's so soothing to see the rain out here. Something about the rain washing over New York City doesn't feel the same. It depresses you. Out here, there's nothing you can do about it, so you just relax and accept it. We played cards."

Their tents were set up near the woods behind the fire. Music played on a boom box, a Doors song, much softer than the party of the previous night.

Joe threw another log on the fire. I mentioned the party. They laughed and said that was no big deal.

"Living in New York, you get used to the noise," Joe said.

"It's weird without it," Dana said. "When I was on this road trip with my mom, some of the places we stopped I couldn't sleep, it was so dark and quiet."

"That's how it was when I went down to Arkansas," Joe said. "It's, like, 'Whoa, it's so dark. Is it always this dark?'"

"Yeah," Dana said. "Why aren't there any sirens?"

Someone brought up that they had seen a news story about the possibility of adding cell service in subway tunnels.

"I'd hate that," Dana said. "That's my one time of day you can't get ahold of me."

"Can you imagine?" Joe said. "Everybody would be on phones. 'WHAT? YOU'RE WHERE? NO, I SAID I WANTED MUSTARD ON IT!'"

A jet passed over, growing louder and louder, then fading into the distance.

"It's interesting to be here," Joe said. "We have a phone signal here, but I haven't used my phone at all. I can turn it off and relax and escape."

I mentioned that the park service is attempting to reach their generation by using technology—creating apps, expanding cell phone coverage.

"I'd say they'd be better off investing in transportation to bring people to the parks," Patrick said. "For me, this happened because Joe and Slim had a car."

You couldn't take the subway to the park. And even if you rode the bus here and got off at the stop near the visitor center, you still had to walk about three-fourths of a mile to the campground. If there was an easy way to get here, they said, they'd be here more often.

They grabbed another round of beers and talked about Cabin Porn, a website full of user-submitted photos of nothing but cabins. Some of the cabins were luxurious; some were spartan. All were in their own way stunningly alluring, especially to people living in New York City.

There was a pause in the conversation. Everyone sat, staring at the fire. Someone pointed out the purple in the center of the fire. Which led to others finding colors in the flames. Blue, fuchsia, maroon.

Dana pointed to the silhouette of a person tending a campfire nearby in the same clearing. It was the campsite basically right behind mine. I had seen a tent set up there, but I hadn't met the camper yet.

"Have you talked to him?" she said. "You should."

HE WAS A New York City cabdriver, a Russian immigrant who was practically living in the campground. After I introduced myself, he started giving me the rundown on the park.

"Have you seen our wildlife?" he asked. "We've got two stray cats, one rabbit, and a raccoon."

He pointed to his tent and a hole in the corner of it. That, he said, was the work of the raccoon.

"He went after my pipe tobacco and thought it was food," he said. "The little piece of shit. Then he went, 'Phew.'" He spat on the ground, illustrating what the raccoon had done after eating his tobacco.

"So he's a snob," he said. "He hangs out here. He's a juvenile. Cute as shit. And we've got a couple of hawks. And a shitload of other birds. And of course the mosquitoes."

A plane flew overhead. I waited for a second for it to pass, then said I had met the mosquitoes.

He told me the key was to have a fire going and a can of Off! And a fiancée who is a fencer.

"When we get in the tent, I just give her a flashlight and she fucking destroys them," he said, doing his impression of a fencer in a tent full of mosquitoes.

He was on his own with the mosquitoes this weekend. His said his fiancée was in Boston, then told the story of how they met, how he picked her up in his cab and ended up falling in love. Which made things a bit complicated because he already was living with a girl-friend.

"Because I'm a gentleman, I paid my ex's last month of rent," he said. "At the moment, I'm kind of homeless."

That's how he ended up as a regular at the Floyd Bennett Field campground.

"It's cheap as shit living here," he said. "And it's fun. You saw the NYPD choppers over there?"

I told him that I hadn't seen them, but I had heard the helicopters and, of course, the jets.

He asked how I got here. At first I thought he meant how did I decide to come to Gateway, but eventually I realized he meant it literally. How did I get here? When I explained that I flew from Florida, got a rental car, and drove to Floyd Bennett Field, he shook his head.

"As we say in Russia," he said, exaggerating his accent, "I'm going to tell you the truth, please do not be offended. It just seems a really fake way of doing it. Shouldn't you load up the station wagon and just fucking ride through the parks and write a whole Bill Bryson–ish story?"

I laughed and explained that as tempting as it was to hit the road for a year, I had a wife and daughter at home who had work and school. I went somewhere for a week or two each month, then returned home.

"So you're trying to keep the family together?" he said. "I respect that."

He said he hoped I could at least include the family in part of the journey.

"Because forcing your recalcitrant wife and children into the car and making them go a thousand miles, isn't that, like, the American way?" he said. "I don't know. I'm a Russian immigrant. But I've watched enough movies I think I know that's how it's supposed to work. The dad's supposed to drive the car off a cliff at some point."

This led him to start talking about cars, specifically the best car he ever owned: a '93 Buick Century. And about how Americans used to make good cars. How that car could haul ass. How you could use the bench seats to lie down and sleep. Or if you had a girlfriend . . .

"I'm sorry, I'm a little stoned," he said, inviting me to join him.

"No, thanks," I said.

"You're a writer and you don't smoke weed?" he said, shaking his head in mock disgust.

He offered me a shot of vodka. I took him up on that.

We stood near his picnic table, a few feet from the fire, jets and helicopters flying overhead. At one point he picked up a long knife, used it to stir the fire or something, then casually flicked it into the wood of the table.

When I asked him his name, he didn't want to tell me his full name. He said his first name was Alex.

He moved to the United States when he was eleven. He recalled when the tanks were in Red Square in 1991, he and his family were about twenty blocks away, crammed into his uncle's apartment, watching it all unfold on CNN. He said when he came to America and learned that the Berlin Wall had fallen in 1989, his first reaction was: What is the Berlin Wall?

"They never taught us this," he said. "I knew a shitload about tanks and imperialistic Americans, though. You guys are evil."

I laughed. I grew up with images of stern Russian men and babushka-wearing Russian women. That was before, among other things, a series of long-legged, short-skirted tennis players tore down that wall and ended up on the bedroom walls of teenage boys across America.

He said being a New York cabby was on his bucket list.

"I love to drive," he said. "And I always felt like anybody can drive in New York traffic for a couple of hours, right? But if you do it long-term, you really see if you're good enough. It's like baseball, where your season has two hundred games."

"One hundred sixty-two," I said.

"Sorry, not my sport," he said. "But you get my point."

He asked where my tent was. When I pointed at the nearby spot, he laughed.

"The rose garden," he said.

He said that when he first came here with his girlfriend, they ended up using some dry roses from bushes surrounding that spot for kindling. And while they were trying to get their fire going, there was a young couple in a tent—where my tent was now—making quite the amorous racket. They'd emerge every so often, chug some protein drinks, return to the tent, and repeat.

"Don't worry," I said. "I won't be putting the rose garden to good use tonight. It's just me."

"I don't know, if you go over to those hipsters with a can of absinthe," he said, motioning to the group of twentysomethings. "I can't do that shit anymore because I'm going to get married. God, that sounds crazy. . . . Tell me the truth, does marriage suck?"

I laughed. "Marriage doesn't suck," I told him. "It can be great, but it's inevitable that things do change. You've got to work at it."

We kept talking for a while, the conversation repeatedly interrupted by helicopters and jets. I said I was starting to come around to the place, but I still was having trouble getting past the planes and the noise.

He shook his head. These planes are beautiful, he said. They aren't trying to shoot at him. And when he proposed to his fiancée, he did it right here, on a night when the planes were flying so low you could feel them.

"You've got to sell this place right," he said. "It's amazing."

AT THE END of the week, I headed to Ecology Village for the Urban Outback program. I waited and waited, eventually calling one of the leaders to see if I was in the wrong place. No, she said. Two families had signed up, but both bailed at the last minute. There wasn't going to be a family camping program tonight.

I was frustrated. It seemed as if the plans I had for Gateway kept falling apart, starting with the sunset cruise and culminating with this. I had come here hoping to sit around a campfire with some New Yorkers and experience this place through them.

I eventually realized I had done exactly that. Not exactly as planned. Maybe better.

As the sun set, I drove back down the now-familiar runway, parked, and headed to the now-familiar path leading to the campground. A huge pile of wood had been dumped at the entrance for campers to use. Maybe it was that wood, or maybe it was all the trees growing in this patch of Brooklyn—poplar, bayberry, gray birches, sumac, tamarack—but it did smell like a campground should.

I was thinking about this, wondering why I hadn't noticed it until now, when I saw the insects. They were all over, darting across the path, dancing in the woods.

Not mosquitoes.

Fireflies.

While I was growing up, fireflies were as much a part of summer as baseball and backyard barbecues. Most evenings my friends and I would play outside, milking every bit of the long days, barely even noticing as the light faded. Then fireflies began appearing, creating something that was simultaneously magical and taken for granted, kind of like childhood itself.

I hadn't seen fireflies in years. And I wasn't alone. I thought about a song by JJ Grey and Mofro, one of my favorite North Florida bands. In "Fireflies," the refrain asks where all the fireflies went: "I heard someone say / They ain't never coming back."

But here they were. Back in, of all places, America's biggest city.

The jets were still flying. The beach was still covered with bottles; there were remains of boats covered with graffiti, broken windows, weeds, and lots of concrete. Jamaica Bay, the city's largest open space, still had a long list of environmental issues. And Gateway National Recreation Area still desperately needed the kind of community support that its twin, Golden Gate National Recreation Area, had been receiving ever since they were born in 1972.

None of that had changed. But in one week, my view of Gateway and Floyd Bennett Field had.

This wouldn't have been Mom's idea of a national park. But she would have gone to the Jamaica Bay Wildlife Refuge, like I eventually did, and walked through what has become a landing strip and runway for hundreds of species of birds. She would have kayaked from Canarsie Pier. She would have found a large piece of Floyd Bennett Field, between the cricket fields and remote control flying field, known as the North Forty. She would have spotted redwing blackbirds as she walked the trails that have been cut through the tall Phragmites. She would have listened to the towering reeds swaying in the breeze.

She would have found beauty here.

She seemed to find it everywhere.

Before the year began, I read some of Thoreau's writings. And even though I now was more than 150 years and 200 miles removed from Walden Pond—or perhaps especially because of that—one journal entry seemed particularly relevant.

"The question is not what you look at, but what you see."

As the JetBlue plane took off, passing over Jamaica Bay, I looked down and saw a place that I wanted to come back to someday. I hoped if I did, it would be dramatically different. And yet I also hoped some of it would be the same. I hoped the fireflies would still be there.

8

*

AUGUST: YOSEMITE

*A*fter Mom died, I went through some old photo albums and found one with a worn red cover. A piece of string held together fragile pages with square black-and-white photos glued on them. A handwritten label said "Woods family, Vol. 1, 1958–1961."

Mom and Dad were married in 1958. I was born in 1961, Lisa in 1965, Beth in 1968. So these pictures, I realized as I started to gently turn the pages, were snapshots of their life before children.

There were photos of them boarding a plane to San Francisco, leaving behind Illinois and heading to Berkeley, where Dad was going to start seminary. Dad was wearing a suit and tie, a handkerchief tucked in his pocket. Mom was wearing a dress.

They looked so young, so happy.

There were photos of their first apartment, their first car (a 1949 Chevy), their first Christmas, and all kinds of other firsts before their firstborn arrived, taking over the final pages of the album and, I'm sure, their lives.

I kept coming back to one page. Atop it was written in Mom's handwriting: "Vacation to Yosemite National Park." I never knew—or if I did, I forgot—they went there three months before I was born.

As best I can tell, they were first-generation visitors to the national parks. They spent much of their childhood within a few blocks of each other in Rock Island, Illinois. Their parents didn't take them to places like Yosemite. But something drew them and many others of their generation there.

Yosemite was one of their first national parks. And it was their last before they became parents. No wonder it always had a special pull for them.

They took us there when we were kids and lived in Reno. I remember one trip in particular, at Christmas. As much as the trip itself, I remember taking pictures—of the Merced River, Half Dome in the distance, draped in snow—and developing them with Dad.

Wherever we lived, he'd take a room—a laundry room, a bathroom, whatever—and turn it into a makeshift darkroom, covering the windows, putting towels at the base of the door. He'd let me help mix the trays of chemicals. Developer, stop bath, fixer.

We'd put a negative in the enlarger, put the photo paper in the easel, flip a switch and count the seconds, using our hands to block the light and burn and dodge parts of the paper. Then we'd slide the paper into the developer and watch the image appear.

It had been forty years since I had been to Yosemite. And yet as I drove into the park it felt familiar, as if the memories were like those prints, appearing gradually, then becoming clearer and clearer.

There was so much rock. Piles of rocks, rows of rocks, slabs of rock, walls of rock. And I hadn't even made it to the valley yet. I was heading to a Climbers Coffee in Tuolumne Meadows, following the winding Tioga Road through the park's high country. When I pulled up to the Big Oak Flat Entrance shortly after sunrise, there wasn't a car in front of me or behind me. No one was in the booth. A sign said to go ahead and enter the park, pay when you leave.

I figured the lack of traffic was because I was arriving early on a Sunday morning. But I couldn't help but wonder if the recent news also was a factor.

On July 30, a thirty-six-year-old man from the San Francisco area had checked himself into a hospital with flu-like symptoms. He died the next day. The cause turned out to be hantavirus pulmonary

syndrome, a disease spread to humans by exposure to rodent drop-
pings and urine. It was traced to a trip to Yosemite in June and a stay
in one of ninety-one "signature tent cabins" in Curry Village.

Death in Yosemite was hardly new or rare. The previous year more
than a dozen people died in the park. And this summer already had
produced headlines about three deaths in Yosemite.

In July, Michael Ybarra, a reporter who wrote about his
extreme-sport adventures for *The Wall Street Journal,* was crossing the
Sawtooth Ridge in the Eastern Sierra when he fell about two hundred
feet. He was forty-five. His sister wrote on her Facebook page, "He
died doing what he loved most."

Then in August, two stepbrothers, ages six and ten, waded into
the Merced River and got swept away. On August 16, searchers were
still looking for the body of one of the boys when the park and the
California Department of Public Health issued the first of a series
of press releases that led to international news coverage about
hantavirus.

When I first heard the news, I got out a map of the valley. My
campsite was in the Upper Pines campground. The campground
included a series of finger-like loops with sites packed closely together. I had purposefully booked something at the end of one of the
fingers. Site 142. I liked that it backed up to a bit of woods and a
road, used only by shuttle buses.

Curry Village was on the other side of that road. I knew I shouldn't
worry. As officials had emphasized, hantavirus isn't a long-lived bac-
terium and can't be passed from person to person. There wasn't a
single case of somebody in the Upper Pines campground contracting
hantavirus. But because of all of this—an adventure writer dying in
the mountains, two kids drowning in the river, an outbreak of a
deadly virus in the valley, and, of course, losing Mom—I arrived in
Yosemite thinking about death.

On the flight to California, I had finished *Gloryland,* a novel by
Shelton Johnson, a Yosemite ranger. I had highlighted what his protagonist, Elijah Yancy, a soldier with African and Indian blood who

finds himself among the park's protectors in 1903, says he learned in his first few months in Yosemite: Death hides in beauty.

> It's pretty here all right, so pretty that you can get stupid looking at it and forget to pay attention to Death, who walks up wearing Yosemite as if it were a fine suit of clothes, and while you're admiring the cloth and color, there's Death standing in front of you and smiling, considering all the ways he's got to kill you. Yeah, death hides in beauty.

IN 1869, JOHN MUIR got his first glimpse of Yosemite's beauty.

Raised in Wisconsin, the son of a Presbyterian minister who demanded he memorize the entire Bible and beat him when the progress wasn't sufficient, Muir had understandably mixed emotions about organized religion. But when he took a job in California helping to drive two thousand sheep through the Sierra Nevada range, he repeatedly used religious terms to describe what he was seeing and feeling. And when he reached Yosemite Valley, he wrote that it was "by far the grandest of all the special temples of Nature I was ever permitted to enter."

He ended *My First Summer in the Sierra* with this: "I have crossed the Range of Light, surely the brightest and best of all the Lord has built; and rejoicing in its glory, I gladly, gratefully, hopefully, pray I may see it again."

He did of course see it again. And less than one year later, in the spring of 1870, he was making the kind of complaint that is often heard in the temple today: There are too many people here.

At the time, Yosemite was a relatively new park and new idea. It was created as a state park in 1864, eight years before Yellowstone became the first national park. With an act of Congress and the signature of Abraham Lincoln, about sixty square miles of federal land were given to California with the condition "that the premises shall be held for public use, resort, and recreation."

The Civil War ended in 1865. The Transcontinental Railroad was completed in 1869. By the next spring, Muir was writing letters to a friend, complaining about the crowds in Yosemite Valley.

There were, he said, about sixty or seventy visitors there. If you can imagine.

Today, if you go to Yosemite on a typical summer day, there might be sixty vehicles circling one parking lot.

Muir predicted what he saw happening was only the start. He was only partly correct. When a friend wrote a letter complaining of "the desecrating influences of the fashionable hordes," he tried to comfort her. He wrote back saying that while the valley floor was destined to be overrun by man, the towering walls that framed the valley would forever remain untouched.

"The tide of visitors will float slowly about the bottom of the valley as a harmless scum, collecting in hotel and saloon eddies, leaving the rocks and falls eloquent as ever . . . with imperishable beauty and greatness," he wrote.

Muir died in 1914, two years before the National Park Service was created. As prescient as he was, he had no idea of the scale and scope of what would happen at Yosemite.

By the end of the century, attendance had topped 4 million in a year, the vast majority of them heading for a valley that remains the same size it was when Muir was lamenting having to share it with a few dozen people: about 7.5 miles long and an average of a mile wide.

Not only was the valley floor teeming with people and vehicles, its towering granite walls were covered with people climbing the walls, people sleeping on the walls, people (illegally) jumping off the walls wearing parachutes and flying suits.

Muir didn't see that coming. And he was a rock climber before anyone used such a term. In that summer of 1869, he climbed Cathedral Peak, an aptly named prominence south of Tuolumne Meadows. To reach the summit, he had to scale a block that is about 30 feet high and steep on all sides. He did it without ropes, by himself.

But it was one thing to scramble to the top of Cathedral Peak. It was quite another to stand in the valley, look up at the 2,000-foot face of Half Dome or the nearly 3,000-foot nose of El Capitan, and think about somehow scaling them.

It wasn't just that people didn't climb these walls for thousands of years. In the book *Camp 4: Recollections of a Yosemite Rockclimber,* Steve Roper wrote that before 1950 no human being even entertained a passing thought about climbing El Cap: "It just sat there, a definition of impossible."

But then, in the summer of 1957, Warren Harding and two others began climbing what is now one of the most famous routes in the world, the Nose.

Harding spent parts of the next eighteen months, with a variety of partners, climbing up the wall, fixing ropes with an assortment of homemade gear, establishing camps, climbing back down and repeating the process. At one point the crowds watching in the valley grew so large, bringing traffic to a halt, that the park service restricted Harding and his crew from climbing until after peak tourism season.

When Harding pulled himself up to the top shortly after sunrise on November 12, 1958, it was official. It no longer was impossible to climb El Capitan. It took Harding and his partners forty-seven days of climbing.

Ever since then, the definition of impossible has been repeatedly redefined. While the list of firsts on the Nose has continued to grow—first solo ascent, first woman, first hammerless, first blind climber, first teen, first preteen, and on and on—the time it takes people to climb from the 4,150-foot start to the 7,050-foot finish keeps shrinking.

The second ascent, in 1960, took seven days. In 1975, it was done in a day. From there, the record dropped to 13 hours in 1979, to under 10 hours in the 1980s, to 4:22 in the 1990s, to 3:59, 3:57 and 3:24 all in 2001, to 2:48 . . . 2:45 . . . 2:43 . . . 2:37 . . . 2:36.

By the time I arrived in the park, climbers were still buzzing about what had happened in the valley two months earlier.

Alex Honnold and Hans Florine began climbing at 5:52 A.M. on a warm June day. They were at the top before most of the people in the valley had finished breakfast—completing the route in 2 hours, 23 minutes and 46 seconds, nearly 13 minutes faster than any previous climb of the Nose.

This same summer Honnold, a twenty-six-year-old from Sacramento, climbed Yosemite's three biggest walls—Mount Watkins, El Capitan, and Half Dome—in less than 24 hours. First, with a partner, then solo, finishing the latter in 18 hours and 50 minutes.

The reason Honnold had been featured on *60 Minutes* the previous year, the reason he had sponsorship deals rarely seen in the climbing world, wasn't just how fast he climbed. It was how he regularly climbed.

Free solo. Without ropes.

When he climbed the three biggest walls in one 24-hour span, he free soloed about 90 percent of it.

Every time I watched footage of Honnold climbing in Yosemite without ropes—relying on his long fingers, sticky-soled shoes, and a Zen-like demeanor—I had an uncontrollable reaction. My palms started sweating.

If the sight of him climbing the rock wall had been in a Hollywood movie, I would have assumed it was some sort of special effect. Maybe the valley below really was a green screen. Or maybe there was a net just below the camera shot. He couldn't be doing this. And yet he was, taking a long history of free soloing in Yosemite to new heights and speeds and raising an obvious question for the future: What on earth will people be doing in national parks in another hundred years?

In 1916, nobody pictured the walls of El Capitan dotted with human beings. But as the park system approached 2016, it wasn't just that there were a few climbers like Alex Honnold. It was that there were tens of thousands of somewhat more mortal climbers who came to rock climbing's mecca every year.

The park service didn't have an exact figure. It gave a rough estimate of annual "climber days" of 25,000 to 50,000. Whatever the actual number, there were concerns about traffic not only on the valley floor but also on its walls.

This is why I planned to go to one of America's busiest national parks in one of its busiest months, to camp in a crowded camp-ground, to think not so much about death, but about the age-old concerns of loving a place to death.

I PULLED INTO the parking lot at the Tuolumne Meadows visitor center shortly before the start of the Climbers Coffee.

Two rangers, Jesse McGahey and Ben Doyle, were setting up six large thermoses on a picnic table. I introduced myself to Jesse. We had been trading e-mails for a few months. He had suggested coming to this, saying it might be a good spot to meet some climbers.

This wasn't just any old parking lot. It had long been a meeting spot for the climbing community. "It's where it goes from blows to bros," one climber said.

Twenty-seven climbers gathered around the picnic table, hold-ing an assortment of coffee mugs and thermoses. A majority of them were men but there were a few women. There was a wide age range. The common denominator seemed to be that they all looked in-credibly fit.

Ben kicked things off by introducing himself and Jesse. He said they needed some volunteers for some work the following week. And he reminded everyone to put the ninth annual Yosemite Facelift—a cleanup done by climbers—on their calendars. He was giving the details when one of the climbers interrupted.

Everyone else had on long pants or tights. This climber was wearing cut-off jean shorts, a sweater, and wrap-around sunglasses. I guessed he was in his fifties.

"It's cool we're picking up litter in the valley," he said. "But have any of you thought about our environment up here? Go down to Tenaya Lake if you get bored. We really have a problem with litter."

He said he had been out there the other day, picking up litter. Someone drove by, recognized him, and figured he must have gotten a DUI.

"I go, 'No, man, it's just something to do,'" he said. "I love this place."

He continued for several minutes, lamenting what was happening to Yosemite, asking what today's climbers are leaving for future generations, getting more and more worked up as he spoke.

He eventually paused.

"If you don't know who I am, I'm Dave Yerian," he said.

One of the rangers thanked Dave, then gave some details about the upcoming Yosemite Facelift. When he wrapped up, Dave said, "I've got something else I'd like to say, if that's okay . . . I've got an issue. It's back to what we leave behind for everybody."

WHEN HARDING MADE the first ascent of El Capitan in 1958, he used 600 pitons, small spikes driven into natural cracks in the rock to hold safety ropes. But there were still many stretches of blank granite. To climb these sections, he hand-drilled 125 holes for expansion bolts.

This amount of bolting led to a debate among climbers that only grew in 1970 when Harding and Dean Caldwell climbed a beautiful but daunting route about 200 feet east of the Nose. The Wall of Early Morning Light was so named because it was exactly that—when the sun rises on Yosemite Valley, one of the first places it illuminates is this wall.

To do the first ascent, Harding and Caldwell climbed for twenty-seven days and used 300 expansion bolts.

When Harding died in 2002 at age seventy-seven, the obituary in the *Los Angeles Times* about one of big-wall climbing's biggest characters included details about the bolting debate. Galen Rowell, a photographer who made a first ascent of Half Dome's south face with Harding in 1970, said: "Some climbers felt that if you couldn't use all the natural features of the rock that you should not do the climb. Warren had a libertarian view of climbing . . . he was very bold and determined and thought climbing was one of the last places in North America where you could be totally free and make your own decisions, and he went for it."

This still was true in Yosemite.

Ever since its creation, the park service had found it necessary to institute all kinds of rules and regulations to attempt to walk the tightrope of its mission. You had to have a permit to camp in most of Yosemite's wilderness. But you didn't need a permit to camp on the side of El Cap. Once you were on the wall, you were legal. And you still could hand-drill anywhere. The question was: Should you?

Dave Yerian was several minutes into a passionate rant about what had happened at nearby Medlicott Dome—"I can't even look at it anymore . . . It makes me sick to my stomach . . . It's an atrocity."

As the climbers discussed this and the rangers packed up the coffee, I ended up talking to a fiftyish couple, originally from Minnesota but now living in Los Angeles. Before we went our separate ways, he wanted to show me something he had in his trunk. His white climbing helmet.

Climbers like to personalize their helmets, he explained. So he had made his look like Wilson, the volleyball who became Tom Hanks's companion in the movie *Cast Away*. He pointed to a signature on it. Aron Ralston. The adventurer who in 2003 got his right forearm trapped under a boulder while canyoneering in a remote section of Canyonlands National Park. Ralston survived by cutting off the forearm with a dull knife, leading to a book and the movie *127 Hours*.

"He was in town for a book tour and I got him to sign it," he said.

He said that while some people like to collect the signatures of baseball players on trading cards, this was his thing. He collected the signatures of rock stars.

"I should have had Dave sign it too," he said.

In the world of rock climbing, Dave Yerian had one of the

ultimate claims to fame. Not his name on a star on some horizontal piece of pavement. His name on a route on a wall in Yosemite. The Bachar-Yerian.

Long before there was Alex Honnold, there was John Bachar. He showed up in Yosemite with his VW bus, wearing calf-high tube socks and short running shorts and looking like a real-life version of a doctor's office poster illustrating all the muscles in the human body. He became famous for using those muscles to free solo.

He once spent an entire season climbing without using a rope. And in 1981, he posted a note in Tuolumne Meadow's message board offering $10,000 to anyone who could follow him free solo-ing for a week.

No one even tried.

That same year, with Yerian, he climbed the route on Medlicott Dome that instantly became legendary, partly because he used only thirteen bolts, all drilled on lead—as opposed to rappelling from the top down—in the five-hundred-foot face. It would be another year before anyone else would even attempt to climb the Bachar-Yerian. And after falling on some of the long stretches between bolts, some of the world's top climbers would walk away from the route, calling it unrepeatable.

Just as El Cap was possible, Bachar-Yerian was repeatable.

But even thirty years later, as Alex Honnold was scampering all over Yosemite like it was a giant playground, the Bachar-Yerian remained as one of Yosemite's serious tests.

John Bachar died July 5, 2009. He fell while free soloing a rela-tively tame rock formation near his home in Mammoth Lakes, California. He was fifty-two.

One of his obituaries included this detail: It was estimated that Bachar had done 1.5 million feet of unroped climbing in his life. But, as the *Los Angeles Times* obit said, he was "perhaps best known for his first ascent of the Bachar-Yerian (5.11c) route in Yosemite's Tuolumne Meadows."

This, I eventually realized, is why Dave Yerian was so passionate about bolts. Or walls free of them. Everybody needs a rock, and his was not far from here.

"After John's death, I kind of represent Bachar-Yerian," he said.

Nonclimbers tend to focus on the danger of rock climbing, the proximity to death. But climbers spend tens of thousands of days on these glacier-polished granite walls each year, and there is an average of about 2.5 deaths a year. And in the next breath after bringing up death, Dave Yerian was talking about life, worrying about what his generation was leaving for the next one.

"This is all we've got," he said, pointing to the landscape beyond the parking lot. "We're using up all the resources. Rock, food, water, air."

I couldn't help but notice that when he rattled off a list of essentials for living, the first thing he mentioned—before food, water, and air—was rock.

KEN YAGER TOOK a seat on one of the benches in Yosemite Village, the congested heart of the congested valley. In my list of people to talk to while in the valley, I had written down Yager's name and, as a reminder to myself, "Mr. Clean." Yager, an accomplished climber, not only started the Yosemite Facelift, he owned a business now that was responsible for cleaning the floors and windows at the Ahwahnee, the luxurious hotel in the valley. He was working odd and long hours, but he said he'd be happy to meet.

He was fifty-three years old, and he looked fit but tired.

"Mind if I smoke?" he said.

I was a bit surprised, not because I thought he'd toss a butt on the ground, but because he had climbed El Capitan dozens of times.

There certainly are more accomplished climbers than Yager in Yosemite history. He will be the first to tell you that. But—and this is why so many people told me I should meet with him—few climbers have cherished that history quite like he has.

He has collected thousands of artifacts, going back to 1869.

He has three of the famed stove-leg pitons—literally legs from a woodstove that were turned into equipment for that first ascent of El Cap.

Yager described how he got hooked on climbing these walls, starting with the first time he touched El Cap. He was thirteen. His family had come to Yosemite for a vacation. They were on the way out of the valley, passing through the meadow, when he made his dad stop the car and wait while he ran up to the base, touched the rock, and stared up at the wall.

"Right then, I knew I wanted to climb it," he said.

At seventeen, he made his first attempt. It was December. The days were short. And he had never spent a night on a wall before. After two and a half days, he realized he was in over his head. He climbed down. But he returned the following summer, and this time he did it. He climbed the Triple Direct route, which he describes as "one of the easiest routes," adding that nothing on El Cap is easy.

He since had climbed El Cap so many times that he lost count. He shrugs this off, saying anyone can climb it if they put their mind to it. When I asked him the hardest part, he didn't point to one section of the wall. He pointed to the whole wall, the intimidation of it.

"You have to break it down, pitch by pitch," he said. "It would be like writing a book. Are you going to start and go, 'Oh, shit, what am I going to write in chapter 28?'"

Knowing my propensity for panic, I said I probably would do exactly that. And I couldn't imagine working my way up El Cap.

He said it's like going on a vacation, the best vacation ever, one that once it ends, you can't wait to do it again. When you're on a wall in Yosemite, he said, it doesn't matter that you have a pile of bills sitting at home, or that your girlfriend just left you, or that you don't really know what you're going to do when you reach the top and go back to the horizontal world. All that matters is what is right in front of you. The wall. The next movement, the next pitch.

He doesn't climb as much as he'd like to anymore. He's too busy. But he's always thinking about it, noticing the light on a wall, picturing new ways to attack different pieces of rock. He says records are going to keep falling here. Someday, maybe soon, somebody will climb El Cap without a rope. Maybe Alex Honnold.

Before going to Yosemite, I wasn't sure what other climbers, especially the relative old-timers, thought of Honnold. Yager pretty much summed up what I had heard repeatedly.

"Oh, he's badass," he said. "There's no doubt. He's the man right now. Who else is going to go up and climb the Northwest Face of Half Dome without a rope?"

He said Alex was handling fame well, keeping a clear head, remaining humble. Then he added something.

"I do worry about him," he said. "I was friends with John Bachar."

I mentioned that I had met Dave Yerian at the Climbers Coffee and learned a little about Bachar and the Bachar-Yerian route. I had wondered if Yerian's understandable attachment to the route led him to inflate what it represents. But when Yager said that decades later the route is "still pretty sporty and heads-up"—so much so that while he had lost count of how many times he had climbed El Cap, he knew exactly how many times he had climbed Bachar-Yerian: none.

"I had a dream I did it once," he said with a laugh. "Then I woke up sweating, like whoa."

That era wasn't the start of the bolting battles, though. Yager pointed out that some trace it to David Brower, considered one of the most prominent environmentalists in American history, and the expansion bolts he used to make the first ascent of Shiprock in northwestern New Mexico in 1939.

"Or if you want to go back even further, 1875, the first ascent of Half Dome, the cables route," he said. "George Anderson drilled that with a single jack and handheld drill."

"The cables route that is still there?" I asked.

"Yeah, nowadays it's not much, but back then it was badass," he said.

For some of us, I said, it still seems pretty intimidating, maybe even badass.

IN THE 1860S, California state geologist Josiah Whitney—the man whose name now is on the highest peak in the Lower 48—did an extensive survey of the state and published a six-volume series titled *The Geological Survey of California* (1864–1870).

This is of note partly because he uses the words "national park" several years before the creation of the first one, and partly because of his description of Yosemite and Half Dome: "It has not the massiveness of El Capitan, but is more astonishing." He wrote that "it is . . . perfectly inaccessible, being probably the only one of all the prominent points about the Yosemite which never has been, and never will be, trodden by human foot."

It didn't take long for someone to access the perfectly inaccessible. In 1875, George Anderson, a Scottish trail builder, hiked to the saddle, a point where others had given up, and drilled a hole in the granite, which rose about four hundred feet at nearly a 45-degree angle. He pounded a spike—an iron eyebolt—into the hole, attached a rope to it, and repeated. He drilled and pounded, five or six feet apart, until his two feet trod the top of Half Dome.

Avalanches eventually ripped Anderson's fixed ropes off Half Dome. But in 1919, the Sierra Club paid for the installation of the first set of cables.

With the cables, you didn't need rock climbing expertise and experience to climb Half Dome. You just had to have the ability to hike to the cables—about an eight-mile hike, climbing more than four thousand feet from the valley floor—and the physical and mental strength to climb a final four hundred feet that, while hardly badass to the men and women dotting the nearby vertical walls, remained daunting to anyone with a fear of heights.

While the hike and its final stretch certainly scared away some Yosemite visitors, it also served to draw many others. The place where Whitney predicted human feet would not trod eventually became so congested—as many as 1,200 people on a busy day and more than 50,000 during the typical May-to-October season—that when I arrived in Yosemite, the park service was using a temporary plan, issuing 400 permits a day to climb the cables, and working on developing a long-term plan.

The process intensified in 2009 after a forty-year-old software engineer from Northern California slipped from the cables on a cold and rainy Saturday afternoon and fell to his death. He wasn't the first fatality on the cables. But his fall caused other climbers to panic and led to what the park service called a "controlled evacuation"—transporting forty-one climbers from Half Dome down to the valley in the middle of the night.

Some wanted the complete removal of the cables. Some wanted them to remain up with no restrictions. For now, the park service decided on a middle ground that upset people on both ends of the debate. The cables would remain, but to climb them would require a permit. Many were snapped up in a preseason lottery. But there also was a last-minute lottery that allowed people to apply for any remaining spots two days in advance.

I put my name in that lottery and got one of the last-minute permits.

It was dark and chilly when I left my tent at 5:30 A.M. I put on my headlamp and walked around the deserted service road to the start of the Mist Trail, leading to Vernal Fall, Nevada Fall, the John Muir Trail, and Half Dome. In a few hours, this first part of the trail would be crowded with people following the pavement—yes, pavement at this point—to the first waterfall. But at this hour, it was quiet and serene. I could see a couple of headlamps in the distance and hear the tinkling of the river next to me.

As I got closer to Vernal Fall and heard the distant sound growing louder and louder, eventually turning into a roar, it brought to mind the experience of rafting through the Grand Canyon, approaching a rapids on the Colorado River.

The sun came up. I passed Nevada Fall and climbed to Little Yosemite Valley, a little over 6,000 feet in elevation, where I went to the Merced River and refilled my hydration pack.

The top of Half Dome, at 8,842 feet, is nearly 5,000 feet above the starting point. It is a challenging hike, comparable to going to the Grand Canyon and hiking from the rim to the river and back in one day. But more than that, as is the case with the popular trails in the Grand Canyon, it didn't become popular merely by accident. This is a trail that can still give you a small taste of the euphoria that had Muir talking to plants and rocks in 1869. ("I asked the boulders I met, when they came and wither they were going.") And as I continued on, I kept thinking that on a hike like this, so much is made of where you're going that the beauty and challenge of getting there often is undersold and overlooked—a metaphor for life if there ever was one.

It had turned into a perfect morning, the sunlight streaming through the tall trees, catching the edges of the branches and leaves.

As the trail climbed higher and the trees thinned, even the sound changed. The roar of the river was long gone, its loud voice replaced by that of the breeze. I think even if I had closed my eyes, I could have told you I now was high above the valley.

Every so often the stillness was interrupted as a jet passed overhead.

The side of Half Dome—the side with the cables—came into view in the distance. I caught up with an older couple ahead of me. They asked where I was from.

"Florida," I said.

He said they were from near Daytona Beach. We talked about how nothing in America's flattest state—highest elevation, 345 feet—can prepare you for hikes like this. They said this was their second attempt at climbing Half Dome. The last time they had tried, they just weren't strong enough. So they had trained for another attempt by hiking back and forth across a bridge.

"You look strong," I said. "Good luck."

I continued on and reached the spot at the base of the subdome with two signs.

"Hiking to Half Dome?" said the top one. "Permit required for travel beyond this point."

"Travel on Subdome and Half Dome is DANGEROUS during and after lightning and rainstorms," said the bottom one.

There wasn't a cloud in the deep blue sky. At this elevation it was cool enough that the sun felt good on my bare arms. The air and rocks were dry. It was hard to imagine better weather for climbing Half Dome.

I scrambled up the zigzagging steps of the subdome, becoming more and more aware of the elevation and exposure, then crested and really saw the cables for the first time.

"No way," a woman near me said. "I'm not doing that."

The two cables are a few feet apart, fixed with bolts into the rock and raised by poles. Between each of the poles, there is a wooden board on the ground, serving as a convenient stopping point.

For rock climbers, this all makes climbing Half Dome laughably easy, like going back to grade school and swinging on the monkey bars. But I always had trouble on the monkey bars. And what was in front of me looked more daunting than I had pictured.

In theory, the slope was roughly halfway between horizontal and vertical. But standing at the base, its DNA sure appeared to be more vertical wall than flat path. And while I had told myself that four hundred feet is basically the length of a football field with both end zones, in this case, pay dirt appeared to be very far in the distance.

I'd tell friends later to picture one of the long escalators that descend deep into Atlanta's airport. Now imagine that instead of the steps, you have a smooth slope that, even when it's dry, is somewhat slick. And that instead of that handrail that glides along firmly, you have two swaying braided steel cables. And that if you slip and fall, you don't stop at the Terminal T station.

I'd also tell them the view is amazing.

I was standing on the subdome with about a dozen people, some who had just come down, some who were working up the nerve to go up, when there was a loud boom, so loud that everyone instantly froze, then turned to whoever was nearby and said the same thing.

"What was that?"

While it sounded a bit like a sonic boom, we couldn't see any planes nearby. There wasn't a cloud in the sky. Plus, it sounded like it had come from below, as if an explosion had ripped through some of the rock in the valley. As it turned out, that's exactly what it was. A trail crew was blasting on the south side of the Mirror Lake trail.

There was a break in the stream of people starting up the cables. So I grabbed hold of the cables and started. I took a step up, then another, and . . . my right foot slipped.

I instinctively gripped the right cable, squeezing it as hard as I could.

It took about ten minutes to reach the top. It felt a lot longer.

When I let go of the cables, I had to pry open each hand.

I took a deep breath and looked around.

The top of Half Dome is huge, about the size of seventeen football fields. There were about two dozen people atop it, most clustered near the end with the cables.

A twentysomething woman was talking excitedly on her phone.

"Dad, guess where I am?" she said. "I'm in Yosemite, but I'm on top of Half Dome."

There was a pause.

"Half Dome," she said.

Another pause.

"Half Dome, Dad," she said, turning to her friends. "People from Ohio don't know what Half Dome is."

I sat down on a large, almost bench-like rock to rest for a minute. I looked to my left and there were two guys, about thirty years old, sitting on a similar slab of rock. Both were looking down. The one closest to me was tapping away on his phone. His buddy was doing something on a tablet.

About ten yards beyond them, a sixtyish man was talking on his cell phone.

Several times during the week I felt like John Muir. And not John Muir the poetic outdoorsman, waxing about the world around him. John Muir the curmudgeon, mumbling to himself about all the people around him.

Until this point, I think the peak of this came when I got a sandwich at one of the restaurants and sat down at a picnic table. At the other end of the table, there was a retired couple from Georgia. The man asked what cell service I had.

"Verizon," I said.

"How's your signal here?" he said.

"Fine," I said.

In some parts of the valley, I could make and receive calls. In other parts, I had no service. And both of those were fine. In fact, by this point of the year, I had begun to prefer places where I didn't have any service.

"I only have two bars," the man said, clearly disgusted by this inconvenience.

Atop Half Dome, I pulled my phone out of my pocket. Four bars. A better signal than I had in my own living room. I shoved it back in my pocket. I was going to stick to my original plan. I wasn't going to call home until I finished the hike.

I headed off to another piece of the summit, doing something I found myself doing often while in Yosemite: smugly judging others, looking down at their idea of a proper national park experience.

Whenever I did this, I eventually realized the absurdity of it. By sleeping on the ground, in a tent, was my experience somehow more authentic and profound than that of the person in the big RV with the satellite dish? There were plenty of people in Yosemite, on the rock walls and beyond, who could roll their eyes at what I was doing. Camping in the valley? Ooh. How far were you from the bathroom and running water? And you did the hike up to Half Dome, using the cables? Isn't that cute?

What did I care if someone else wanted to spend some of their time atop Half Dome updating their Facebook page or posting something to Instagram?

I'd tell myself to stop judging others. And then thirty seconds later, I'd do it again. This, I realized, is why I don't like going to crowded parks. It's not just that I don't like all the other people. I don't like the person I become.

It didn't take much to get some breathing room in the thirteen acres atop Half Dome. I wandered to the other side, passing the piles of rocks that people had set up. In one case, someone spelled out a message: "It Ain't Easy."

I thought about what Half Dome must have been like when more than a thousand people climbed it in a single day. I had seen photos of the cables crammed with people between them, as tight as a New York City subway train during rush hour. When I decided to head down, there wasn't a single person in the top two hundred feet of the cables.

As I carefully scooted down, taking small steps while gripping the cable, a young boy and his father came flying up the cables. I asked the boy how old he was.

"Ten," he said with a smile.

A few minutes later, I came to the older couple I had talked to on the way up. They had made it to the cables. And they clearly had something in common with the ten-year-old boy. They were exhilarated, proud, and maybe unlike the boy, a little tired.

When I made it to the bottom, I once again pried my fingers open, then began heading back to the valley. On the way down, I took the slightly longer route, including more of the John Muir Trail.

I ended up hiking part of the way with a man I had seen atop Half

Dome. He also was doing the hike by himself. He was in his seventies, dehydrated and struggling. I gave him one of my gels. He said the last time he did this he was in his fifties, and it was much easier.

I wondered if I'd be able to do this in another twenty years.

ANYONE WHO WATCHED all six parts of *The National Parks: America's Best Idea* probably remembers Shelton Johnson. Even if you don't remember his name, you remember him, an African-American ranger with an earring. During the series, he talked about the Buffalo Soldiers, the African-American troops who defended Yosemite in the early 1900s; described his own personal journey from childhood in inner-city Detroit to getting off a bus in Yellowstone; and, in perhaps my favorite two minutes of the entire twelve hours, recalled one ordinary winter morning delivering the mail by snowmobile and being mesmerized by the bison.

Before going to Yosemite I contacted Shelton—even via e-mail he has the kind of personality that quickly puts you on a first-name basis—and we figured out a time and place to meet. We spent a couple of hours talking one afternoon. I went to his weekly Buffalo Soldiers presentation. And at the end of the week, I tagged along as he led children on a Junior Ranger hike, helping me understand why Dayton Duncan, the writer behind the PBS series, said Shelton might be a modern-day Muir.

In one way, he may be better.

If there is a gaping flaw in Muir's legacy, it is that as he fell in love with the High Sierra, he consistently and willfully ignored its history. Or at least one significant piece of it. The man-made part. People were living in the Yosemite area for thousands of years before a white man stumbled on the valley in the 1830s. And the natives were still living there when Muir arrived in 1869.

When Muir wrote of the natives he encountered from Wisconsin to Florida to California, he sometimes expressed admiration for their connection to the natural world, but he frequently wrote of them with disdain. They were unclean, he said, and undeserving of a place as hallowed as Yosemite. ("They seemed to have no right place in the landscape, and I was glad to see them fading out of sight down the pass.")

Shelton, while certainly echoing much of Muir's love of the rocks and trees and rivers, had done quite the opposite with history. He found pieces of the past that were overlooked and lost, dug them up and breathed life back into them.

And while Muir wrote letters to Teddy Roosevelt and convinced the president to come camp with him in Yosemite, Shelton had his own letter-writing success. He wrote to one of the richest, most influential people in America. And because of his letter, Oprah Winfrey came to Yosemite.

"My entire career I have been bothered by the lack of African-Americans visiting national parks," he wrote. "It has bothered me when I look out and I meet people from Germany, from Spain, from Africa. And yet, I can't find an African-American from Chicago or from Boston or from Detroit. I need your help spreading the word."

So Oprah and her best friend, Gayle King, included Yosemite in a road trip. And while she certainly could have stayed in the Ahwahnee Hotel like a long list of rich and famous visitors before her had—Queen Elizabeth II, Dwight D. Eisenhower, John F. Kennedy, Ronald Reagan, Steve Jobs, Lucille Ball, Charlie Chaplin—Oprah chose to camp. At the end of the show, Oprah gave the pop-up camper that she bought for the trip to the lone African-American she met in the campground.

"I recommend the national parks," she told the studio audience. "Everybody should go there once in a lifetime."

A key word: once.

Shelton's story was quite different. His life was changed the day he stepped off a bus in Yellowstone and saw a bison walk by. He was just taking a summer job during grad school to wash dishes. But he knew then and there he wasn't going back to finish his master's in poetry (or, as he jokes, in unemployment). When I met him, he had been a park ranger for twenty-six years, the last nineteen at Yosemite. He was fifty-four, a few years older than me but infinitely wiser and deeper.

One thing in particular he said stuck with me. He said that while Yosemite typically is captured in big, sweeping landscapes—picture an Ansel Adams photo, a moment beautifully frozen in time—the park is the antithesis of a static place. Everything here is constantly changing.

"Life into death, death into life," he said.

And when he talked about the future and the parks, he didn't use the word "relevancy," as so many others had. His words were stronger, more forceful. And they applied to much more than any one demographic.

"I think the survival of humanity is completely dependent on our ability to reconnect with the earth," he said. "We are becoming the first species . . . that is intent on making itself alien to its own ecosystem, its own habitat."

Later in the week, I went to the Nature Center at Happy Isles, on the east end of the valley. I had asked Shelton if I could record him reading a section of his book. He said he couldn't do it while he was on the NPS clock, but suggested that we meet during his lunch break. So I decided to tag along when he led a Junior Ranger hike before lunch.

About a dozen children, plus their parents, had gathered outside the nature center. Shelton arrived wearing his work attire—the NPS ranger uniform, including the iconic flat hat—and asked all the young people, the Junior Rangers, to come forward.

He introduced himself, asked how many of the children had been to a national park before and how many were in one for the first time.

"I want you to feel like you're home, because this is your home," he said. "This is part of your property. You're just checking in to see how it is. . . . So we're going to start. And the first thing I'd like you to do is just close your eyes and listen for ten seconds."

The children closed their eyes. So did some of their parents.

There was a slight breeze, rustling the nearby trees. But another sound, a little farther away, was more prevalent. Water.

This hike was about trees, but without the water, he said, these trees wouldn't be here. And without water, we wouldn't be here, either. Water is life, he said. So the sound of water is the sound of life.

Midway through the hike, he gathered the Junior Rangers, pointed at a nearby tree, and asked, "What color are these leaves?"

"Green," shouted several kids.

"What color are these leaves," he repeated. "Look carefully. Are they all green?"

The children looked closer and saw that some of the leaves were pinkish.

"So what's happening?" Shelton said. "What temperatures are we getting lately in the morning? Has it been hot or cold?"

"Cold," answered the Junior Rangers.

He explained some basic science that I learned in elementary school but had long since forgotten. It wasn't so much that new colors were appearing in the leaves. It was that they were coming out of hiding. The chlorophyll, the green pigment, was starting to break down, allowing the anthocyanins (reds) and carotenes (yellows) to come out.

This tree was a dogwood, he said, and these leaves were one of the first signs of fall in Yosemite Valley.

As he and the rest of the group moved on, I stood there for a moment, looking at one pinkish leaf, feeling like I had been punched in the gut. Fall was around the corner? Already? How did that happen?

"Junior Rangers, Junior Rangers," Shelton said a few minutes later. "All good things must come to an end. I'm afraid at this point, there's only one thing left. I'm afraid I'm going to have to give you your patches."

He asked them to form a line in front of him.

"Remember, know your trees and you'll be connected to the earth just like they are," he said. "That's what this is all about, connecting you to the earth and Yosemite. Because one day this hat will be yours."

He took off his hat and put it on the girl standing in front of him.

The parents applauded.

I don't think any of them knew that their guide had been the star of the PBS series or that Oprah came here because of him. They just knew that beyond getting a refresher course in things like photosynthesis, and learning how to identify the incense cedar and ponderosa pine, they felt even more connected to this place.

We walked back to a path near the nature center. I pulled out my copy of *Gloryland*, turned to page 212, and asked Shelton to read the paragraph that started on the bottom of the page.

We were back close enough to the Merced to hear the sound of its water. He cleared his throat and began reading the words he put in the mouth of Elijah Yancy.

> God is everywhere, but I'm thinking he prefers some places more than others. I'm thinking he spends a lot of time in these mountains. That means my mama's bound to be happy, cause I'm finally a churchgoing man. Every day in Yosemite is like Sunday, and I finally don't have to dress right or mind my manners. All I got to do to be in church is open my eyes in the morning. Every day here is a kind of prayer, and every night the prayer is answered. I can hear a sermon in the leaves whenever the wind blows. I can hear an amen when the rivers answer. When it rains, the world is singing what was sung at the beginning of creation, and at night before I close my eyes again I can hear it sounding in the ground under my head, in the rocks, the trees, the creeks, and deep in my bones, the same thing sung softly all night long.

It wasn't until later, when I went back and reread the paragraph, that I noticed the next paragraph, in which the book's protagonist is trying to figure out what to make of nature's sermon. Considering I was about to leave Yosemite, it felt particularly fitting.

"I can never quite make out the words, and I'm afraid I'll have to leave Yosemite before I understand what God is saying to me, and what I should be saying back."

In another hundred years, visitors will come to Yosemite not only to experience the place in the twenty-second century but also to look back. They will read John Muir's words. They will look at Ansel Adams's photos. And I hope they will hear Shelton Johnson's voice, talking about the Buffalo Soldiers, the trees, and the water and about how nothing really is static. Especially not Yosemite Valley. Life into death, death into life.

I came here to think about loving a park to death. I ended up quite often thinking simply about death. Not just because of hantavirus, drownings, and climbing accidents. And not in a dark, depressing way. Yosemite—and perhaps all national parks—makes one both keenly aware of death and dying and grateful for life and living.

It took me forty years to make it back to Yosemite. I didn't know when I'd return. I could relate to what John Muir wrote in 1869 about leaving—saying he prayed he might see it again—and what Shelton Johnson echoed nearly 150 years later. Once he arrived here, he didn't leave, because leaving was one of the saddest thoughts in the world.

It helped to know where I was going next: one of America's newest parks, a place where death didn't hide in beauty, a place where beauty emerged from death.

9

*

SEPTEMBER: FLIGHT 93
NATIONAL MEMORIAL

The winding two-lane road, part of America's first transcontinental road for automobiles, rolled through the hills of Pennsylvania between Pittsburgh and Shanksville. Lori Guadagno sat in the passenger seat of a rental car, unable to stop coughing. She was on her third round of antibiotics, trying to knock out a lingering case of bronchitis.

Lori kept apologizing and fretting about what she was supposed to do the next day—give a speech at our destination, a place that at the end of the previous century would have been one of the last places in America you'd have pegged as a future site for a national park.

This part of Pennsylvania certainly did have a bucolic beauty to it, especially at this time of year, past the scorching days of summer and before the first freeze. And when the Lincoln Highway was finished in 1913, it passed right by our destination—at the time a mix of woods and farms and rolling landscape common to Somerset County.

But by the end of the twentieth century, pretty much everything there, including the beauty, had been stripped away to get at what was beneath the surface. Coal.

As was the case in other parts of Pennsylvania, West Virginia, and Kentucky, the land became more valuable for large-scale mining than for family farming. Companies bought the land and started tearing it apart.

Trees and topsoil were mere obstacles. The sounds of nature were replaced by the grinding and coughing of massive pieces of machinery. The scent of leaves and flowers and grass were replaced by the smells of mining. Surface mining. Underground mining. Whatever it took to get to the coal, until that was nearly gone too.

Shortly before the end of the twentieth century, the last surface mine closed, and a reclamation project began.

On September 11, 2001, there still were massive pieces of mining equipment above ground and some men working underground.

If on that morning you had tried to predict where national parks might be added in the twenty-first century, you might have pointed to the long-running debate about Maine's north woods. Or maybe to something to commemorate the Buffalo Soldiers that Shelton Johnson brought to life. Or perhaps to Delaware, at the time the only state in America without a National Park Service site.

But this place? When the sun rose on that bright September morning in 2001, not one person in America would have predicted that this place would join Gettysburg, a hundred miles to its east, as part of our National Park System.

Then a plane plunged into the edge of the surface mine.

There were forty-four people onboard, none of whom expected they would end up here. Four were hijackers, apparently intent on flying the plane to Washington, D.C., perhaps directly into the Capitol. Forty were crew members and passengers who boarded United 93 in Newark, New Jersey, thinking they were on a routine flight to San Francisco.

Lori's younger brother, her only sibling, was one of those passengers.

RICHARD GUADAGNO WAS thirty-eight. He would have turned thirty-nine two weeks later. As we drove through rural Pennsylvania, Lori mentioned that this September he would have turned fifty.

"Hard to believe," she said, shaking her head.

They grew up in New Jersey. She was two years older than her brother. He was, she once told me, a bizarre kid. A cool but bizarre kid. She tried to explain what she meant. While she and all the other kids in the Jersey suburb were doing typical kids-in-suburbia things, her brother would hang out with two old Italian men in the neighborhood and learn about gardening. One summer, he grew twenty-three varieties of lettuce in the family yard.

He loved plants and rocks, butterflies and frogs. Especially frogs.

When he was five or six, the family went to a restaurant on the Jersey Shore. He looked at the menu and saw frog legs. He started crying and wanted to leave immediately.

When his father took him golfing, Richard had little interest in the game. But he loved exploring the places most people try to avoid while on a golf course—the tall grass and woods and ponds. He'd come home excited, not because he had birdied a hole, but because he had found tadpoles and cattails.

"From the get-go, he definitely followed his own path," Lori said.

That path inevitably led into the woods. When they were growing up, they didn't take grand family trips to Yellowstone or Yosemite. But many Sundays, after church, they would go to Cadwalader Park, a hundred-acre park designed by Frederick Law Olmsted in the 1880s. And on Saturday mornings, after their father dropped Lori off at her art class, he sometimes would take Richard to Washington Crossing Historic Park.

The park was created because of its place in history. It's where George Washington crossed the Delaware on Christmas Day 1776. But this isn't necessarily what stuck with Richard and Lori. It was the adventure of quickly leaving their urban and suburban world and heading into the woods, hiking to Bowman's Hill Tower, climbing to the top of it and, on a clear day, being able to see for miles and miles.

While at Rutgers University, Richard volunteered at Great Swamp National Wildlife Refuge. When he graduated, he began working for a private consulting firm. After about six months, Richard decided he was working on the wrong side of land-use debates. He didn't want to help people take down trees and develop land. He wanted to stop them. He wanted to take back land that had been damaged and restore it.

In 2001, he was in his seventeenth year with the U.S. Fish and Wildlife Service. The job took him to Delaware and Oregon and California. Wherever he went, he was passionate about protecting the land and encouraging people to use it—but only in the right way.

Even his mom wasn't allowed to break the rules.

One of the favorite family stories comes from when Richard was managing the Baskett Slough National Wildlife Refuge in Oregon. The 2,492-acre refuge was created to provide a wintering habitat for dusky Canada geese. But it also is a place where the sky-blue wings of the endangered Fender's blue butterflies float between the purple of Kincaid's lupine. Richard loved this place and knew every inch of the trail that meandered through it.

When his parents, Jerry and Bea, came to visit, they went for a walk and his mother started to pick some of the wildflowers. Richard instantly went from son to ranger.

"He yelled at me not to pick the flowers," Bea said years later, her vision gone, but the memory still clear. "I said, 'Don't holler at me, these flowers are going on our dining room table.'"

He always grew his own wildflowers for such purposes. He did that when he moved to Northern California in the spring of 2000. He was managing the Humboldt Bay National Wildlife Refuge, a fragile and rich complex of wetlands and dunes. He was living in an A-frame house surrounded by two hundred trees he had planted, his eight guitars, his taxidermy, his surfboard, his telescope, and his German shepherd.

He was, Lori said, a renaissance man. He was sentimental yet tough. He ran seven miles every night. He lifted weights. He carried a gun for work. And as part of his training, he took a course that taught him, among other things, what to do if he was on a plane that was being hijacked.

His big sister rolled her eyes over that one.

"When are you ever going to need that?" she said.

THE LAST TIME she saw him was September 9, 2001.

She paused before driving away from her parents' house in New Jersey. It was Sunday, the end of a weekend of celebrating her grandmother's hundredth birthday. Family had come from all over the country.

That morning, before leaving, she had given her brother a big hug and whispered something in his ear. He was going back to California. She was preparing to move to Florida from Vermont. She wasn't sure when they'd see each other again. So she squeezed him tight and said, "Of all the good-byes, this is the hardest."

When she pulled away from the house, she saw that the family was continuing the tradition of gathering at the window. Everyone was smiling and waving, except Richard. He was standing there, looking the way she felt.

She drove away crying. And she cried for a good, long time. But while she was on the turnpike, a song came on the radio. U2's "Beautiful Day."

She looked outside. It was one of those perfect fall days in the Northeast. Brilliant blue sky. Sun shining. It was indeed a beautiful day. And not just because of the September weather. As adults, she and her little brother had bonded in a way that you can't when you're kids. Sometimes he'd tell her, "I'll never make it to forty."

She'd get so mad when he said that. She'd tell him to cut the fatalistic nonsense. Even with all the crazy stuff he did—and he was always finding new ways to test his mind and body—he was going to be around for a long time.

She told him, "During our lives, we'll have our lovers, our husbands, our wives, but in the end, there will be the two of us, sitting in rocking chairs, whining and complaining."

When the sun rose on September 11, 2001, splashing across

Cadillac Mountain, then making its journey west, it was another beautiful day. That's one of the details that people always seem to remember.

Lori was in her classroom in Vermont, working with special-needs children, when another teacher came in and said something weird had happened. A plane had flown into the World Trade Center.

Her reaction wasn't shock. She figured some pilot flying a small plane had gotten lost and flown into the building. When she lived in New York City, she remembered crazy things like that happening every so often.

She went back to working with the children. Then the other teacher came back in. It had happened again.

She remembers walking to the library to see the television coverage, still not thinking this was much more than what you might see on the nightly news any other day. Then she saw the images. And she did what all of America did. She gasped. She froze. She cursed.

She started to do an inventory in her head. Who works in the World Trade Center? Who might be there?

She was busy worrying about friends and strangers when the broadcaster said something that made her hair stand on edge. A plane flying from Newark to San Francisco was unaccounted for.

"It doesn't look good, Lori," her father said when she reached him. "It doesn't look good."

The rest is mostly a blur. The drive from Vermont back to New Jersey, on an empty freeway, passing signs that said, "New York City. Closed." The gathering at her parents' house, seeing her brother's name scrolling across the bottom of the screen, thinking that it has to be a mistake. This doesn't happen to our family. Our family is boring. Our family doesn't make the news.

That night, unable to sleep, she went into the living room at about three A.M.

Her brother didn't die, she kept telling herself. He's in that wooded area near the crash site. He's hurt, but he's a survivalist.

But even as she thought this, she also thought about how she should move back to New Jersey, to be there to help her parents cope. But she didn't think she could do it. She wanted to—maybe even needed to—go ahead with plans to move to Florida and start a program at Wolfson Children's Hospital and Nemours Children's Specialty Care in Jacksonville.

It was called Art with a Heart in Healthcare. The plan was to use art to help children who were sick and dying. She believed in the power of art. It couldn't cure cancer, but it could offer them some comfort. And, as she sat in the living room that night, she hoped it could do the same for her.

Her father walked into the living room. And when she told him this, he told her to go to Florida, to try to start that new life.

In the days and weeks after 9/11, memorial services were held all over the country, in churches and cathedrals, in some of America's most historic buildings. Richard's family and friends held a small gathering in a historic park, the one where George Washington crossed in 1776 and Richard explored as a boy.

One of their neighbors, a practicing shaman, led a small ceremony.

When Lori and her parents described it to me years later, they laughed. Here you had a bunch of Italian Americans, most of them Catholics, and a practicing shaman. It made for quite the scene.

"But it was the most rational send-off we could think of at the time," Lori said. "It had to be a park. And this was the park where it all started."

A picture of Richard was placed near the base of a tree. They each approached the tree and left a rock next to the photo. Everybody had a rock for Richard.

The 1.7-mile path in Oregon—the one where he chastised his mother for picking flowers—eventually became the thousandth national recreation trail in America. It was named the Rich Guadagno Memorial National Recreation Trail.

The visitor center at Humboldt Bay National Wildlife Refuge was named after him. Near the building, there is a large rock with a plaque. And then there is the rock in a field in Pennsylvania.

It was placed in the field shortly before the tenth anniversary of September 11.

It's a massive rock, so large that it kept snapping a chain that a construction company was using to move it.

When New Enterprise Stone and Lime Company, a Pennsylvania construction company, was hired to build an entrance and road leading to the place where the plane crashed, the company was asked to place a rock in the field. It did that for free. And when the chain kept snapping and a park official suggested that maybe a smaller rock would do, the construction crew insisted that no, they would get this one there.

"They deserve this stone," the foreman said.

The crew regrouped and eventually moved a seventeen-ton sandstone boulder to a spot at the bottom of a hill, near a grove of hemlock trees on the edge of a reclaimed strip mine.

This is the approximate impact spot of Flight 93.

This rock is the headstone for the crew and passengers.

This is where Lori and I were headed. To a field in Pennsylvania, another rock and one of the newest pieces of our National Park System. The Flight 93 National Memorial.

I FIRST MET Lori, her parents, and Ross Bratlee—Lori's longtime boyfriend and a close friend of Richard's—shortly before the fifth anniversary of September 11.

My newspaper editor asked if I had any ideas for a story, something with a local angle that the paper hadn't done yet. At the time, bumper stickers saying "Remember 9/11" and "Never Forget" still could be found on cars all over America, especially in a city like Jacksonville with a strong military history and presence. But in five years, it felt like people already were remembering 9/11 as the day the

Twin Towers fell, and forgetting that there were two other planes, one of which never made it to its hijackers' target.

I had seen a passing reference in a story about Lori and Art with a Heart to her brother's being on United 93. I decided to call her.

I don't remember what kind of introduction I stumbled through. I just remember that Lori said she hadn't done many interviews, but she appreciated some of the columns I had written (hardly a given). She spoke eloquently about her brother and Flight 93 and then said I would be welcome to spend time with her family in Pennsylvania.

After I had spent several days there, Lori's mother said, "You're a part of the family now." Lori shrugged and said with a smile, "You're stuck with us."

Through the years, our relationship went from that of journalist and subject to friends and, as they kept telling me, part of the family. And even if we didn't talk regularly, we did stay in touch. If nothing else, every September there was a very obvious reminder to call Lori and try to meet them at Jacksonville Beach, where they often gathered to remember Richard on September 11 anniversaries.

I never knew Richard, but as more years passed, I felt like I did.

The more I learned about him, the more I felt we would have been friends. We both loved the outdoors, running, books. I was born in 1961. He was born in 1962. And the rest of the details on his Fish and Wildlife ID—five-eight, 150 pounds, brown eyes, brown hair—were almost identical to the ones on my driver's license.

I never said this aloud to Lori or her family, but I looked at Richard and saw some of myself in him. A much better version of myself. One that had a full head of brown hair, could bench-press more than twice his weight, play the guitar, fix things, save wildlife, and if necessary, maybe help overtake some hijackers.

In my first phone call with Lori, I had asked something about cell phone calls. Did they hear from Richard? It was the one time I remember feeling as if I had touched a nerve or said something I shouldn't have. In time I realized why this question bothered Lori and her parents. The initial narrative about what happened on

Flight 93 was built around the phone calls from the plane to family, friends, and authorities. Thirteen people placed thirty-seven calls. In the immediate aftermath of September 11, the story of Flight 93 quickly became the story of Todd Beamer saying, "Let's roll!" and then a few heroic men rushing the cockpit and preventing the hijackers from reaching their target.

Richard sometimes was included in this narrative. When *USA Today* ran a story with a headline that said, "Passengers likely halted attack on D.C.," it included head shots of six men, including Richard. As time went on, the narrative often was narrowed to the story of four men, former athletes who made calls to loved ones, then thwarted the hijackers.

It wasn't that Richard's family wanted to take anything away from what others did on that flight. To the contrary, they want those four or five passengers at the heart of the early narrative to be remembered long after we're all gone. But in the process, they didn't want everyone else on the plane to be forgotten.

"It bothered our family and others to hear presumptuously that this person took down the flight, that this person rallied everyone . . . and, yes, I was incredibly resentful," she said. "We felt like we had lost Richard once, and we were losing him again."

AMERICAN HISTORY IS full of stories that are as much myth as fact.

There are so many examples it's hard to figure out where to start. Perhaps with one of the most famous stories of American heroism, a night in 1775 when historians say about forty men rode their horses through the Massachusetts countryside.

Eighty-five years later, Henry Wadsworth Longfellow wrote a poem that began, "Listen, my children, and you shall hear, of the midnight ride of . . ."

Quick, name one rider other than Paul Revere.

It's not that Revere wasn't a key part of what happened that night. But he was hardly alone. William Dawes started the ride with him. And the only rider who made it to Concord was Samuel Prescott.

The common denominator in our flawed narratives is often patriotism. Intentionally and unintentionally, we clean up stories, we connect dots when we shouldn't, or we embellish when often no embellishment is necessary.

And if there was any place and any story in modern-day America where that could happen, it was a field in Pennsylvania.

We know so much about what happened that day. But there are many things we will never know.

So how do you tell that story? What do you do with that place?

While my plans for the year changed, one piece remained constant. In September I was going to the Flight 93 National Memorial. Lori and I already were making plans when she called me to say she had been asked to be part of a panel at a program at the park three days before the anniversary.

It was going to be held at the future site of a building called the Learning Center, next to the future visitor center, atop a hill looking down the plane flight path, leading to the memorial wall and the impact site.

The title of the program: "9/11 and the Next Generation."

WE FLEW ON to Pittsburgh, through Washington Dulles, on United Airlines.

I hadn't thought twice about which airline we were on when making the reservation. But it hit me when we met at the Jacksonville airport. When the gate agent told Lori she couldn't carry on the poster-shaped box she had with her—which she had just told me she wasn't letting out of her sight—I wanted to tell the agent the story behind the box. I wanted to say that this woman's brother had been on a United flight on September 11, 2001, and this was a framed shadow box containing something found at the crash site. His badge.

It was more than a month after 9/11 when Ed Ryan, an FBI agent who had been working long days at the American 77 crash site at the Pentagon, decided to decompress by riding his motorcycle to Pennsylvania. He went to the site of the Flight 93 crash and spotted something that others had missed in the hemlocks just past the impact site. A gold badge.

There was no name on it, but blue letters and highlights said, "Department of the Interior, U.S. Fishing and Wildlife Service, U.S. Refuge Officer. 1038."

It was Richard's badge. While there were all kinds of mementos of Richard in his parents' house, his badge might have been their most cherished. The family had had it framed, along with four white Department of the Interior ID cards, set against a blue background. And now Lori was taking this back to Pennsylvania, giving it to the National Park Service.

The gate agent in Jacksonville assured Lori they'd take good care of it, and that when we landed in Washington Dulles, she could get it and carry it to our next flight.

When we changed planes in Washington, D.C., the televisions in the concourse showed images of President Obama delivering his convention speech the previous night, followed by an update on hantavirus in Yosemite. Park officials were saying as many as 22,000 visitors might have been exposed. I hadn't been feeling well for a couple of weeks. Hypochondria set in and I called a hantavirus hotline. After asking me some questions, the woman on the other end basically said there probably was another reason I was having flu-like symptoms—because I had a flu-like illness.

So as I drove the rental car on the Pennsylvania Turnpike, we coughed and caught up.

The leaves were starting to turn. I told Lori about how the sight of a single dogwood leaf in Yosemite had made me feel melancholy. She said that growing up in New Jersey she always felt the same way—and now, even though she lived in Florida, she struggled every year as September approached.

"How are you doing?" she asked.

I told her that I wasn't sure, but that this trip now felt even more important to me than when the year started. It was hard to lose my mother, but we'd had 144 days with her after her diagnosis. We were with her when she died. We got to say good-bye. Lori and all the other family members of the Flight 93 passengers never got to do that.

The sky was mostly clear, with streaks of clouds. It was a beautiful day.

At Somerset, we got off the Pennsylvania Turnpike and took Pennsylvania Route 281 to the Old Lincoln Highway. We passed cornfields and barns. A sign in front of a church said, "Back to school? How about back to church?" Several homes had American flags flying out front.

We passed white fences and horses, a cemetery with a stone wall, signs for fall mums, an American Legion post, a junkyard with cars and cars, stretching into the distance.

Shortly before we arrived at the entrance to the Flight 93 National Memorial, we came to State Game Lands 93.

The land across the road from the park was acquired in 2006 to preserve the natural setting and view. When it was dedicated in 2010, one piece of the 665-acre site, which included man-made wetlands and a nature trail, became the Richard J. Guadagno Habitat Area.

In the distance, towering white windmills turned slowly, a reminder of something Lori had pointed out when I came with her family for the fifth anniversary. The wind always seems to be blowing here. She said the wind felt different here. It reminded her of being out west, at places sacred to Native Americans.

When we approached the land, Lori gasped.

The field next to the entrance to State Game Lands 93 was full of sunflowers, Richard's favorite. Hundreds of them, still tall with bright yellow heads, but starting to wilt. With all of their heads bent forward, it didn't take much imagination to look at them and see an entire field of plants bowing toward the entrance of the Flight 93 National Memorial.

As I turned off U.S. 30 and onto the 3.5-mile road leading through the park and to the memorial wall, we tried to orient ourselves.

When I came here with the Guadagnos for the fifth anniversary, there wasn't a permanent memorial. There was just a makeshift temporary one on a forty-foot-long fence atop the hill that Flight 93 passed over, upside down, before plunging into the ground. An estimated 750,000 visitors had visited there, leaving behind every conceivable kind of trinket on the fence and the ground near it. Flags, crosses, flowers, toys, patches, Bibles, medals. Every so often, the park service cleared away the items, cleaned them up, and stored them.

Lori looked at the memorial with an artist's eye. It was like an ever-evolving, kitschy, yet beautiful and raw piece of pop art. And while others kept talking about what kind of monument should be built here on this hill and below, she liked the idea of just letting nature take over. And to a degree, that was what was happening now.

While there already had been all kinds of man-made features added to the 2,200 acres, and much more was planned for the future, the dominant feature was becoming the landscape itself.

We drove the winding, undulating Approach Road. The architect wanted those who visit here to begin with a decompression period, where they leave behind the anxiety of travel and the concerns of everyday life, getting in the memorial frame of mind.

When Lori first came here, two draglines—enormous pieces of mining equipment—still dominated a landscape remarkable for its bleakness. Not only didn't she like what the place was in the immediate aftermath of the crash, she worried about what it would become in the future.

"It could've become a circus, a tacky, overly patriotic kind of thing," she said.

I said I was picturing a monument version of a Toby Keith song. A place where the Statue of Liberty shakes her fist every morning; the fountains rain down red, white, and blue every afternoon; and the gift shop sells "We'll Put a Boot in Your Ass" bumper stickers.

"Oh, it so easily could have become that," she said.

Some of those fears were allayed when this place was put in the hands of the National Park Service. Still, there were understandably many different opinions on what exactly would be fitting. A design competition drew more than a thousand entries. They were narrowed to five finalists. And on September 7, 2005, the winner was announced: Paul Murdoch's *Crescent of Embrace*.

Almost immediately there was controversy.

Some felt that the idea of a crescent-shaped pathway, lined with red maple trees and following the bowl of the landscape beneath the hill, was a nod to Islam. Murdoch explained that wasn't the intent. "We called it a crescent because it was a curving landform," he said. "We called it *Crescent of Embrace* because of the symbolic gesturing of embracing this place."

Lori said she got to the point where she was done with all of it.

"I was like, 'Just throw out the seeds and let it be wild,'" she said.

Eventually the design was modified. The crescent became a circle. And seeds were thrown out. Lots of them. Fields were full of wildflowers. More than fifteen thousand trees had been planted in the April, May, and June before we arrived in September.

As the landscape was coming back to life, wildlife also was returning. One of the rangers said it was routine to see and hear wild turkeys, deer, geese, bullfrogs, crickets. Black bears had been spotted.

Lori said it was starting to feel like a national park.

"Sublime is the word that comes to me when I think of a national park," she said. "And somehow this park evokes that kind of feeling. Even though it wasn't birthed the same way as other national parks and came out of such a tragedy, there is just this sublime quality."

We reached the hill where the temporary memorial once stood and where the visitor center would be in the future. On this

anniversary, it was the site of a giant white tent, set up for the program the next day.

We continued past it, onto the Ring Road, a swooping one-mile
semicircle that drops down into the bowl where the plane crashed,
passing wetlands and wildflowers before reaching the parking lot for
the Memorial Plaza.

Lori wanted to go to the crash site when we first arrived. She
knew that in the next few days, as the anniversary approached, the
atmosphere here would change. It would become busier, noisier.
Helicopters would bring Secretary of Defense Leon Panetta on September 10 and Vice President Joe Biden on September 11. There
would be groups of motorcycle riders, buses with schoolchildren,
television trucks.

And while all of this is good—she wants people to remember
what happened here—she relishes coming here when the park is
quiet. As it was on this afternoon.

There were just a few cars in the parking lot. The sun was shining, the air was unusually still. We walked toward the Memorial
Plaza. The entrance to the plaza includes interpretive panels and a
small visitor shelter, where people can pick up brochures and leave
a personal note tacked up on a board. We had barely gotten out of
the car when one of the volunteer "ambassadors" saw Lori. They
greeted each other, hugging like old friends.

We began the quarter-mile walk to the primary man-made
destination in the park: the Wall of Names.

The wide walkway is coal black. A short, angled wall separates
you from what is beyond it, yet encourages you to be aware of it—
grassland and the hemlocks, part of the final resting place for those
aboard Flight 93. Some said this monument wasn't monumental
enough, that it was too simple, too stark. But Lori was among those
who liked it for exactly those reasons.

"It's quiet, it's simple, it's minimal," she said as we walked toward
the wall. "It's total dignity."

At one point, Lori took a deep breath. It wasn't a deep breath of preparation and trepidation. It was a deep breath of appreciation—of the setting, the day, the serenity.

A few geese flew overhead, honking.

From a distance, the white wall popped out of its surroundings, the black walkway and the blue sky.

The Wall of Names isn't one solid hundred-foot wall. It is a collection of forty panels of white marble from Vermont. Each one is 8 feet high and 2½ feet across, weighs about a thousand pounds, and has a name etched into it.

Between each panel and the next one, there is a small space. They zigzag along the final path of Flight 93. And as ranger Brendan Wilson explained, "Each panel represents an individual, but together they create a larger element that reminds us that these forty people took action as part of a combined and unified effort."

When we reached the wall, Lori walked to the panel that had Richard's name engraved in it.

She leaned against it, patting the rock and smiling.

She straightened up, looked at her brother's name, then placed her left hand on RICHARD and her right hand on GUADAGNO and slowly ran her fingers across the indentations.

She stepped back and looked at the wall. I followed her to a gap in the wall between the final name—Deborah Jacobs Welsh—and a panel with the date. Behind the wall, a path surrounded by bright yellow wildflowers led to a gate. A butterfly fluttered in front of us.

A ranger unlocked the gate for us. It creaked open. And we walked through the field, toward the boulder marking the crash site.

The end farthest from the wall was nearly as tall as Lori. She walked around it, clockwise, her right hand gently touching the rock.

There were flowers and three small American flags in front of the boulder. On top of it there were items left by loved ones, including a small flag, flowers, a 9/11 token, some seashells, and—the most common item atop the big piece of sandstone—much smaller stones.

I thought about the cairns I had seen in other national parks, from the trails in Acadia to the top of Half Dome in Yosemite. Rocks leading your way. Rocks marking an accomplishment. And here was this, rocks being used in a way that dated back thousands of years. Marking the spot where loved ones were buried.

After circling the boulder, Lori turned to the hemlocks beyond it.

"Well, I'm going to brave it back there," she said. "If I can find it, it will be a miracle."

She started wading through the waist-high grass.

At the first anniversary, she and Ross had wandered back into the woods to get away from the chaos in the field. They took some sticks and leaned them against a hemlock tree, building what she described as "our little totem." So every time she came back here, this was one of the things she wanted to do. Go into the hemlocks to check on the trees, the totem, and the ground beneath them.

We walked into the woods and the sound changed. It became quieter, more insulated, but far from silent. Every so often there was the chirping of birds above, mixing with an almost constant high-pitched backdrop of insects.

One of the many details that stuck with me from the stories about 9/11 involved what the first responders heard when they arrived on the scene here.

Nothing.

There undoubtedly was the noise they made, the sirens and sounds of men and women rushing to the scene of a plane crash. But the site itself was quiet. There wasn't even the sound of insects.

The spot instantly became sacred ground. And the hemlocks just beyond the impact site became a thread running through the memorial.

"There it is," Lori said.

She pointed to the branches arranged around the hemlock. They were still there, arranged the way they were when Lori and Ross set them up ten years earlier. She took comfort in finding their totem standing unchanged. But she seemed to take even more comfort in finding change throughout the area, including here in the woods.

As we walked through the woods, every so often she stopped, knelt, and plunged her fingers into the ground.

"It smells like soil again," she said, recalling how it had still smelled like jet fuel those first few trips here. "I keep on thinking I'm going to find something I'm going to recognize. You just have to dig now a little deeper than before. But it's still there. You can find a spot and put your hand in the earth and something comes up."

She said this is where she feels closest to Richard. When she is out at the formal memorial, she wants to be back here. We walked for a while, but before we left the hemlocks, she knelt down again.

"I have to do one final little dig," she said. "It's just this obsessive thing."

She kept pulling up handfuls of dirt, then turning her hand over and letting the soil sift through her fingers.

I asked her about that first time here.

"It just didn't feel. . . . It just didn't feel clean," she said. "It still had the stain of everything on it."

She started digging again while talking.

"I hated being with all of these other people," she said. "I felt so resentful that I had to share this moment and this place with other people. Because I just wasn't there yet in the whole healing process. I was far from it. And I never had an opportunity to share with other people, because I was in Florida. I wasn't with other people in New York. And then coming here and having all of these families that are a part of my story? I remember being, like, 'Just get away.' I remember being back here and building that with Ross and just wanting to hide back here."

She recalled wandering back into the grass near the woods that day—at the time low and dry—and looking up and said, "Oh, God, Richard if you can hear me, please, just give me a sign because I can't take this shit. This is horrible. This sucks. I am lost here. Where are you? Just show me a sign.'"

She had looked down and found a bird's nest at her feet. She picked it up and, cradling it, ran toward her mother and father, saying she had found Richard.

"I was just like the lunatic," she said with a laugh. "Anyone else must have thought this woman absolutely went off her rocker. And I'm sure I did in my own little way. But not really, because to me that was the most tangible sign I possibly could have received from him. And it just shifted the rest of my experience here. I came out of the woods blessed or something, sanctioned by his presence, and it made it feel a little bit better."

She paused and gazed around at the trees. Sunlight streamed through at a low angle. A few mosquitoes circled around us.

I told her that it reminded me of a childhood spot. I had never been here before the fifth anniversary. And yet these woods felt familiar.

"Absolutely," she said.

For her, coming here was like being transported back to one of the parks in New Jersey that she and Richard spent many hours exploring.

"It wasn't the grandeur of being in the West, being in the mountains, that type of thing," she said. "But it was something that I could totally relate to, because we were in places like this. . . . This feels more like home."

She stuck her hand in the ground again. And this time she found something.

She turned her palm up and brushed the dirt off of two short pieces of wire. One red, one blue, tattered and wrapped around each other.

"That," she said, "could easily be a piece of the plane."

She said this with more of a sense of wonderment than of horror. And then she explained that maybe what she had just done—jumping from the serenity of the moment back to the violence of the past—encapsulated the experience of coming into these woods, maybe even of coming to this national park.

There are moments when you can forget where you are and why you're here and just relish the serenity. And then something will jolt you back to thinking about what once happened here. Back and forth.

"I think that's the dance that you're always going to have to do in this place," she said. "And I think that's what you want here."

The sun was low in the sky as we walked out of the woods, through the tall grass, past the boulder, and through the gate behind the wall.

As we retraced our steps back to the parking lot, Lori saw a park ranger, then one of the ambassadors. In each case, they greeted each other like old friends.

For her parents, this was a place of solace and comfort right from the start. For her, it was an evolution. But that initial resentment she felt about sharing this place with others had gradually changed, reaching the point where part of the lure of the place was the people here. The other Flight 93 families. The park service staff. The locals who had become involved with taking care of the memorial, its visitors, and its story.

We stopped at the visitor shelter. Inside of it there was a black bulletin board and a stack of white cards that said at the top: "Leave Your Message: Please share your thoughts about Flight 93 and September 11, 2001. Your response will become part of the Tribute Collection."

There were twenty-nine cards tacked up on the wall. Another woman was reading some of them and composing her own. Lori took a card, wrote something, then tacked it up on the wall.

> *I love you Rich. You are with me always. I hope tomorrow I will make you proud.*
> *I miss you every day.*
> *Tomorrow is for you.*
> *Lori*

———

THE NEXT MORNING the weather was dramatically different. The sky was overcast. The wind was whipping, shaking the big white tent atop the hill.

Jeff Reinbold, the superintendent of the park, began the "9/11 and the Next Generation" program.

Reinbold, in his mid-forties, had spent more than twenty years working for the park service. For him, this wasn't just another stop. He was a Pennsylvania native. While studying geology at the University of Pittsburgh at Johnstown, he started his career by becoming a seasonal ranger at the Johnstown Flood National Memorial—a site dedicated to remembering the day in 1889 that a dam failed and 2,209 people were killed.

He recalled preparing for the tenth anniversary at the Flight 93 National Memorial, holding forums, talking with staff, discussing what could be added to the memorial.

"It became clear to us nobody was really talking about children," he said.

He described a frequent scene when families came here. Parents would come here and start tearing up.

"We're not building this memorial just for us," he said. "It's for those generations who are going to come, who don't have the same personal connection and remembrances of September 11 that we do."

After Joy Knepp, the fine-arts director at a nearby school, told the story of her memories of that day—and how her students have remembered it in the years since—it was Lori's turn.

She talked about what she was doing on September 11, about driving back to her parents' house, asking her father if it was okay if she moved to Florida and started Art With a Heart.

Since its creation, she said, the program had served more than thirty thousand children. And these weren't children who had bro-ken bones. They had debilitating diseases. Some of them didn't sur-vive. She explained that art helped these children and their families to not only express themselves but also live in the moment. And as art helped them, it saved her.

This place, she said, also has that kind of power. "There's something so profound here at this site and this memorial," she said. "It has taken something that was so horrible and so tragic and so senseless, but it can be turned into something that can teach, that can inspire."

SEPTEMBER 11 STARTED out chilly. As a line of vehicles wound its way down the Ring Road into the bowl beneath the hill, fog hung from the trees and steam rose from the ponds. It was another beautiful morning.

I had driven Lori back to the Pittsburgh airport so she could fly home and spend the anniversary with her parents, but her extended family invited me to sit with them, in a section of chairs set up close to a stage near the wall. They gave me a button with a photo of Richard, his name, and "1962–2001." I reluctantly put it on, not feeling worthy of the button or the seat.

There wasn't any wind. A harp played. Some of the relatives of the passengers went up to the wall. Some placed objects at the base of the wall. Some just stood there and looked at a name, the sun behind them creating shadows on the wall.

There was a moment of silence.

A generator hummed nearby. Cameras clicked.

A bell tolled. A half hour earlier, one passenger's mother had been joking about getting frisked by a Marine. Now she was wiping away tears as the bell tolled forty times and forty names were read.

Patrick White spoke. A cousin of one of the passengers, he became involved in making this place evolve from mine to memorial. And as he noted the coolness of the morning and the change of seasons, the crowd was beyond still, almost frozen. It felt as if by not moving a muscle, not fidgeting, not checking electronic devices, they had temporarily become a living piece of the memorial.

When Secretary of the Interior Ken Salazar spoke, he reminded people that this now is a piece of the National Park System, along with places like the Grand Canyon and the Everglades. But he said we come here for something that is less visible, something that he described as "a journey into the depths of our own thoughts."

The ceremony ended with the vice president and family members heading to the boulder. The harp played "Try to Remember (The Kind of September)."

AFTER THE CEREMONY, the public was allowed to approach the wall again. People milled about, pointing at names, touching the stone, talking quietly.

Parents tried to explain to children why they were here, what had happened, what it meant—things that many adults still were trying to figure out.

There were several groups of schoolchildren. One class, middle school students in uniforms, had an assignment. The students were standing in front of the wall, writing down answers to questions.

I glanced over one of their shoulders. The first question asked what had happened on September 11, 2001.

The student's answer: Terrorists flew planes into the Twin Towers.

I looked at another paper and saw a similar answer.

They were on a field trip to *this* field, and when asked about September 11, they wrote about New York City.

I eventually left the wall and followed the walkway back toward the parking lot. Another group of schoolchildren, all dressed in white and blue, was gathered near the flagpole at the plaza. They were from Pittsburgh. Their leader said that she had been bringing a group of children here to perform every year.

They sang and took turns reciting short biographies of each passenger. When it was Grace Traynor's turn, the fourteen-year-old stepped to the front, stood tall, and started speaking confidently.

"Richard Guadagno," she said. "Richard was a renaissance man . . . His interests varied from reading and the arts to science and math. Most of all, he loved nature and he fought to protect it. He had a wonderful smile. And he loved to take long hikes with his dog."

I wished Lori had been there for that. But in many ways the atmosphere changed as the day wore on.

As people headed to the plaza, they passed a small First Amendment area where a couple of tables were set up. Several people were standing behind one offering "FREE PATRIOTIC LITERATURE" and a collection of books such as Sarah Palin's *Going Rogue*. A few yards past that, one person, a middle-aged man, was standing behind a table with a large sign that said "FLIGHT 93 WAS SHOT DOWN."

He had been there all week, holding out flyers, telling people they could get "the truth" about September 11.

I had stopped at his table the day before and taken one of the flyers. I noticed that one part of it said "Relatives of Flight 93 Victims Demand Answers." It mentioned the families of three passengers, including Richard Guadagno.

When I told Lori this, she was dismayed. In the days and months after 9/11, of course they had wanted answers. And they had said so. But to get from there to supporting the conspiracy theories about Flight 93 being shot down . . . "It's crazy," she said.

I introduced myself to the man and told him that the Guadagnos—and I'm guessing maybe others—didn't want their names on his flyer. He seemed surprised.

He said his name was Oleg. He was fifty-five. He seemed awkward, almost meek. He said he lived twenty miles away and he first did this at the fifth anniversary in 2006. But he had been coming here regularly since July, setting up his table, handing out pamphlets and DVDs about this and other conspiracies. A woman from New Jersey stopped to look.

"I'll take whatever you've got," she said.

I asked him why he was doing this.

"I figured if I had been on Flight 93, I would want someone like myself telling the truth about what really happened," he said.

The truth is that there are a lot of things we will never know.

Whenever that's the case, it's tempting to fill in blanks and connect dots. Oleg and others had done that to come up with a variety of different "truths." And while that was a mistake, so was something the park service had done in the past at other historic sites—connecting dots and filling in blanks to make tidy, gripping stories.

That wasn't necessary here.

I looked at the acres of wildflowers stretching into the distance, up toward the hill where the visitor center would be in the future. It was a beautiful place, one that, like all the other parks I had visited, made me proud to be an American. And not in the we'll-put-a-boot-in-your-ass way, although as this day progressed some visitors certainly brought their boots.

AS OLEG WAS handing out his material, a twentysomething guy stood near the flagpole at the Memorial Plaza entrance, playing a guitar and singing a country song about how, if you questioned the wars that followed 9/11, you obviously had forgotten how it felt that day.

I walked away and called Lori. I told her that it was probably for the best she left when she did, best that she was spending the day with her parents and Ross at Jacksonville Beach, putting notes in a bottle for Rich.

We agreed that while there are reasons to come here on September 11, there's something to be said for what the place feels like every other day, when the wind and the wildflowers do most of the talking.

THERE WAS SOMETHING I wish Lori had been there to see and hear. People had gathered near the plaza entrance to listen to Brendan Wilson, the ranger who had greeted Lori at the wall when we arrived, give one of the park service's interpretive talks.

This one was titled "Planting Seeds."

As the wind whipped across the field, he began by telling the story of what this place was before September 11. He moved on to some of the details that we do know about that day. How the plane crested the nearby ridge. How it was traveling at 563 miles per hour, descending at a 40-degree angle, almost completely upside down.

He described what the land looked like then, and how it has changed since. And then he told a little bit about a few of the passengers, and why they were on the plane.

Donald Greene was going to the Lake Tahoe area to hike and bike with his three brothers.

Don and Jean Peterson, the only married couple aboard, were going to meet Jean's parents and brothers at Yosemite.

Two buddies, Joe Driscoll and Bill Cashman, also were making an annual trip to Yosemite.

"A nephew of Bill's said he loved the idea of being in nature, the fact that you could feel so small and insignificant before something that is so large," Wilson said. "A friend once noted that for Joe, hiking was a spiritual quest as much as a fitness endeavor. He would stand in a valley surrounded by sheer mountains and proclaim this is the greatest cathedral in the world."

The ranger said that there were people on the plane who devoted their lives to advocating for public lands. Alan Anthony Beaven was an environmental lawyer who during his career had sued the National Park Service for not moving swiftly enough. Christine Snyder of Hawaii was a certified arborist who had been at a forestry conference.

He held up a photo of Richard and told his story.

Then he brought everything full circle, back to the field where the park visitors were sitting and standing. We built a wall to remember them. But it's more than that. We've been planting seeds in their memory, he said. The trees on the ridge. The wildflowers blooming on the slope. The wetlands. The return of migratory birds and black bears, snakes and snapping turtles. Nature was returning to this place. And this, he said, was just the beginning.

10

*

OCTOBER: OLYMPIC
NATIONAL PARK

Gordon Hempton bent over and picked up a large maple leaf.

We had barely begun hiking into the Hoh Rain Forest in Washington State, but already the sounds of the visitor center parking lot—the slamming of car doors, the beep-beep of alarms, the murmur of conversation—had faded and been replaced by the sounds of the rain forest. Which on this afternoon didn't include rain. Sunlight was streaming through the trees.

Gordon, who describes himself as an acoustic ecologist, used a handheld device to measure the sound. We were less than a hundred miles from downtown Seattle, and it was one decibel quieter than Benaroya Hall when the symphony wasn't playing.

"Quiet enough to hear a single leaf drop," Gordon said as he let go of the maple leaf.

It floated through the air, swishing back and forth, falling slowly, before landing with a soft scrape and a muted clap.

This, Gordon said, was just the beginning.

"Very soon . . . comes the final applause," he said, whispering. "See the maple above us? Those leaves will dry further and then a breeze will come through after a still night, that first breeze of the morning, and we'll hear the final applause of the season."

He smiled, laughed, and said in his normal voice, "And then begins the deluge we call winter. Thirteen feet of water."

He turned and started hoofing it back down the trail he had

walked hundreds of times, leading us to the place where in 2005 he had taken a small red stone, placed it on a log, and proclaimed a spot in Olympic National Park to be the One Square Inch of Silence.

Some people fight to save trees or bison or air. Gordon had spent most of his adult life not only recording natural sound but fighting to save it.

His quest didn't involve answering the age-old question: If a tree falls in the forest and nobody is there to hear it, does it make a sound? Gordon would say that of course the tree makes a sound. Lots of them. Cracking, groaning, whistling, and crashing with a thud. Does the tree make a sound? That's a silly question, kind of like asking if the sun rose on the Grand Canyon and nobody was standing on the rim, would the view still be beautiful?

Gordon's quest and question were more like: If a leaf falls in the forest and you are standing right there but still can't hear it—if all you hear is a jet—what happens to the sound of that leaf? And beyond that, what happens to you?

He said he was losing the fight, that silence had become an endangered species, that by his own standards for a quiet place—fifteen minutes or longer during daylight hours without interruption by man-made noise—fewer than a dozen such places remained in America. And he was leading us to one of them.

WHEN I ARRIVED in Washington, I was acutely aware of sound and light.

A few days after returning home from Shanksville, I went for a bicycle ride and crashed, breaking my left collarbone, cracking my helmet, and ending up with some of the classic symptoms of a concussion.

I spent about a week on the couch, my shoulder wedged against a cushion. I tried watching *Breaking Bad* and decided it was too depressing. I tried watching some cable news and found it to be even more depressing than *Breaking Bad*. I eventually put in a DVD of

The National Parks: America's Best Idea. There was one story in particular I wanted to find, about a Japanese immigrant who was put in an internment camp during World War II. Chiura Obata coped by painting. And after he was released, he went back to his life as a professor at UC Berkeley and became a painter best known for capturing Yosemite on his canvas.

But when Obata talked about the High Sierra, he often didn't describe it in visual terms. He talked about its stillness, its sound.

"In the evening, it gets very cold; the coyotes howl in the distance, in the mid sky the moon is arcing, all the trees are standing here and there, and it is very quiet. You can learn from the teachings within this quietness. . . . Some people teach by speeches, some by talking, but I think it is important that you are taught by silence."

I turned off the TV and listened to tree branches scraping against the roof.

I thought about Mom. She craved silence more than anyone I know. And not just the kind of silence you get when you sit inside and turn off the television and phone. That kind of silence often feels lonely and hollow.

The silence that Mom craved was far from silent. It's what she got when she walked in the desert every morning. It's rich and full, and when you listen to it, you don't feel alone. You feel like you're a part of something infinitely bigger than yourself.

After Mom died, I wandered through her house, looking at what was on the walls and shelves. In a hall near the guest room, there was a small framed poster that I hadn't paid much attention to before: "Desiderata," written by Max Ehrmann in 1927.

"Go placidly amid the noise and haste and remember what peace there may be in silence," it begins, winding its way through a guide for life before finishing with another reference to sound. "And whatever your labors and aspirations, in the noisy confusion of life, keep peace with your soul. With all its sham, drudgery and broken dreams, it is still a beautiful world. Be careful. Strive to be happy."

A couple of weeks before the trip to Olympic, I went to a fol-low-up with the surgeon. I asked if I could still do the trip, if I'd be okay flying and driving and going for some hikes. Sure, he said. Just be careful not to fall, and don't put weight on the shoulder held to-gether by a plate and screws.

I told him that part of the plan was to put a backpack on my shoulders—nothing too heavy, maybe twenty pounds—for a hike into the Hoh Rain Forest.

"That ain't going to happen," he said.

This is how I ended up buying a fanny pack. Not that I ever referred to it as such. Yes, it rested on my hips and had one strap that went over my one moderately good shoulder. But when I called the longtime friend who lived in Tampa and was going to be meet-ing me in Seattle for the week, I didn't say I had bought a fancy fanny pack.

"Jimmy," I said, "I got a lumbar pack."

We met more than twenty years earlier, when I lived in Tampa. Jimmy's real name isn't Jimmy. It's David DeLong. But we had stopped calling each other David and Mark years ago. I called him Jimmy. He called me Jimmy. We had been doing this so long that I didn't even think about the roots of it anymore, an episode of *Sein-feld* where a character in the gym named Jimmy always refers to himself in the third person. Jimmy will see you around. Jimmy likes Elaine. . . . Jimmy has a fanny pack.

A friendship that started out because we lived nearby and ran about the same pace grew as we aged and became fathers. When I moved, we stayed in touch, talking pretty much every weekend, planning trips. We kept returning to the Grand Canyon. When we weren't there, we talked about getting back. And when we were there, we were looking for The Spot.

We noted that there probably was a time in our lives when The Spot would have referred to the place we dreamed about ending up with a female hiker who looked like she stepped out of a Patagonia catalog. But now we were husbands and fathers and, in a sign we were aging, The Spot referred to the place where we wanted our ashes scattered.

Now we were headed to a spot in a rain forest.

WHEN WE LANDED, people kept telling us how many days they had gone without rain. Sixty, sixty-four, seventy. The numbers varied, but now that it had started raining, they all agreed, it probably wouldn't stop for a long time.

It was raining as we took one of the ferries from Seattle to the Olympic Peninsula. The next morning it was still raining as we drove toward Port Angeles, the town where the park headquarters are located.

Before meeting Gordon at his home in Joyce, I had an appointment with Barb Maynes, the park's public information officer.

It was a fascinating time for a park that President Teddy Roosevelt originally preserved as Mount Olympus National Monument in 1909, in part to protect the declining herd of elk that now bears his name.

It often is billed as three parks in one—glacier-capped mountains, rugged coastline, temperate rain forest. With two dozen plants and animals that exist nowhere else on earth, from the Olympic marmot to Piper's bellflower, it was recognized as a Biosphere Reserve and a World Heritage Site. But what truly defined this park more than a century after its creation wasn't something it still had. It was what it still didn't have in the middle of its nearly 1 million acres.

A road.

If you look at a map of Olympic, you see roads circling its perimeter, but only rivers and trails cutting through its heart. In 1988, more than 95 percent of the park was designated Olympic Wilderness. And yet one enormously significant piece of the park wasn't wild, or at least not nearly as wild as it had been for thousands of years.

In the early 1900s, two dams were built on the Elwha River to provide electricity to a paper mill in Port Angeles. State laws requiring fish passage facilities were ignored. And the salmon that had long filled the river—some weighing up to a hundred pounds— no longer were able to swim upstream to spawn. More than seventy miles of habitat was blocked.

This is why what happened a couple of months before I arrived at the park was a big deal.

The salmon could be seen and heard splashing their way back up the Elwha.

In 1992, legislation was signed to begin the largest dam removal in U.S. history. Twenty years later, the 105-foot-high Elwha Dam, located about five miles from the mouth of the river, came down. By August, adult Chinook salmon were spotted upstream, in the park. And by October, the Glines Canyon Dam, about eight miles more upstream, was nearly gone.

One afternoon, Maynes drove us to what remained of it. We put on yellow hard hats and orange vests and walked out on the abut- ment. We had to speak loudly, partly because of the construction equipment, but mainly because where the dam had once stood 210 feet tall, about 50 feet remained, a waterfall roaring over it.

The reservoir that used to be behind the dam, known as Lake Mills since the 1920s, was almost gone, the Elwha River snaking its way back through the muddy valley. The salmon would follow. Downriver, sediment was restoring a beach at the mouth of the river. And when Lake Caldwell, the reservoir behind the Elwha Dam, was drained, it revealed a sacred spot for the Klallam tribe, a stone considered to be their creation site.

"It's all very exciting," Maynes said.

Throughout our time in the park, she was helpful, patient, re- laxed. Except the time when I asked about Gordon Hempton and the One Square Inch of Silence.

Her body language instantly changed. She stopped smiling. Her tone became more official, with a touch of weariness.

When I first heard about the One Square Inch of Silence a couple of years earlier, I had assumed that, because it was in Olympic National Park, it was a park service site. I had since realized that wasn't the case. It was the site of an ongoing battle between the park service and Gordon Hempton.

On Earth Day 2005, he set down a stone at one particular spot in the Hoh Rain Forest and declared it the One Square Inch of Silence. He said it was one of the quietest places in the United States but that it was endangered, inadequately protected by many entities, including the park service. He said if that one square inch could be made 100 percent free of loud noises, such as planes passing overhead, then many square miles around it would also be protected.

In the view of the park service, this would be a bit like if I went to the Dry Tortugas and designated one coral reef as ground zero for climate change, then successfully promoted it, getting ink in national publications and airtime on NPR.

"Certainly Gordon's called a lot of attention to the value of natural sounds," Maynes said. "That part's great. The part that has not always been so great is kind of the destination he's created. And I know his website still says he has a little jar out there, a little jar where people are supposed to write their thoughts."

"I read about that," I said.

"It should not be there," she said. "It is wilderness. And there have been times where a social trail has developed from the main trail to this one square inch."

She said that the bottom line is, they want to protect all resources at that spot and throughout the park. Yes, natural sound is important. But so are the elk habitat and vegetation. She said that the park service already has a division devoted to preserving natural sound; in fact it was an important part of Olympic's most recent general management plan.

"I don't remember what the actual figure is, but somebody actually figured out how many square inches of silence we have in the park," she said, smiling again. "It's more than just the one."

GORDON LIVED IN Joyce, on the north side of the Olympic Peninsula, just a couple of miles from the Strait of Juan de Fuca.

David and I had lunch at the Blackberry Cafe and stopped in
the Joyce General Store, the only grocery store, gas station, and post
office for miles. When we pulled down the gravel driveway leading
to Gordon's property, I knew we were in the right place when I saw
the light blue '64 Volkswagen van parked under a carport. In the
summer of 2007, Gordon took the VW on a cross-country trip and,
along with John Grossman, wrote *One Square Inch of Silence: One
Man's Search for Natural Silence in a Noisy World*.

We were admiring the van, reminiscing about old-school road
trips, when Gordon appeared. He was wearing jeans and a gray
and white sweater that matched his beard and closely cropped hair.
At fifty-nine, he was a few years older than David and me. But
from the moment he stuck out his hand and grinned, I was struck
by how he somehow came across as both wise old man and wide-
eyed kid.

"Let me give you a tour," he said.

He had purchased the six-acre piece of land a few years earlier.
When he said it had once been someone's private pitch-and-putt
golf course, I could almost picture it—perhaps with a tee box up
where Gordon now had a yurt, hitting down the hill, toward a
creek and woods.

As we stood at the crest of the hill, he recalled the first time he
stood here, with a real estate agent. "I could hear the creek singing
to me," he said. "I turned to the real estate agent and said, 'Full price,
no contingencies.'"

Three weeks later, they were at the closing and the agent said,
"And isn't that a beautiful cottage down by the creek?"

We started walking down the hill as Gordon continued the
story, laughing as he explained that he had been so busy he hadn't
even been back to the property and didn't even know there was a
cottage there.

The little cedar structure had been the previous owner's version of a man cave, a clubhouse for him and his buddies, complete with a wet bar. Gordon had ripped out the plumbing, redone the interior, and put a claw-foot tub right next to the creek, bringing to mind a Cialis ad.

"There's really no finer experience than getting it all stoked up and looking up into that giant big-leaf maple and listening to the music of this beautiful place," he said.

The clubhouse had been converted into what he called the "Christmas cottage." He explained that for him, the feeling of being here reminds him of being a young child on Christmas Day. He opened the door, reached inside, and turned on the lights. Christmas lights.

It was a tiny cottage, basically just room for a large bed.

"So if you choose to stay down here at the cottage instead of in the yurt—it doesn't make any difference to me—you can drive right on down here," he said. "This ground will stay solid probably for another two weeks."

David and I looked at the romantic setting—the bathtub, the cottage—and apparently were thinking the same thing: Does he think we're a couple? Because almost in unison we blurted out, "The yurt would be great."

"Oh, you prefer the yurt?" Gordon said.

We proceeded to overcompensate by talking about our wives and children and the beautiful woman who had served us our espresso that morning. Which eventually led us to overcompensate for our overcompensation and basically become the *Seinfeld* episode where the recurring punch line is, "Not that there's anything wrong with that."

We headed back up the hill to the yurt. The circular, domed tent-like structure had a couple of steps leading to a door made of wood and glass. Its white exterior was decorated with a string of multicolored prayer flags, giving it a Tibetan vibe.

Inside, it felt more cabin than tent. Beams of Douglas fir, a wood floor, couches, lamps, bookshelves filled with titles such as *The*

Noise Manual, The Singing Life of Birds, Stillness, and *The Acoustic Sense of Animals.*

It was starting to rain again. And the sound of the rain was amplified by the yurt.

Gordon started to explain that he built the yurt a couple of years earlier when he returned from a recording trip where he slept outdoors for months.

"It took me a long time to get comfortable living inside a traditional structure," he said. "And I usually . . ."

He paused as a plane passed overhead. "Oh, yeah," he said with a laugh. "We'll get to that."

He said we were standing in a membrane structure twenty-seven feet in diameter. And just like the surface of a microphone vibrates as it captures sound, the membrane structure of the yurt also vibrates. He can hear a passing crow or eagle. When the salmon start coming up Salt Creek, they splash so loudly they'll wake you up at night.

"Now the downside of a yurt is it doesn't discriminate," he said. "So when a jet passes overhead, or in the morning when the logging trucks start at three o'clock, it's actually louder inside the yurt than outside."

He showed us around the rest of the yurt, pointing out the camp stove hooked up to propane, the kegerator, and—out back in the woods—the bathroom.

That evening we made chili and rice on the camp stove. Gordon opened a bottle of scotch. As the membrane above us amplified the rain, we talked about our mothers, our kids, and the power of the nearby national park that he called the "listener's Yosemite."

TO EXPLAIN HOW his mother is part of his story, he starts by going back a bit, to the fall of 1980 and a long drive to Wisconsin for graduate school. He was studying botany, planning to be a plant pathologist. He pulled off I-90 and went down a side road.

While he was lying in a Wisconsin field, a thunderstorm rolled over.

He describes listening to the thunder and rain and crickets as if it were a religious experience, nature speaking to him, telling him that this was what he was supposed to be doing with his life. Listening.

"I was twenty-seven years old and had never truly listened before," he said.

He decided not just to become a better listener, but to record what he heard. He bought his first recording equipment. It was, he said, "mind-expanding." It also was like an addictive drug. He wanted more. He decided he wanted—needed—the best equipment in the world, a Nagra reel-to-reel recorder made in Switzerland. It cost $10,000. He was a bike messenger in Seattle making an average of a dollar a delivery. He asked himself if a recorder was worth 10,000 deliveries. He decided it was.

When his parents made a trip to Switzerland, he asked his mother to pick up the recorder at the factory. She didn't try to convince him it wasn't the best use of his money. She got the recorder and delivered it to him in Seattle. He hooked it up. The first thing they listened to was the sound outside his window in the Queen Anne area. It was the sound they would have heard any other day if they had opened the window. And yet it was completely different.

"She understood then what I was trying to do," he said. "She was my only fan for the next couple years."

She died of cancer long before he won an Emmy for a PBS documentary; before he called himself "The Soundtracker" and said that while most people around here earn their living with a chainsaw, he lives by his ears and a recorder.

He paused. "Yeah," he said. "But if you're ever going to have a fan of a career—a career that didn't even have a name—you'd want it to be your mother."

———

DAVID AND I spent a day going to see—and, of course, hear—some of Gordon's favorite spots.

We went to Rialto Beach and listened to the roar of sixteen-foot swells coming ashore, crashing into the rocky beach, creating a knee-deep layer of sea foam, then retreating back over the stones.

We went to La Push and found a giant piece of Sitka spruce driftwood, the cavity in it large enough to walk into. "Ears of wood," Gordon called the old-growth logs.

On the morning of October 17, we headed for the Hoh River Valley.

We stopped in Forks, a town made famous by the *Twilight* books and movies. There were Twilight-themed restaurant menus (Werewolf Burger, Vampire Shake, Bella Banana Split) and a Vampire Threat Level sign (the arrow pointed to green/low).

At the visitor center, in addition to "Twilight Information," there was a pole with a red arrow at the seven-foot mark. "Forks Rain," it said.

The rainy season had started. But after wimping out by staying in hotels and going "glamping" in Gordon's yurt, David and I were glad to finally be putting our tents to use. In a forest where the average annual precipitation is thirteen feet, it *should* be raining.

Yet as we made the eighteen-mile drive on the Upper Hoh Road, entering the park through a tunnel of towering trees, it stopped raining. And when we parked at the visitor center, the sun was shining.

Gordon was waiting for us. We went to the small, unstaffed visitor center and handled the self-serve backcountry permit. With me and my lumbar pack, and David carrying a backpack crammed full of half my stuff, we weren't attempting anything too ambitious. The One Square Inch was only a little more than three miles into the valley. And we were taking in a site Gordon recommended that was on the way.

Before beginning the hike, he wanted to say something.

He said he had been sitting on the bench, thinking about his day leading up to this point. He wanted us all to do a little exercise, related to the value of quiet—the first part now, the second part when we left the Hoh Valley.

"Right now all you do is be aware of yourself," he said. "Just feel yourself. Take a breath of air."

He inhaled deeply, then exhaled.

"My chest feels like there's a book on top of it," he said. "There are thoughts on my mind about business, about family. How do you feel right now?"

Neither David nor I said anything right away.

"You don't have to use words," Gordon said. "Just feel it."

The sound of birds chirping mixed with the noise of the parking lot. Voices in the distance. The sound of footsteps and car doors and alarm beeps.

"Take time to memorize it," he said. "Now you're going to experience the quiet of the Hoh Valley . . . And when you leave, when you're still in the forest, ask yourself how you feel."

He said he had a question for us.

"There is not a single place in the world where aircraft is off-limits for civilian purposes, not one quiet place designated by any government," he said. "Is it possible we can have one? Is it possible? I'll tell you what my answer is right now, and the way I'm feeling is—to tell the truth, I don't know if it's possible. I want you to ask yourself that question after we've been . . .

A hand dryer cranked up in the visitor center restroom, nearly drowning out his voice.

". . . in the quiet," he said. "Tell me what the quiet tells you."

With a beep, the hand dryer shut off.

"Okay?" he said. "Let's go."

Gordon was wearing a felt hat. He had on boots that reminded me of the galoshes I had as a kid, his jeans tucked into them. He grabbed his backpack, an umbrella sticking out of it.

We started walking toward the trailhead and David's backpack did something that made us give each other a look, as if to say we were surprised Gordon didn't end the hike right then and there.

With each step, David's backpack squeaked loudly.

If we hadn't been hiking with Gordon, I'm sure the first thing I would have noticed about the Hoh River Trail would have been visual. It wasn't just green. It was greener than anywhere I had ever seen. Every inch in every direction was saturated, as if someone had taken a big box of crayons, pulled out all the shades of green, and gone to town.

I thought about how Barb Maynes had described it a few days earlier. She grew up on the East Coast. And she said the first time she walked into the Hoh, it felt like she was standing in the middle of one of those dioramas in the American Museum of Natural History.

Only, of course, this place felt very much alive. And what gave it that life—what gives so many places in national parks life—are the things that go beyond the visual. The smell of the place. The feel of the air. The sound of it.

We had barely started down the trail and Gordon stopped. One of the Roosevelt elk, with a big rack of antlers, was about twenty-five yards off the trail. Another, a female, was nearby. Gordon said there were probably more, not far away.

"The elk are good listeners," he said, whispering. "They do not see particularly well. So if you ever want to be invisible to an elk, just stop moving."

We watched them work their way through the brush before Gordon eventually said there was enough distance for us to go ahead on the trail.

"Listen to the antlers, the way they hit the branches," he said. "The sound tells you a lot about the quality of the antlers. Nice and solid."

He took off walking. Quickly. David and I scrambled to keep up.

The rhythm of our footsteps (and the squeak of David's backpack) mixed with the chirping of birds and the rustle of the maple leaves, the ones that Gordon said soon would be falling in the final applause of fall.

In New York City, Floyd Bennett Field and Gateway National Recreation Area.

The Amelia Earhart section of the Floyd Bennett Field campground, Gateway National Recreation Area, New York.

Park ranger John Warren at Dead Horse Bay and the place unofficially known as Bottle Beach, Gateway National Recreation Area, New York.

Dave Taft, a Brooklyn native and head ranger of the Jamaica Bay unit of Gateway, walks through the grasslands near the campground, talking about the beauty of this park. Gateway National Recreation Area, New York.

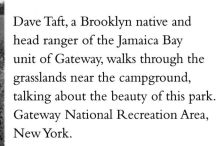

Park ranger Dan Parker, right, and Brooklyn native Anthony Sadasiva lead a kayaking trip from Canarsie Pier, Gateway National Recreation Area, New York.

In Yosemite National Park, California, a view from the John Muir Trail.

On the subdome of Half Dome, the cables in the background leading to the place Josiah Whitney predicted would never be "trodden by human foot." Yosemite National Park, California.

Park ranger Shelton Johnson leading a Junior Ranger hike and telling the young park visitors: "I want you to feel like you're home, because this is your home." Yosemite National Park, California.

A field of sunflowers near the entrance of the Flight 93 National Memorial, Pennsylvania.

Lori Guadagno at the spot on the Wall of Names with the name of her brother, Richard Guadagno, who died on 9/11. Flight 93 National Memorial, Pennsylvania.

Lori at the seventeen-ton boulder marking the crash site of Flight 93 on 9/11. Flight 93 National Memorial, Pennsylvania.

Lori holds the wires from Flight 93 that she found while digging in the dirt in the hemlock grove near the crash site at Flight 93 National Memorial, Pennsylvania.

Park ranger Brendan Wilson with a photo of Richard and his dog, Shadow—one of the photos Wilson uses in an interpretive talk about United 93 passengers and their ties to nature. Flight 93 National Memorial, Pennsylvania.

Family members of LeRoy Homer, first officer of Flight 93, bow their heads at the wall before an anniversary service on the morning of September 11 at Flight 93 National Memorial, Pennsylvania.

Olympic National Park, Washington: Gordon Hempton reflects at the spot in the Hoh Rain Forest that he dubbed the One Square Inch of Silence.

Gordon measures the decibel level of a plane passing overhead, Olympic National Park, Washington.

The rock Gordon placed on a log in the Hoh Rain Forest, marking the spot he calls the One Square Inch of Silence, Olympic National Park, Washington.

David DeLong talks to Gordon at our campsite in the Hoh Rain Forest, Olympic National Park, Washington.

Another visitor celebrates the sunset from atop a piece of Sitka spruce driftwood in Olympic National Park, Washington.

The end of a cross-country road trip: Jacksonville, Florida, Round Marsh and the
Timucuan Ecological and Historic Preserve.

A flashback to a trip with Mom in her camper van on the way to Arches National Park, Utah, in 2007.

Mom on a hike in Arches National Park, Utah, 2007.

Chris Burns on the road to Chisos Basin in Big Bend National Park, Texas.

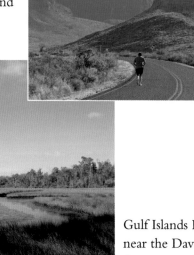

Gulf Islands National Seashore near the Davis Bayou Campground in Mississippi.

Last sunset of the year: the summit of Haleakalā, Haleakalā National Park, Hawaii.

Modern-day *paniolo,* a Hawaiian cowboy and cowgirl, head into the volcanic crater of Haleakalā, Haleakalā National Park, Hawaii.

Nan Cabatbat greets the sun with a chant atop Haleakalā, Haleakalā National Park, Hawaii.

A silversword (*'ahinahina*) near the summit of Haleakalā catches some of the last rays of sunlight of the year. Haleakalā National Park, Hawaii.

Natives called this sacred space Kua Mana (the land above the clouds), Haleakalā National Park, Hawaii.

A trip with Mia and Toni to a park in our backyard, Cumberland Island National Seashore in Georgia, 2014.

Toni rides through the oaks during a trip to Cumberland Island National Seashore, Georgia.

Mia at our site in the Sea Camp campground, a short walk from eighteen miles of unspoiled beach, Cumberland Island National Seashore, Georgia.

Gordon stopped again. A plane was in the distance, getting closer. He started taking decibel readings.

"We're having a hiker approach us," he said. "That's why I'm taking the reading at a distance, not waiting for the peak value."

The hiker, a young woman, passed by us, then stopped. "Are you Gordon Hempton?"

"Yes," he said.

"Hi, I watched your TED talk yesterday," she said. "I'm in the class that's here."

"Oh, Evergreen," Gordon said. "Terrific. I'm sorry the park denied the permit for me to accompany you."

Gordon had told me before I made the trip that he might be leading a class from Evergreen State College, located south of the park in Olympia, into the Hoh. I hoped to tag along, seeing how a generation that grew up connected by technology would react to being disconnected in the rain forest. But the park service denied the permit. One longtime park employee sent Gordon a note saying that it was presumably because the group was larger than the limit of twelve. Gordon invited her to tag along for our hike. She already had plans but thanked him and added, "UNOFFICIALLY I so support your project."

Gordon and the Evergreen student were chatting about mushrooms—the student had a sketchpad full of her drawings—when another plane passed overhead.

"Let's just be still again," Gordon said.

We stood there listening. Gordon glanced at his reading and his watch.

"Why is this happening?" he said. "I don't have an answer for that. Why shouldn't it happen? The answer is down the trail."

When we crossed boardwalks, the cedar slats became what Gordon described as "outdoor xylophones."

We could hear the Hoh River off to our right. We stopped at our campsite, just off the right side of the trail, next to the Hoh. David and I set up our tents, then continued heading down the path.

Whenever a plane passed over, Gordon stopped and wrote down the time. After one registered at fifty-eight decibels, he compared the man-made sounds that disturb national parks to other kinds of pollution.

"It's like sewage," he said. "It doesn't have a smell. It has a sound. . . . It's damaging to wildlife. The animals don't have cell phones, right? They have one way of delivering their message. This is how they attract a mate, establish territory, do all kinds of things."

I had read that scientists found man-made sound was causing birds to change their communication. Louder, higher-frequency calls were being rewarded. Nature, I decided, was evolving a bit like cable news and column writing.

I asked Gordon sort of the flip side of the "what's your favorite park?" question. What parks that people think of as pristine have been sonically disappointing?

He mentioned the Grand Canyon and all of its overflights. And the Everglades. If having Miami International Airport nearby wasn't enough to spoil it, there was the sound of boats carrying across the water. But there was one national park in particular—a place that Gordon had long imagined as a sound mecca—that left him disappointed, frustrated, and, in a way, inspired to preserve the place we were in now.

"Yosemite," he said. "That was the crown jewel for John Muir. Yosemite changed his life. But even then John Muir complained about the noisy tourists and their mules."

Several months before the trip, I traded e-mails with Gordon. He gave me some homework of sorts. He said to read Muir's writings, to pay attention to how much Muir focused on the sounds of nature. He said that the turning point in Muir's life was when he suffered an eye injury while working at a carriage factory in Indiana-polis. After recovering from the injury that left him "temporarily blind," Muir began his thousand-mile walk to the Gulf.

Gordon sent me two images of Muir. One a photograph, one a painting. He noted that the painting seemed to correct flaws in the one eye. He didn't have any proof, but he speculated that Muir was forever visually impaired—and that he lived in a period when you would downplay, even hide, such an issue.

"If Muir was in fact visually impaired, this would explain why his writings are so sonically rich and accurate, far more than any other naturalist before or since," he said. "As noise pollution increases, our culture stops listening to anything outside of what we produce—music, speeches, television, radio. We stop listening to the real world. It becomes mute."

He spent one summer in the 1990s searching for the sounds Muir described. He concluded that an alarming chunk of them were gone. At the time, the park service had begun studying plane noise and its effects.

The gathering of data was presumably the first step toward change. A 1986 midair crash over the Grand Canyon led Congress to pass the National Parks Overflight Act a year later, requiring the park service and Federal Aviation Administration to work together to resolve "the significant adverse effect on natural quiet" caused by overflights. In 2000, Congress passed another act, the National Parks Air Tour Management Act, and the park service established a natural sounds program. In 2011 it was elevated to a division—the Natural Sounds and Night Skies Division.

While some were frustrated by how little progress had been made on the act in a decade, Gordon had another kind of criticism. The act itself—and much of natural sound preservation—focused on air tours. With three hundred overcast days a year, there weren't many air tours at Olympic.

"We have four jetways—these amount to interstates in the sky—which jetliners travel at cruising altitude through Olympic National Park," he said. "Those are the four jetways I'd like to have moved off of Olympic National Park so that this can become the world's first place off-limits to all aircraft. . . . With the single exception of search and rescue for human life. I'm not being an extremist here."

He laid out an elaborate argument for this, calculating operating costs for planes to go around Olympic, saying it would cost less than a dollar per passenger and that the payoff for the entire region would be enormous. Olympic could be maintained and marketed as what he believed it already was—one of the last great quiet places in America.

Shortly after the three-mile mark on the trail, Gordon stopped and turned to face David and me. He took a deep breath. When he started talking, his tone was different. He was serious and, it seemed, a bit agitated.

"We've arrived at the point of access, the access trail to the One Square Inch of Silence," he said. "This will be the last place we'll be speaking to each other, and I have a number of things that I want to say."

He looked at his watch. "Okay, it's 2:26, a good time to be here," he said. "I have to leave all of my concerns, all of my worries behind at this point. I have to say that I am surprised that it appears that the National Park Service, since they are the only objectors to One Square Inch of Silence, have blocked the entrance."

He pointed to a Sitka spruce a few yards off the left side of the trail. It had a natural tunnel at its base, sort of an upside-down wishbone, large enough to take shelter in during a storm or walk through with a bit of ducking.

Not that anyone would be walking through it right away.

The opening was filled with branches.

Gordon walked over to the tree and began yanking them out. David helped him. I did what I came to do—record the sounds of the Hoh, which at this moment was the cracking and snapping of branches.

"Is it like this every time?" David said.

"First time it's happened," Gordon said, tossing the last of the branches.

He stepped back and exhaled. "The tree looks much nicer now," he said, patting his backpack. "I also brought along a special treat today, which is the jar of quiet thoughts."

He said that when we got to the One Square Inch, he would set the jar beneath the log.

"There's one rule: that none of the thoughts can be repeated," he said. "It will be at the site only for half an hour until I'll put it away. You can choose to read it. You can choose to contribute to it."

He pulled out a red stone.

When he first decided to mark one spot in this forest, he placed a similar stone, given to him by David Four Lines of the Quileute tribe.

"If the stone is there, then you may keep this as a reminder to yourself that it's been here," he said. "You can remind yourself what it's like to be here amidst silence, and perhaps the silence will speak to you and share its wisdom. So I'll give this to you."

He handed me the stone. "If the stone is not there, I'll point my finger and that's where you can give it up," he said. "Let's see. Anything else I need to cover? Cell phones off."

He took out his own cell phone and put it in a setting that seemed both fitting and ironic: airplane mode.

HE LED THE way, walking through the opening in the tree.

We meandered through the woods for a couple of minutes, following a narrow path, stepping over a coaxial cable, a miles-long remnant from when rangers at distant outposts used it for communication.

We stepped on some logs to cross a low muddy area, climbing to a slightly higher elevation and arriving at the spot.

I didn't realize this until Gordon pointed at the chest-high, moss-covered log. No rock.

I pulled the stone out of my pocket and put it on the log, at this one square inch in the rain forest.

If I expected something instantly to happen, like in a fairy tale, I would have been disappointed.

I looked around. Yes, looked. Instinct. It was a beautiful spot—a mix of towering trees, fallen ones covered in moss and open space—but no more beautiful than many other places in the park.

Gordon pulled a glass jar out of his backpack. On top of the somewhat rusted lid, it said "Jar of Quiet Thoughts." Inside there were pieces of paper with writing on them and a pencil. He set it under the log, then seemed to go into One Square Inch mode, relaxing, soaking it all in.

I initially kept busy doing something. Recording the sounds, taking a photo of the rock on the log. But eventually I stopped doing and started listening.

I closed my eyes.

The first thing I heard was what was in the distance, the white noise of the Hoh River. There were birds chirping, high above us, all around us.

I thought about how Dad would talk to the birds, making calls and sometimes getting them to call back. I thought about how Mom could identify birds without seeing them. I had no idea what kind of birds these were. But just by listening to them and to the occasional rustling of the trees—it was mostly still today—I could get a sense of the size of the place around me.

I kept listening and heard something close to me, something I had completely missed when my eyes were open.

Drip, drip, drip.

Water was slowly dripping. By itself, it was an interesting sound. But mix it with everything else—the river in the distance, the birds overhead, the trees all around—and there was a depth and richness that I was pretty sure no recording equipment, no matter how expensive, could capture. It was like trying to take a picture of the Grand Canyon that did it justice.

That's what I was thinking when I heard a hum in the distance. It was a fraction of the volume of the planes that flew over my tent in New York. But somehow it seemed exponentially more intrusive.

I opened my eyes. Gordon was getting ready to measure the sound.

It passed over. The natural sound returned. Then there was another plane.

As the quiet returned, David picked up the jar Gordon had left under the log. He wrote a note, put it in the jar, and returned the jar to the spot. I still wasn't sure about the Jar of Quiet Thoughts. It seemed a little New Agey, like something they'd do in Sedona. But Gordon seemed to care about it, and I appreciated him playing host and tour guide. So I grabbed the jar, set it on top of the log, and twisted the lid.

It opened with a loud creak. I pulled out some of the pieces of paper and read what others had written. Then I took my own notepad, still not even really sure what to say. I eventually wrote:

> Mom,
> Thanks for
> giving me
> the gift of
> (appreciating)
> silence.
> Love, Mark

When I tucked the note back in Gordon's little Jar of Quiet Thoughts, I felt a lump in my throat. I forced it to go away. And as if to help, a plane passed overhead.

We stayed at the One Square Inch for about an hour before Gordon began packing up, retracing the path out. David and I followed, heading back through the Sitka spruce and onto the trail.

We didn't immediately begin talking. To the contrary, we remained silent for a moment. David shook Gordon's hand. I shook Gordon's hand.

He began to talk, but in a whisper.

"Because we did have a noise-free interval of twenty-five minutes, that does place us on the list of the last great places," he said. "It exceeded the standard by ten minutes. So that's great news. The bad news is . . . the noise-free interval is shrinking. And unless things change it will disappear entirely, possibly even in our generation."

WHEN WE REACHED our campsite, David and I said good-bye to Gordon. We cooked dinner, talked for a bit, then crawled into our tents.

I lay there listening to the Hoh River, thinking not only about this place but about every place I had been to this year. I realized how much sound had been a part of each one.

There had been the cracking of the wind atop Cadillac Mountain in Acadia; the stillness of the desert on the King Canyon Trail in Saguaro; the way the Grand Canyon even *sounded* vast in the dark; the gentle rhythm of water lapping at the wall around the fort in the Dry Tortugas; the rustling of tall reeds in Gateway; the hissing and gushing of geysers in Yellowstone; the roar of the waterfalls in Yosemite; the chirping of the insects near the Flight 93 memorial wall.

But as I ran through the trips in my head, I realized that at every place there also had been sounds that interrupted, detracted, and remained a part of my memory of that place.

The drone of air tours near Hermits Rest in the Grand Canyon. The ringtone of a cell phone atop Half Dome. The rumble of the generator at Fort Jefferson. The roar of a raft engine on the Colorado River. The jets and garbage trucks and everything else at Gateway. The pop-pop-pop of hunting near the Flight 93 Memorial. The jets that kept flying over the Hoh River Valley that afternoon.

All I could hear now was the sound of the river, mixed with the swaying of tree branches overhead and . . .

I was asleep before I knew it.

When I woke up the next morning, the first thing I thought was that I had just experienced the best night's sleep I'd had since breaking my collarbone. The second was that it was morning in the rain forest and it still wasn't raining.

We cooked breakfast, lingering a bit by the river. We were less than three miles from the parking lot, a laughably short distance for backpacking. And yet it was a reminder that you don't have to go far to get away.

We eventually packed up. I put on my lumbar pack. David crammed half my stuff into his backpack. We started hiking, slower than the day before, partly because Gordon wasn't taking off down the trail in front of us, partly because I think we just wanted to make the short hike last.

We talked about The Spot, how the places we wanted our ashes scattered still were in the canyon, but we could see adding a few spots here too. Somehow during our conversation with Gordon, he brought up that he had thought about this too. He said he was torn between two spots: Rialto Beach and the One Square Inch.

A jet roared overhead, much louder than any the previous day.

"Did he forget his keys or something?" David said. "I could feel that."

"I know, it reverberated," I said.

"It's so noticeable here, more noticeable here than a lot of places I've been," he said. "But maybe not. Maybe I just haven't been aware."

Gordon had told us a story about someone he took to the One Square Inch. Months later they had run into each other and this person had said that the experience had opened his ears. Everywhere he went, he noticed the sounds. Which was both good and bad. He heard beautiful sounds that in the past he had completely missed. But he also realized that some of the places he thought were quiet were far from it.

So when he saw Gordon, he said, "Thank you and f-you."

At one point, I had asked Gordon who he thinks are the modern-day Muirs. He said they don't exist; they can't exist, because the world that shaped Muir no longer exists. I hope he's more wrong than right.

Muir is often referred to as the "father of our national parks."

But it's worth remembering that he and many others—David Brower, Edward Abbey, Rachel Carson, Marjory Stoneman Douglas—not only ardently supported the preservation of these places but also often questioned, confronted, pushed, pulled, and annoyed the people responsible for that preservation. In that way, Gordon Hempton seemed like a descendant of Muir.

David and I continued walking. As we got close to the parking lot and started noticing the sounds of cars and people, we joked that we wished Gordon was there so we could say thank you and . . .

And then it started to rain.

Before I saw the rain, I heard it.

Before I felt drops on my skin, I heard them slowly, sporadically, plunking here and there on the canopy high overhead. When they started to fall harder, their pace and pitch rising, I closed my eyes and heard sounds that reminded me of a campfire crackling. And when the water eventually started to cascade through the trees, the individual drops turning into a collective chorus, the only thing I heard was the bittersweet refrain of one of Olympic's greatest hits, green noise in the rain forest.

Listening to it, I thought about Gordon dropping a maple leaf at the start of our hike, saying that any day now a wind would blow through, creating the final applause of fall—and setting the stage for the deluge of winter.

11

*

NOVEMBER: ROAD TRIP

I hadn't cried since Mom died.

It wasn't that I had some macho idea that real men didn't cry. When my mom was dying, I cried all the time. In the car after she told me the news. While hiking through the desert. While hugging her in the kitchen. While pacing around her bed some of those final nights, listening to her gasping for every breath.

But then she died and . . . nothing.

Not that morning when I stepped outside and watched the sun rise on another day. Not at the memorial service. Not on the flight home. Not while in Gateway, Yosemite, or Olympic.

At some point I realized I had this unintended tearless streak going. I kept reminding myself that so many other people were dealing with much tougher losses. If you live long enough, you no longer have your parents. Death is a part of life. But sometimes I wondered. Was I coping with this too well? Or was it the opposite?

Some apparently thought it was the latter. Toni gently suggested I see a counselor. A close friend mentioned that counseling had helped him work through some things and asked if that might help me too. Maybe, I said. But I didn't have time for that. Maybe I just needed a good cry.

One night I took what, for me, had always been a laxative for tears. I watched the final scene in *American Beauty,* where Kevin

Spacey calmly narrates what flashes before the eyes of his character, Lester Burnham, the last second before death.

> First of all, that one second isn't a second at all, it stretches on forever, like an ocean of time . . . For me, it was lying on my back at Boy Scout camp, watching falling stars . . . And yellow leaves, from the maple trees that lined our street . . . Or my grandmother's hands, and the way her skin seemed like paper . . . And the first time I saw my cousin Tony's brand new Firebird . . . And Janie.

In the past, the images of Janie, his daughter—as a teenager, as a young girl dressed in a princess outfit and holding a sparkler—inevitably pushed me over the edge. And by the time Lester was talking about letting go and feeling only gratitude for every single moment of his stupid life, the floodgates were open.

But this time . . . nothing. Dry eyes.

It wasn't until I was standing in front of a room full of people on the first day in November that I started to choke up.

It was Pint Night at Black Creek Outfitters, a local outdoors shop. Joe Butler, the owner, had decided to have a series of events involving someone speaking or playing music. I was surprised when a few hundred people showed up, until I remembered there was Intuition Ale. They weren't there to hear me talk. They were there for the beer.

I put together some of my photos from the year. I planned to end the presentation with a collection of family photos through the years, set to Marc Cohn's "The Things We've Handed Down."

I hoped when people saw these Kodachrome images—no longer the nice, bright colors that Paul Simon sang about, but now faded like the memories themselves—it might bring back some of their own memories of family trips.

I planned to wrap up the talk by saying that being an advocate for the parks doesn't mean you have to do something extreme. You don't have to chain yourself to a redwood. You don't have to be able to donate a bunch of money. If you want to help the parks, the most important thing you can do is simply to go to them—and take someone with you.

I had picked out some of Dad's photos from the 1960s and 1970s and some of mine from the last few decades, matching the images with the "Things We've Handed Down" lyrics.

I started it with a picture of Mom and Dad before they were parents. They're standing facing each other, holding both hands, as if preparing to say their vows. Only they aren't in a church. They're in the woods, wearing backpacks. I don't know who took the picture or where it was taken. I just know they look like they fit one of the opening lines in the song, "We've been doing fine without you . . ."

From there I went to a series of photos of my parents with me and my two sisters. One of Dad, a face full of stubble, a different kind of pack on his back, to carry one of my sisters. One of me and my two sisters eating pancakes at a picnic table. One of me holding up a book about rocks, a huge grin on my face, as if it was the greatest gift I could ever get. Which at the time, it probably was.

I matched photos to the lyrics about things that get handed down. Mom smiling. Mom kneeling, showing Mia something in the desert. And so on. Leading to a few pictures I had taken of the things that my parents—all of our parents—handed down. The granite atop Cadillac Mountain. A river full of moss-covered rocks in the Smokies. The colors of the springs in Yellowstone. The rocks and waterfalls of Yosemite. The view from the South Rim of the Grand Canyon. The plaque there with Teddy Roosevelt's words.

Keep it for your children. Your children's children.

When I put this together, I worked on it for several hours late one night. I'd tweak something and play the entire slide show again. I must have watched it several dozen times from start to finish. I did not cry once.

But here I was, in front of a room full of people, and even

before I hit play, I felt a catch in my throat. I was starting to explain that when I was growing up, my parents didn't have a lot of money, but they took us to places like this. And how I now realized some of the things they gave us. And how I had lost my mom during this year. And . . .

I looked at the first image on the screen—Mom and Dad facing each other, holding hands—and I felt the catch get bigger. I swallowed and tried to continue. I shook my head, thinking, This is going to happen now? I quickly wrapped up the introduction, stepped back, and watched.

A FEW DAYS later I flew to Philadelphia to have another surgery, an attempt to get up and running, literally. That, I figured, was the only therapy I needed. A good, hard run.

It was outpatient surgery. I'd have the surgery in the morning and spend the night at a Philly hotel. I already knew that I had a good friend in Chris Burns, a Jacksonville attorney whom I had been running and biking with for years. But when Chris volunteered to go with me to Philadelphia, so Toni could stay home with Mia, I didn't know what to say other than "Are you sure?"

Chris insisted that he was, saying it would be fun. I questioned his idea of fun.

The surgery was the day of the presidential election, Barack Obama running for reelection against Republican challenger Mitt Romney. Once upon a time, I thought covering a presidential race would have been the ultimate assignment. But the way elections and coverage had evolved made me glad to spend this year repeatedly retreating to the places in America that remained wonderfully free of a cell signal or Wi-Fi.

I had the surgery first thing in the morning. By five P.M., I still couldn't pee. So I was sent back to the hotel with a catheter. I watched the election results lying in a hotel bed, still groggy from the drugs, a tube running from my penis to a bag hanging from a nearby chair.

This will be my lasting memory of that election night. This and watching Karl Rove having an on-air meltdown.

Three months before the election, the National Parks Conservation Association and the National Park Hospitality Association conducted a poll of 1,004 registered voters and found that nearly 90 percent said it was "extremely important" or "quite important" for the federal government to support and protect national parks.

In a time when it was hard to find much of anything that people agreed about—let alone at such high levels—this was one of them. Americans still loved their national parks.

I didn't doubt that the national parks were still significantly more popular than the national politicians. In any era, that wasn't saying much. But I did worry that while this poll illustrated that the parks still had public support—and therefore, the NPCA argued, the parks deserved their sliver of the budget (1/14th of one percent) and more—it didn't capture a troubling shift.

Midway through this year, nearly 20 percent of the votes in the House of Representatives had sought to undermine environmental protections, prompting the Sierra Club to produce a graphic for its magazine with a heading that said: "Worst. Congress. Ever." And while it was tempting to say the politicians in Washington weren't paying attention to the will of the people, my fear was that was exactly what they were doing. Some of the same protections that had been put in place with bipartisan support, signed by presidents from both parties (people often forget that the Clean Air Act has Richard Nixon's signature on it), and applauded by the majority of Americans were being dismantled not because politicians were ignoring public sentiment, but because they were following it.

Some politicians were calling for states to take over federal lands, including national parks. And at one point in the presidential campaign, former senator Rick Santorum said the president adhered to "some phony theology, not a theology based on the Bible." He wasn't saying, as others had done, that President Obama was a Muslim. He was saying Obama was beholden to "radical environmentalists" with a world view "that elevates earth above man."

Beyond this being an interesting take on the president's first three years—some environmentalists were disappointed he didn't do more—it was the kind of statement that made me sometimes think my father preached from a different Bible than the ones politicians and pundits kept citing.

Dad and Mom cared deeply about the environment, not in spite of their faith, but very much because of it.

Dad wrote prayers that were full of nature. And going for a hike with Mom was a spiritual act. Not because she cited Bible verses while strolling through the desert. Because she quietly and reverently appreciated the natural world around her. She saw life the way John Muir had a hundred years earlier: "Everybody needs beauty as well as bread, places to play in and pray in, where nature may heal and give strength to body and soul alike."

HOW DO WE hold onto a loved one once they're gone? What pieces of them do we hold on to? What possessions of theirs do we cling to?

I returned to Tucson—along with my sisters and our families— to scatter Mom's ashes and answer such questions. I initially wanted to keep Mom's house. It wasn't just a structure built on a hill on the west side of Tucson. It was her. It was a place full of memories of eating meals, playing board games, watching days start with the sun rising over the mountains in the distance and end with the sun turning those same mountains all kinds of colors.

But we eventually decided that keeping the house was too complicated. Once that decision was made, I told myself that I didn't want anything that was in the house, other than a few pieces of art and some books. They were just objects. They weren't Mom.

I would have taken Wally if Abe didn't want him. After Mom

died, sometimes I'd find Wally sitting in her office. Before this, I wasn't sure I believed dogs mourn. After this, I was convinced they do. But Abe wanted Wally, which was good. I'm sure he needed Wally as much as Wally needed him.

More than anything, Mom's life made me think about what I wanted in my life. And I didn't want things. I wanted to *do* things.

Which is why I eventually decided I wanted the most expensive thing, other than her house, that she owned—her 2001 Pleasure-Way Traverse camper van.

Mom kept the receipts for seemingly everything. And after she died, while we were going through files full of paperwork, I found the one for the camper van: $45,505.50. In the world of recreational vehicles, that's not much. But in the world of Mom's purchases, this was huge.

She was born in 1938, the tail end of the Great Depression. I rarely made that connection when I was growing up. In my mind, she was more a product of the 1950s. But when I looked back at some of her habits—not just the way she saved money, the way she saved and reused seemingly everything—the connection seemed fairly obvious.

She didn't buy bags to line wastepaper baskets or pick up dog poop. She used the plastic bags from the grocery store.

She would take a piece of paper that I would have tossed without thinking twice—a piece of junk mail, for instance—and use the blank flip side, perhaps even cutting the paper into smaller pieces and using them for notes.

She used the same water bottle for hikes for years. When I'd walk into her house and see it hanging there, I'd be embarrassed by just how many different hydration devices—bottles, packs, bladders—I had experimented with through the years.

One time I was talking to a neighbor with parents of a similar age and he said his parents did many of the same things. We decided that maybe our parents weren't just the greatest generation. Maybe they also were the greenest.

In retirement, while she still pinched pennies on some things, she was happy to spend money on things she cared about. She had a beautiful home and a busy itinerary. She and Dad had planned to spend their retirement traveling the country, making it to parks they hadn't seen yet, revisiting ones they fell in love with long ago. So maybe it shouldn't have come as a surprise when, five years after Dad died, she bought the Pleasure-Way Traverse—a silver Ford E-250 converted by a Canadian company to a camper van.

One of the last places she and Abe had taken it to was the redwoods for my fiftieth birthday get-together.

When Mom was dying, she asked her three children if any of us wanted the van. Each of us said no. Seeing camper vans in Yellowstone changed my mind. Especially an old blue VW Westfalia parked near a stream.

It reminded me of when Mom and I took her van—basically a modern spin-off of a Westfalia—and headed to Utah for the rafting trip, camping in Arches National Park beforehand.

Equally as powerful as the memories of trips taken, though, were the thoughts of trips not yet taken, the dreams of leaving behind the daily grind, hopping in a vehicle, and hitting the road. Maybe these were idealistic, naive thoughts. But they were powerful, all the same. And I clearly wasn't the only one having them.

In 2011, Foster Huntington had a good job in New York, working as a menswear designer at Ralph Lauren. But he found himself spending his lunch breaks, sitting at his desk, looking at websites, hoping to find a van. He bought a VW Vanagon Syncro, quit his job, and headed on a meandering road trip. Along the way, he started taking photos of other vans and their owners, posting them online with the hashtag #vanlife. He created a website and Kickstarter campaign for a book devoted to the idea that *Home Is Where You Park It*.

THANKSGIVING MORNING IN Tucson, I woke up before everyone else and went outside to watch the sun rise over the mountains.

It was going to be hard to drive away from this place. But I took comfort in knowing we'd always have the place where we were going later to scatter Mom's ashes—the desert behind the visitor center at Saguaro National Park.

Eventually everyone got up. We ate breakfast and everyone piled into Abe's Chevy Silverado and Mom's van. Even though it was now legally mine, I still thought of it in those terms, which made me even more upset when I backed the van out of the garage and veered slightly off the driveway, running over a small cactus that Mom had planted and brushing against the branches of a larger tree.

I got out of the van and saw that I had put a scratch on the side of it. Great. Mom had managed to keep it looking pristine after a hundred thousand miles. I hadn't even driven it a hundred feet and I'd already damaged it.

At the visitor center, we stood at the overlook where we held Mom's memorial service, then walked on the same short trail we did that morning. Only this time we weren't being silent. We passed the sign that said "Javelina Wash Trail."

"Before Mom moved here, I wouldn't have known how to pronounce 'hah-vuh-lee-nuh,' " I said.

"Or wash," Beth said.

Mom was incapable of pronouncing wash without an *r*. It was always worsh. Make sure to worsh your hands. I just put some clothes in the worshing machine. Do you remember when we went to Worshington, D.C.?

When I was a teenager, this bothered me. I mean, really bothered me. Why couldn't she just say wash like everyone else? But you eventually give up and just accept your parents' quirks. And then when they're gone, you find yourself missing even those quirks.

As we walked into the desert, our footsteps crunching on the path through the wash, someone was sitting near the visitor center, playing a flute.

We stopped. Beth tried to figure out how to open the brightly colored cylinder of ashes, eventually getting the top off.

Abe picked up the container. While Mom was dying, he rarely showed his emotions. But in this moment, his voice cracked.

"Lord, we ask you to take our spirit of Nancy into your arms and take care of her just like she took care of the desert," he said. He took the bag out of the container and shook it, pouring some ashes into the dry air.

Beth poured some ashes near a cactus. Lisa tossed some in the air. I reached into the bag, grabbed a handful and sprinkled around a bush.

The flute continued to play, switching to "Amazing Grace."

We stood there for a moment, then turned around and made the short walk back around the side of the visitor center. Trying to make sure memories were planted in Mia's head, I talked about how when I watched Nana take her on hikes, pointing out all kinds of things, it brought back memories of my own childhood.

"Some things I wasn't very interested in," Mia said. "No offense. Like flowers."

I told her that I remembered thinking the same thing when I was her age. Mom would show me these flowers and birds and trees and I'd think, What do I care? And the names and details about most of those flowers and birds and trees didn't stick. But the pull of them did. And I hoped that someday Mia would feel the same way.

BEFORE THE YEAR began, Mom said I could use the van for all my trips. I said I didn't want to waste too much time driving.

The months since then had reminded me of many things. Plans change. Life's short. And there's something to be said for a long drive.

When I was growing up, we made all kinds of long drives, covering thousands of miles, and hitting nearly every one of the Lower 48. But I hadn't done that kind of trip since Mom decided to move from Wisconsin to Arizona and I agreed to make the trip with her.

I wasn't thrilled about burning a week of vacation to drive

two thousand miles with my mom. But it seemed like the right thing to do. And as it turned out, it was a memorable thing to do.

The pace of a long drive allows you to talk about things in a way that few other venues do. You can't have lunch with someone, even someone close, and have a fifteen-minute pause in the conversation. But if you're driving across the heart of America, a long stretch of road fading into the distance, you do that all the time.

We talked about things I had forgotten but wanted to remember. How did she and Dad meet? What was their first date? How did they end up in California, then Michigan, Minnesota, and Wisconsin? And we talked about things I never knew. About things Mom struggled with early in the marriage. How their relationship evolved. How now that he was gone, she was sad and afraid, but ready to start a new chapter in her life.

More often than not, though, we just sat there, the radio off, the hum of the wheels on the road filling the car with white noise, a broad landscape and big sky spread out before us. It was, I eventually decided, quite a relaxing way to spend a week.

I thought about that as I drove the van to the Tucson airport to pick up Chris Burns.

He said he'd fly from Jacksonville to Tucson after Thanksgiving and help drive the van back to Florida. As grateful as I was for his offer, I kept trying to give him an out. And he kept insisting he wanted to do it, that it would be fun. If he was comparing the road trip to going to Philly with me for surgery, I suppose that was true.

I picked up Chris and said that if he came this far, he had to at least get a little taste of Saguaro National Park. We headed to the east half of the park, drove the Cactus Forest Loop road, and did a short hike on the Tanque Verde Ridge Trail.

By the time we got on I-10 and started heading east, the sun was setting behind us. We didn't have a specific destination in mind. Just drive until we got tired.

We made it to El Paso, about 320 miles away, at about eleven

P.M. When we pulled off I-10 and into the parking lot of a Holiday Inn, I called home to say good night.

"You have the van and you're going to stay in a hotel?" Toni said.

I said we planned to stop in a national park the next night, but it was late so we'd probably just crash at a hotel this evening. But after we hung up, I decided to at least look at an iPad app that showed nearby camping spots.

There was a place just off the previous exit: a Walmart.

It wasn't my idea of camping, but it did seem silly to spend money just to have a hotel bed for a few hours. Chris said he was up for whatever. It would be just another part of the adventure, right?

I turned the van around and headed back to the Walmart.

The parking lot was surprisingly full and bustling. And when we went inside, we walked into a chaotic buzz. The beeping of checkout scanners, the clatter of shopping carts, and the chatter of conversation. When I saw dozens of abandoned carts haphazardly arranged near the customer service desk, some empty and some full of items, it hit me.

This wasn't just any Saturday. This was the Saturday after Black Friday. At Walmart.

I parked the van at the far end of the parking lot, in a row near where Christmas trees leaned against the sign that said "Garden/ Outdoor."

I popped the top to the van, creating a bunk above the backseat that folded down to a bed. I told Chris I'd take the bunk, partly because I'm shorter than he is, but mainly because if he was willing to do this drive with me *and* to spend the first night at the El Paso Walmart, the least I could do was let him have the bed.

I will say this about camping there: It made me miss Floyd Bennett Field.

I fell asleep to the sound of cars and sirens in the distance, then woke up to the sound of music blaring from a car in the parking lot. I looked at my watch. It was 2:50 A.M., and I had to pee.

As I walked inside wearing pajamas and slippers, there were a few customers shopping. Nobody seemed to bat an eye.

When we got out of the van at 7:30 in the morning, the place already was starting to hum with shoppers.

As we headed east on I-10, to the south was the ramshackle edge of Ciudad Juárez. All around stretched a landscape that, in the hazy morning light, reminded me of the look Steven Soderbergh created for some scenes in *Traffic*. Brown, bright, bleak. I always thought he had taken filters and artfully exaggerated reality. Looking at this landscape, I thought maybe he had captured it.

I'm sure this edge of Texas has its own history, charm, and character. But passing through it, I was glad to see the speed limit: 80.

Before the trip, a native Texan told me that, even when the speed limit here increased through the years, Texans still viewed the numbers on signs more as suggestions than laws. And as if to confirm that, as I eased the van up to eighty miles per hour and put it on cruise control, several vehicles with Texas plates blew past on my left.

We could have headed northeast from El Paso and fairly easily gotten a taste of two national parks—Guadalupe and, just across the New Mexico border, Carlsbad Caverns. Or we could detour to the south to Big Bend, the park named for part of its southern edge, a large sweeping curve in the Rio Grande along the border with Mexico.

"You pick," Chris said when I asked him which option he'd prefer.

I picked Big Bend. I remembered asking Darla Sidles, the superintendent at Saguaro, the question: What's your favorite park? Without hesitation, she said Big Bend. She recalled going there often as a teenager, getting in a little boat, and crossing into Mexico in the pre-9/11 days and climbing to the top of Emory Peak in the Chisos Mountains, seeing as far as the eye could see.

"You felt like you were in the middle of nowhere," she said, adding that there was a reason for that. You *were* in the middle of nowhere. "It's truly a destination. You have to want to go there."

I wanted to go there partly because of that middle-of-nowhere location. The park service, the state of Texas, and the communities near Big Bend had taken some of the darkest, clearest night skies in America and made them even clearer and darker. Nine months earlier the International Dark-Sky Association, a Tucson-based organization, designated Big Bend as an International Dark Sky Park—the largest in the world at the time.

It was about 290 miles to the park. If everything went as planned, I figured we'd get there shortly after lunch and have some time for a hike.

After about 120 miles on I-10, I exited onto U.S. 90 South. While the landscape changed slowly and subtly, the vibe changed almost instantly. From four-lane divided highway to two lanes. From eighty miles per hour to seventy miles per hour. From cars in your view and rearview to looking at nothing but empty road, big blue skies, and wisps of mountains in the distance.

At one point, a tumbleweed about three times the size of a basketball rolled across the road in front of us. And another. A third one didn't make it to the other side of the road. It rolled in front of a car coming from the other direction and seemed to disintegrate and disappear upon impact, which made what we saw a few miles later even more interesting.

A tumbleweed was stuck in the grill of an oncoming car, flattened and looking like some sort of Texas-style Christmas ornament.

There was a relaxing monotony to the landscape and the long straight road, the telephone poles flicking past to our right. And then, still more than twenty-five miles from the town of Marfa, we could see something else on the right side of the road.

A small building. A storefront. No actual store. Just the front. White stucco walls, two windows with purses and shoes inside, and a sign that said "Prada Marfa."

Neither of us knew what to make of it. But thanks to Google and a cell signal, we quickly got the backstory that we had missed: It was a permanent sculpture—"a pop architectural land art project"—dreamed up in New York by German artists Michael Elmgreen and Ingar Dragset and installed here. As *The New York Times* wrote in 2005, "Texas, as big as it is, does not have a Prada store . . . But come Saturday it will look as if a tornado had picked up a Prada store and dropped it on a desolate strip of U.S. 90 in West Texas."

Even knowing that, we weren't sure what to make of it.

We passed through Marfa and then entered Alpine. I was intrigued by these places, which seemed quite different from Dallas and Houston and also from the Odessa and Midland described in *Friday Night Lights,* West Texas towns north of I-10 where everything revolved around oil and football.

Here they were mixing cattlemen with culture, saloons with art, Friday night lights with dark sky regulations.

McDonald Observatory was located in Fort Davis, not far north of where we were driving on U.S. 90. A new law had gone into effect at the start of the year requiring that counties within fifty-seven miles of the observatory enact outdoor lighting control to help preserve dark skies.

As we left Alpine, I realized I had missed the turn to Big Bend. I was mad at myself for setting us back even further.

Chris shrugged and said it was fine whenever we got there. All part of the adventure. He was calm, relaxed. Which made me kick myself for making it this far into the year, into life, and still letting something like this bother me.

We decided to just continue on U.S. 90 another thirty miles to Marathon, where we could take U.S. 385 south to the park's north entrance.

We stopped in Marathon (pop. 430) to get lunch. Chris got out of the van wearing his version of comfort travel wear that could be worn for a run once we got to the park—shorts, knee-high compression socks, and lime-green running shoes.

He managed to draw a few stares, which takes some doing in Marathon.

On the way to the French Company Grocer, we walked past what had once been a staid white Mercedes, now painted with a pattern of blocks of bright colors and adorned with an owl on the trunk.

We picked up a couple of sandwiches to go. When the dark-haired woman at the cash register started to ring up our items, it was clear from her accent that she didn't grow up here.

Chris struck up a conversation, asking her where she was from. Slovakia, she said. But she had traveled all over the world, eventually ending up here in Marathon, Texas.

It turned out she also helped run a nearby hostel with about a dozen bright-colored, wild-shaped structures built out of adobe, papercrete, and assorted found objects. The result was sort of a Pueblo Revival meets Dr. Seuss style of architecture. As a cyclist passing through Marathon about the same time wrote on his blog after staying there, "It's not so much a hostel but an evolving art project and a way of life wrapped up into one."

On the way out of town, we stopped at a gas station and filled up. Two men with a traditional Texas look—cowboy boots, jeans, flannel shirts, cowboy hats—were standing out front talking.

I was still worried about making a wrong turn. So Chris, wearing his compression socks and green shoes, walked over to the two men. I wished I had my camera handy to capture the looks on their faces.

"Is Big Bend National Park near here?" Chris asked.

"Yep," one of them said. "Just down that road."

"Like it says on that sign?" Chris said. "Sixty-seven miles?"

"Yep," he said.

To locals, sixty-seven miles was just down that road.

We reached the north entrance of the park by midafternoon. Chris wanted to go for a run. A ranger inside the visitor center told him that they discouraged "jogging" in the park.

A mountain lion had attacked a twenty-nine-year-old hiker from Spain the previous week. From the scant details in news stories, it sounded like the woman was fine. But as rangers searched for the mountain lion, that remote part of the park was temporarily closed to visitors. It was the second mountain lion attack of the year, after nearly a decade without a single attack.

"The drought has caused problems," the ranger said.

The park's website advised visitors who encounter mountain lions to hold their ground, wave their arms, throw stones and refrain from running. Chris decided he'd play it safe, which meant instead of running on a trail, he would run on the road.

"Can you drop me off six miles from the campground?" he said.

That turned out to be right near a large sign that said, "Bear and Mountain Lion Country." The road climbed three thousand feet in five miles, then descended for a mile, zigzagging into Chisos Basin, the late afternoon light splashing across it, the rocky walls circling around it.

Chris made it safely. I was relieved. And jealous.

After dinner, we watched the sun set and the moon rise. It was big and bright enough—three nights later it would be full—that the skies were far from their darkest. But there were still stars. Lots of them. Along with the moonlight, they outlined the peaks of the rock wall. And once everyone settled in for the night, this mountain bowl in the middle of nowhere was quiet.

Before this trip, I read Edward Abbey's description of an adventure to the southern edge of Texas. He wrote, "I'd rather be broke down and lost in the wilds of Big Bend, any day, than wake up some morning in a penthouse suite high above the megalomania of Dallas or Houston."

I'd add that I'd rather wake up in Chisos Basin, any day, than in an El Paso Walmart parking lot.

In the morning, it was overcast. Instead of heading back to the north entrance, we left the park on the road I had meant to enter it on. Large spiders crossed the pavement and dark clouds filled the sky behind sunlit mountains. When it started to rain lightly, I rolled down a window and the air smelled familiar, like Mom's backyard during a rare Tucson rain.

I spent less than twenty-four hours in Big Bend National Park.

And as we left, I wanted to come back, stay longer, and see the night skies with a new moon.

We spent the next night at the house of Chris's in-laws in Houston, then continued on I-10 the next morning, hoping to make it to Gulf Islands National Seashore by sunset.

As the van rolled past miles and miles of dark water dotted with bald cypresses, we continued the conversation that already had gone on for days. We talked about our parents, kids, careers, spouses, religion, college, college girlfriends, bikes, camping gear, running shoes, and road trips. Not so much the trips we'd already taken. The ones we wanted to do someday.

We talked about biking around Crater Lake, hiking in North Cascades, stand-up paddleboarding on a pristine lake. I said that someday I wanted to take a boat to Isle Royale in Lake Superior, the island in Lake Superior where my parents spent one of their anniversaries.

But for now, we were looking forward to checking out the Mississippi section of Gulf Islands National Seashore. When we exited I-10 near Biloxi, a rattling noise came from somewhere on the right side of the van. It got louder and louder, slowing when we slowed, stopping when we stopped.

It now officially was an old-fashioned road trip. We had vehicle issues.

It was getting close to five P.M., but we found a shop willing to look at the van.

I tried to remember something Gordon Hempton had said over breakfast one morning on the Olympic Peninsula, recalling his own cross-country trip in his VW bus. He said a friend had told him there is a difference between a trip and a journey. A trip is about getting from Point A to Point B. There's always something to worry about because there's always something that could sidetrack the trip. With a journey, he said, "You never have to worry about what will happen next, because *something* will always happen next."

It sounded good. But I wasn't the best at embracing it. As I was worrying about what would happen next—imagining a major issue that could take days and cost thousands of dollars to fix—one of the mechanics came out of the garage, wiping his hands off with a rag.

The rattle was just some loose bolts on the running boards. They replaced them and we were on our way, to one of the most visited sites in the National Park System.

Gulf Islands National Seashore spreads over two island chains in Florida and Mississippi. Its white sand beaches and historic forts were on their way to drawing nearly 5 million visitors for the year, making it the ninth most visited NPS site that year—ahead of the Grand Canyon, Yosemite, and Yellowstone.

We pulled into Davis Bayou Campground after dark, looping around the fifty-one campsites, most already filled with large RVs, some of them flickering with the glow of large TVs inside.

We picked campsite No. 40, mainly because it backed up to some trees. The temperatures dropped into the thirties overnight. In the morning, we boiled water for coffee and watched as some of our neighbors got in their vehicles and drove to the restrooms, less than a hundred yards away.

Even with all the visitors and nearby development, the park still was home to an array of wildlife. A board in the visitor center tallied what had been spotted: Acadian flycatcher, yellow-rumped warbler, pied-billed grebe, juvenile red fox, dolphins, box turtle, alligator, kingsnake, fiddler crab, blue crab, and periwinkle shrimp.

When I walked through the park, what struck me most was that with the marshes and forts and wildlife it reminded me of Northeast Florida, particularly of one of my favorite places in it—Round Marsh in the Timucuan Ecological and Historic Preserve.

It even had the same earthy, salty smell.

We were getting close. By the end of the day, we'd be home.

Somewhere near the Mississippi/Alabama border, we made one last stop, at a Texaco/McDonald's, filling up with gas and getting a drink.

Wherever we went, Chris struck up a conversation. As he was

ordering an iced tea at McDonald's, he asked the cashier, a teenage girl with dyed red hair poking out of her cap, about the tattoo on her right wrist.

"Is that new?" he asked.

"I got it last night," she said.

It said "Marley." She explained that it was her daughter's name. And that her daughter's father had picked the name, saying he had a cousin named Marley who had died. And that she had since learned this wasn't true, that he had picked the name because of Bob Marley. And that when she went to the tattoo parlor the night before, she hadn't even planned to get a tattoo.

"I wanted to get my tongue pierced, but it was too short," she said.

Chris nodded and smiled, as if there was nothing unusual about this conversation.

When we climbed back into the van, we agreed: You don't get these kinds of memories when you fly across America. It's not just that you see and hear and feel things on a drive that you'd never see and hear and feel from a plane. It's how the road unfolds slowly, how on a truly good road trip the unplanned is part of the plan.

We drove from Tucson to Jacksonville, 2,314 miles with the detours, without listening to the radio. I had loaded my iPod with music and NPR podcasts. But the only time we even turned on the radio was to put in a cassette tape I found at Mom's house. Yes, the van had a cassette tape deck.

A label on the tape said it was recorded in 1979, when Dad spent a summer at a church in England. I was hoping to find Dad's voice. Instead, I heard English accents, garbled by the tape's degradation.

I ejected the tape and we drove on, talking about anything and everything, often saying nothing, just listening to the whoosh and hum of the road.

I can't drive home from work without impulsively turning on the radio, but somehow we went across the country with it off. The journey itself became the ultimate mix tape. The saguaros and sage-brush, the El Paso Walmart and Prada Marfa, the moon over the Chisos Basin, the swamps and marshes of Louisiana and Mississippi, the girl with a Marley tattoo, the sign that said we were entering the city limits of Jacksonville, nearing the end of I-10, nearing the end of the year.

12

*

DECEMBER: HALEAKALĀ NATIONAL PARK

I woke up in my tent, the final sunrise of the year still a few hours away.

I imagined panning back from where I was lying, my tent quickly becoming a speck in the corner of the crater of a dormant volcano; panning back farther and this crater becoming the crown atop a mountain that rises 10,023 feet out of the ocean; farther and this mountain becoming part of a string of islands poking out of the water; farther, much farther, and this water stretching for more than two thousand miles in every direction, making this the most remote archipelago in the world.

While a million people were expected to gather later in New York to watch the ball drop, I came here—Maui's Haleakalā—to watch the sun set and to start the final day of the year in a place that might be the antithesis of Times Square.

I lay there, trying to stay still and not rustle my sleeping bag. I wanted to hear a sound. Not a specific sound. *Any* sound.

A slight breeze had been blowing earlier. But now, nothing. It felt like if I unzipped the tent and peeked outside, I'd find that the surreal setting I last saw in the fading daylight had disappeared, replaced by something even wilder, some sort of deep-space nothingness.

I had read that when it is like this here—the air calm, the birds sleeping, the helicopters grounded—it's one of the quietest places on earth, with ambient sound levels at the threshold of human hearing.

In other words, there were sounds out there. I just couldn't hear them.

I eventually heard one thing, only one thing. A persistent thump-thump, thump-thump. My own heartbeat in my ears. And the more I thought about it, the louder it seemed to get. Loud enough that I started to *feel* the heartbeat in my ears.

With no lights, no sound, and no cell signal, I felt disoriented, as if everything had stopped, maybe even time itself.

I sat up and unzipped my tent, making a *zzzzz* sound that seemed loud enough to carry across the crater floor—a nineteen-square-mile area Mark Twain described in 1866 as large enough to "make a fine site for a city like London."

Twain had slept at the summit of this mountain a half century before it became part of a national park. And when the sun rose through the clouds, he wrote: "I felt like the last man, neglected of the judgment, and left pinnacled in mid-heaven, a forgotten relic of a vanished world. . . . It was the sublimest spectacle I ever witnessed, and I think the memory of it will remain with me always."

That was one of the reasons why I was here, a copy of Twain's *Roughing It* tucked in my backpack.

I glanced at my watch. Forty-three degrees. Outside the tent it probably was in the thirties, far from what people picture when they think of Hawaii.

I crawled out of the tent and into the cold air, aware of every noise I made. The scuffling of my feet in the dirt, the rustling of my jacket.

As my eyes adjusted, I looked around.

In the moonlight, the volcanic landscape looked even more otherworldly.

I slowly turned around 360 degrees, thinking about how this giant geological bowl made Big Bend's Chisos Basin seem small and cozy. The rim, outlined by the moon and night sky, gave a sense of the size of the crater—7.5 miles long, 2.5 miles wide, more than 2,500 feet deep—but that was only one sense.

There were quieter places on earth. Labs in Minnesota and Washington were battling for that title, designing chambers that not only were insulated from outside sound but capable of absorbing the sound within. The negative decibel race created places where, if human beings tried to stay in them in the dark, they quickly became uncomfortable.

This crater, with its concave floor of dried lava and soft cinders, was nature's echoless chamber.

A few days earlier, a local woman had told me that when people enter the crater for the first time, sometimes it rattles them. They think they know what silence sounds like. They picture the quietest place they know and expect something similar. But they have no idea. If they close their eyes and let their other senses inform their brain, sometimes they feel like their body is floating. And sometimes they aren't sure whether to stay or run.

Standing there, looking at this expanse in the dark, hearing nothing but my own breath and heartbeat, I was aware that this was different from the quiet of the Olympic rain forest. This was simultaneously awe-inspiring and unnerving, a reminder that the difference between "sacred" and "scared" is a couple of transposed letters.

WHERE DO I END?

Back when the calendar still was as white and inviting as new snow, I knew where I wanted to begin the year—atop Cadillac Mountain, watching the first sunrise in America—and I had a pretty good idea where I would go every month after that. Except for the last one.

After Mom died, forever making June 30 more than just a midpoint on the calendar, the question of where to end seemed even more important. I no longer was solely trying to figure out where the national parks were headed in the future. I was trying to figure out where I was headed.

I thought about ending in Denali. But the more I pictured December in Alaska, the more Hawaii sounded like a good idea. Throughout the year when I told people I started the year with a sunrise in Maine, they asked, "So are you going to end with a sunset in Hawaii?"

I'd laugh and say maybe. Then I started to think about it.

Part of what I loved about being in the parks, spending more time sleeping under the stars than I had in decades, was how it boiled life down to the simplest of things. Perhaps even more liberating than what you control is being keenly aware of what you don't.

In a typical year, I don't see many sunsets. In this year, even when I wasn't watching one, I was aware of the light changing and another day turning to night.

The beauty of another sunset wasn't merely the sight; it was the sensation of being a small, irrelevant part of what Muir called the eternal grand show.

"It is always sunrise somewhere," he wrote in a journal. "The dew is never all dried at once; a shower is forever falling; vapor is ever rising. Eternal sunrise, eternal sunset, eternal dawn and gloaming, on sea and continents and islands, each in its turn, as the round earth rolls."

As I thought about where I wanted to be when the round earth rolled through another year, one sign after another kept pointing to a volcano in Hawaii.

There was the shared birth date. Like Acadia, Haleakalā's national park roots go back to 1916. Just weeks before the birth of the National Park Service—and forty-three years before Hawaii became a state—a park originally known as Hawaii National Park was created. At first it consisted only of the summits of Kilauea and Mauna Loa on the Big Island and Haleakalā on Maui.

Haleakalā became a separate national park in 1961, at the end of a week that was quite significant for Rex and Nancy Woods. They became parents.

There were the words of Jack London, written in his 1911 travel book, *The Cruise of the Snark*. Go to this mountain, he said. "Haleakalā has a message of beauty and wonder for the soul that cannot be delivered by proxy."

There was the name. In Hawaiian, Haleakalā means "House of the Sun."

There was the controversy, an ongoing legal battle that pitted sacred traditions against state-of-the-art technology. Haleakalā remained such a spectacular place to watch the sun—perhaps the best place on Earth, some said—that there were plans to build the world's largest solar telescope atop it. Ever since the National Science Foundation announced in 2009 that it had selected Haleakalā over Big Bear Lake in California and Spain's Canary Islands, some native Hawaiians had been protesting, saying adding this 143-foot-tall telescope to the ones already at the summit would defile a sacred place.

If all of this—the birth date, the meaning of the name, the day and night skies, the tug-of-war between the past and future, the sound of silence—wasn't enough to convince me I was supposed to end up in Haleakalā, there was the story behind the name.

According to ancient legend, the sun used to sprint across the sky. The days flew by quickly, making it difficult for those on Earth to finish tasks and enjoy life. No sooner had Hina, the mother of Maui, laid out her kapa cloth to dry in the sun than it was turning dark again.

One day before sunrise Maui crept to the summit of the mountain and lassoed the sun. When the sun begged for its freedom, Maui made the sun promise to slow its daily rush across the sky. The sun agreed. And ever since then, the sun has moved slowly and the days have lasted longer—especially atop Haleakalā.

A son lassoing the sun for his mother, extending the day.

That was it. I was going to finish the year in a volcano.

A FEW DAYS before I left, I saw a story in my newspaper. It was on Page B-8, right next to the obituaries. The headline said: "Happiest nations? Survey surprises."

Gallup had asked people in 148 countries questions designed to measure their happiness. The happiest people weren't necessarily in the wealthiest countries. The United States—a place with the "pursuit of happiness" enshrined in the Declaration of Independence—came in thirty-third, far behind the likes of Panama, Paraguay, El Salvador, Trinidad and Tobago, Ecuador, and Costa Rica.

I circled one quote. Luz Castillo, a thirty-year-old surfing instructor in Guatemala, gave his explanation for why people in his country smile so much: "Despite all the problems we're facing, we're surrounded by natural beauty that lets us get away from it all."

I was ready to get away from it all.

The news of the day was a mix of what happened less than two weeks before Christmas in Newtown, Connecticut—a gunman walked into an elementary school and killed twenty children and six adults—and what wasn't happening in Washington. A political stalemate, the latest in a series of them, was walking the country toward a December 31 fiscal cliff.

It seemed like a good time to go into a volcanic crater.

On a plane somewhere over the Pacific, I realized everyone else seemed to be with someone—beginning a vacation, starting a honeymoon, heading home. I was alone and . . . what? Ending something that I didn't want to end?

I wouldn't exactly be re-creating Jack London's journey to the top of Haleakalā, a trip that involved six days on a steamer from San Francisco to Honolulu, an overnight boat to Maui, and a horseback ride to the summit. I would be driving about thirty-seven miles of pavement stretching from near sea level to 10,023 feet.

There are roads in the world with steeper ascents, but few have a combination of gradient and distance quite like what now leads to Puʻuʻulaʻula, the summit of Haleakalā. The road opened in 1935, three years after drivers started traveling the Going-to-the-Sun Road in Montana's Glacier National Park. With dozens of steeply banked switchbacks, it was billed as the "Speedway to the Sun."

Before leaving Kahului, I stopped at a grocery store and got what had become the usual supplies. Food, fuel for my stove, water, local beer, ice, and a cheap cooler. Even though much had changed since the park was created, once you were through the entrance gate at about 6,500 feet, there wasn't any food for sale. No café at an over-look or hotel at the top. No snack machines. Just places to fill water bottles at a couple of visitor centers and the Hosmer Grove camp-ground, where I planned to spend the night. I'm sure some people complained about this, but I liked it.

The sun was beginning its descent when I headed inland and began the gradual ascent through farmland and fields. At Route 378, the road truly began its climb. In the next twenty-two miles and thirty-two switchbacks, it would rise seven thousand feet.

The landscape seemed to change around every corner. It re-minded me of a drive I did several times with Mom in Tucson, to the top of Mount Lemmon, and how the desert quickly disappeared, replaced by ever-changing vegetation. Grassland, woodland, oaks, pines, firs, and finally, at the top, forests.

The transition here was even more dramatic. From lush coast to rocky mountain. From humid subtropical to subalpine desert. When I talked to Matt Brown, the acting superintendent, he said a clima-tologist described the park's 33,000 acres as the steepest precipitation gradient in the world. There are wetter places on the planet, and there are drier places. But in no place, he said, is it so wet and so dry so close together. From one edge of the crater, a rain forest drops thousands of feet down to the coast.

"There's a line," he said. "You can stand on a ridge and put your hands out and it's raining on your right hand and it's dry on your left hand. It's crazy. Where else do you get that?"

By the time I reached the park entrance, clouds were rolling in. I stopped and took a picture of the entrance sign. Behind it, farther up the mountain, was a thick, dark cloud.

I debated whether to just head to the campground, down a nearby road, or to keep heading up the mountain. Even though it didn't look like there would be much of a sunset, I decided to stop briefly in the campground and then keep going up the road.

The visibility kept getting worse. I was considering turning around when I rounded a corner into the most dramatic transition yet.

Sunshine and blue skies.

The clouds hadn't suddenly disappeared. I was above them. A big, nearly full moon was rising.

I found a place to pull off the road.

To stand on the side of this mountain, looking down at an ocean of clouds, was to understand why the natives considered this sacred space and called it Kua Mana (the land above the clouds). What I had just driven through was an everyday thing, the mauna lei, a lei of clouds forming around the mountain.

I headed back partway down the mountain to Hosmer Grove, the free campground located just inside the park boundary. When I stopped there earlier, it was a symphony of surround sound, created by some of the island's one hundred thousand birds and the nearby forest. Whistles and chirps overhead, whirs of flapping wings and—when the wind picked up—the creaking of Hosmer's eucalyptus trees rubbing together, sounding like the door to a haunted house opening.

But now it was quiet, and the clouds had disappeared.

I wandered into a nearby field and looked up.

A shooting star darted across the dark sky.

HOURS BEFORE THE 7:02 A.M. sunrise, I watched red taillights snake up the road, making the mountain look like the world's largest Christmas tree. I got in line and followed them to the top.

About three hundred feet below the actual summit, a couple of hundred people gathered along a railing next to the visitor center, overlooking the crater, which the rangers repeatedly reminded visitors isn't really a crater. It's an erosional valley.

The temperature was in the mid-forties, not nearly as cold as it could get here, but still a long way from the beaches where many started their day. Most came prepared, wearing down jackets, caps, and gloves and wrapping themselves in blankets. Some wore shorts and flip-flops and shivered.

As the darkness gradually faded, people stared off into the distance or held up iPads and smartphones, waiting for the sun to appear.

A woman wearing a name tag (Nan) and a jacket over a gray fleece vest with a logo (Hawaii Pacific Parks Association) stood a few yards behind them. Every so often she lifted her left sleeve, turned over her hand, and looked at the watch on her wrist. At one point, she closed her eyes as if while others were waiting to see the sun, she was waiting to feel it.

Then, at the right moment, Nan Cabatbat began a loud chant.

> *E hō mai*
> *Ka ʻike mai luna mai e*
> *ʻO na mea huna noʻeau*
> *ʻO na mele e*
> *E hō mai,*
> *E hō mai,*
> *E hō mai*

As she repeated this three times, asking for knowledge and wisdom from above, the sunlight began to reach her. First the top of her head and her graying hair. Then her light brown eyes. Then her entire face. By the time she was finished, she and everyone else on the rim was bathed in sunlight.

Nan softly said something else in Hawaiian, then belted out a welcome. "This is your sunrise!" she said.

People applauded. Some began to head to their cars, perhaps to warm up, perhaps because they had checked "Haleakalā sunrise" off their list and were ready to leave the park.

She added one more thing, her voice still booming but now carrying the tone of a teacher.

"The state of Hawaii makes up 2/10ths of 1 percent of the total land area of the United States," she said. "Yet we are responsible for more than 70 percent of all lost known species. That is why Haleakalā became a national park. Not because we have a pretty viewing area for sunrise and sunset, but because we have insects, animals, birds, and plants that can be found only here. To this end I ask: Take responsibility for your national parks. Returning to the parking lot, there will be no cut-shorting through the rocks. We have two insects that can be found nowhere else in the world."

Afterward, she answered a few questions, explaining to one man why it was important to protect an insect—saying that everything is connected, and when we lose even small pieces, we risk losing everything.

When she finished, we got in her car and headed down the mountain a couple of miles, turning into the parking lot for the Kalahaku Overlook. She had said it would be a quieter place to talk. And, sure enough, when we walked to the overlook, there wasn't anyone else there.

Nan grew up on Maui. When she was young, she wanted to see what it was like to live away from water. She ended up in Oklahoma, but eventually returned to Hawaii. She had been working in the park for twenty-four years.

I told her I wanted to get a native perspective on this place—and the plan to add the world's largest solar telescope to the summit.

She started by giving one of the arguments that some made for the telescopes. In a way, they said, the Haleakalā Observatories continue an ancient tradition of using the skies for wayfaring. Early Hawaiian elders took their sons to the summit to teach them how to use the sun and moon and stars to find their way. The new telescope—ninety-two feet long with a main mirror thirteen feet in diameter—would stand fourteen stories high and allow man to follow the sun in unprecedented detail.

While the height was at the heart of much of the criticism, Nan pointed to what would happen beneath the ground. To build this telescope involved digging five stories deep.

"The planet we live on, we refer to as Papa—earth mother," she said. "Would you let someone that you don't know, who doesn't understand your background, cut up your mother? . . . I just hope that when they start to dig, we have a conversation with our mother."

I knew not every local felt quite this way about having telescopes atop Haleakalā. When I was at the summit, one of Nan's co-workers had come out of the visitor center and, spotting one of the telescopes open, began bowing toward it. He grew up on Haleakalā, just down the road. He talked reverentially about the island, the history, the geology, the night skies. But he also thought some of what happened at Science City was "pretty cool." He said that open telescope tracked thousands of pieces of space debris, ensuring he didn't miss his NFL playoffs, hockey updates, baseball scores.

So when he saw it open, he bowed to it. Sort of a mock bow. Still, I had a feeling I wouldn't see Nan doing the same.

Our conversation didn't feel like an interview. It felt more like I had come to the mountaintop and found the proverbial wise old man with the answers to life's questions. Only in Haleakalā's case, as is often the case, wisdom came from a woman.

When we first sat down, even though there was nobody else around, even though we were on the edge of this massive open space—or perhaps because of that—she whispered.

"It's quiet here," she said. "We tell people, close your eyes and just listen."

She told a story about the first time she went to visit her oldest son in Winnemucca, Nevada. She felt disoriented, unsure of where she was in the universe. One night her son took her to the top of Winnemucca Mountain. He set a towel on the ground and told her which direction was west. She lay down on the towel, her feet pointing west, and looked into the night sky.

She found it, an orange star, the brightest in the northern night sky.

When Polynesian colonists first sailed large double-hulled canoes more than 2,500 miles of ocean from the South Pacific to Hawaii, they navigated with the wisdom of elders and the signs of nature. Birds, currents, winds, tides, and stars. Especially Arcturus, or Hokule'a.

When Nan looked up into the Nevada night sky and found Arcturus, she sat up and said, "That's home."

Ever since then, she said, she hasn't felt off-kilter when she visits her son.

"I know where home is," she said. "As long as you know where home is, you can go anywhere."

I HAD A dream about Mom, the first time that had happened since she died.

I was hiking on a trail. I rounded a corner and there she was.

"Hi," she said, like it was no big deal that we bumped into each other.

I stood frozen for a moment.

"Are you okay?" I said.

"Yes," she said. "Are you okay?"

"Yes," I said. "Yes . . . no . . . I don't know."

I woke up, a bit shaken. A strong wind was blowing in Hosmer Grove. The trees no longer were creaking. They were roaring.

I wrote down the details of the dream, then lay there listening to wind and the trees.

Mom never set foot on Haleakalā or, for that matter, Hawaii.

She had been to nearly every other place I went during the year. Acadia, Dry Tortugas, Saguaro, Glen Canyon, Grand Canyon, Yellowstone, Yosemite, Olympic, Big Bend. She hadn't been to Floyd Bennett Field in New York or the Flight 93 National Memorial in Pennsylvania. But that was about it.

When I spent time at these places, I took comfort in knowing I was experiencing what she had experienced, standing where she had stood, smelling what she had smelled, hearing what she had heard.

This was different. She had never been within two thousand miles of here.

Before arriving, I had wondered if that was going to be the big flaw in ending the year here. If she and Dad had never been here, how was this place going to make me feel connected to them? Or was that exact reason to be here, to experience something without that connection and start moving on?

I realized now both of those questions were misguided.

I felt connected to them at every turn. And not just by a dream. By something more powerful: memories.

When I spent an hour taking a picture of a Haleakalā silversword—waiting for the light to change, moving around the rare plant, trying to frame its shiny leaves in the foreground and the crater in the background—I was doing exactly what Dad would have done. When I closed my eyes and forced myself to be in the moment, listening to the birds in Hosmer Grove, I was doing exactly what Mom would have done.

When I headed to the Halemauʻu Trail to hike into the crater for a night, I was doing what they would have done, once upon a time, before my sisters and I came along, before we grew up and they grew older, their bodies suddenly vetoing their minds' plans. First Dad, then Mom.

As I began the hike, I was well aware of my own mortality, or at least the screws in my left shoulder and the incisions in my groin, remnants from two surgeries in three months.

I had barely covered the first few hundred relatively flat feet of the Halemauʻu Trail and my body already was saying it was a good thing I chose to get a backcountry permit for Holua—at 3.7 miles from the trailhead, the shortest hike to wilderness camping.

I got a later start than I had planned. The afternoon clouds had rolled in. The trail wound through mist and shrub land for the first mile, dropping, then climbing slightly as it passed a brown sign with white lettering and an arrow:

Haleakalā Crater

I was thinking about how even the official sign didn't describe the crater as an "erosional depression" when I reached the edge of it—a surreal entryway.

The path continued straight ahead on a ridge seemingly extending into the crater. Off the left edge of the path, clouds swirled and rolled and hovered, the visibility changing by the second. To the right, there were no clouds, just the cliff dropping a thousand feet to the expanse of the crater floor.

I crossed the ridge and snaked down the cliffside switchbacks, reaching a metal gate and hitching rail on the crater floor. Beyond the gate, the trail headed a flat mile through landscape much different from the crater near the summit. With knee-high grassland, it felt pastoral.

By the time I passed the Holua cabin—a family with a few small children had the coveted reservation for the night—and climbed to the rocky plateau where camping was allowed, it was nearly five P.M., about an hour from sunset.

The park service set a twenty-five-person limit for the area, but as I started to wander through the rock and native scrub dotted with small yellow flowers, I wondered if anyone else was here. I eventually figured out there were seven people scattered about the plateau: two twentysomething guys from Oahu, a young couple from Belgium, an older couple from the Czech Republic, and me.

While setting up my tent, I thought about how my green little home had traveled from Maine to Maui, ending up everywhere from a tropical island beach to New York City to a rain forest. Now this. A dormant volcano.

I sat on a rock and ate dinner. Darkness started to fall on the crater. The only bit of sunlight left was on the rim in the distance.

A cloud covered half the rim. Where the sun met the cloud, a rainbow appeared. The wind faded a notch, and the crater got a little quieter.

I pulled my audio recorder out of my backpack, knowing that maybe this was a silly exercise. The idea of recording sound here seemed a bit like taking a picture of a room with no windows and the lights turned off.

Yet, when I stopped and listened, there still were a few sounds. The breeze itself touching my ears. The horses in the corral occasionally snorting. People talking nearby.

I ended up standing in the middle of the plateau with the Belgium couple, Peter and Elizabeth. They said the trip to Maui had taken forty hours.

"I think if you dig a hole in the ground, you end up in Belgium," Elizabeth said with a laugh. "But it's worth it. It's so pretty."

She glanced around, looking at the towering cliff behind us and the expanse in front of us, all of it gradually turning dark.

"In Belgium, you see lights everywhere," Peter said. "Everywhere. The horizon is always orange from the lights from cities. I lived in the desert once for half a year. That was the first time I experienced it. It was just then that I realized I had never experienced a decent sky."

"I saw a shooting star last night," I said.

"We saw one as well!" they said in unison.

"Did you make a wish?" Peter added.

"I didn't," I said. "Can I still make one?"

I made a wish. I wished I could lasso the sun when it came up the next morning and make this year last a little longer.

As the breeze continued to soften, so did the conversation. At one point, I realized we were whispering. And then we stood there watching, the air quickly turned cold and the stars started to come out, slowly at first, then like popcorn, exploding and filling the sky.

They said good night, heading back to their tent.

I thought the sky was as full as it could get. But with each blink it seemed that more stars appeared. I remembered being in Acadia, walking out to the rocky coastline and having my breath taken away by the stars. This trumped that. This trumped any night sky I had ever seen.

I WOKE TO honking.

After the middle-of-the-night experience—venturing out of my tent and hearing overwhelming nothingness—it was comforting to hear something, anything, especially this. A couple of nene, Hawaiian geese, passing overhead.

I had the backcountry permit for another night, December 31. Ever since getting into the crater, I had been debating: Should I end the year here? Or should I go to the summit and watch the sun set there?

I boiled some water and made a cup of coffee.

While sitting there, I heard something in the distance, the far distance. I couldn't see it. Helicopters weren't allowed to fly in the crater. But for several minutes I could hear the hum coming from somewhere beyond the crater. And then it was quiet again.

I eventually decided I would pack up and hike out.

Being in the crater had hit me differently than I had expected. Yes, it was beautiful and peaceful. But, as Nan had predicted, it also made me feel surprisingly on edge.

As I climbed out of the crater, the calendar said it was the end of the year. But there are other calendars. Nan told me that her people live by three of them.

"The stars tell us what to do," she said. "The moon tells us when to do these things, and the sun gives us the light to do."

When the sun sets, she said, it isn't the end of the day. It's the start. It's a time to talk about what happened before the sun set—good, bad, otherwise—and figure out how to learn from it.

So maybe the sunset I had been dreading, picturing as the end of something, actually was a beginning.

If that was the case, this day was supposed to start at 6:01 P.M. And when I reached the summit about a half hour before sunset, there were only about two dozen people there. The clouds below us were big and dramatic, like mountains themselves. And the air was surprisingly temperate and calm.

I thought about New Year's Day at Acadia, huddling behind a rock, trying to stay warm as the wind whipped across Cadillac Mountain and the fog turned sunrise into a pink glow.

Here the visibility seemed infinite. People posed for pictures, the sea of clouds behind them, their arms raised as if on top of the world.

When I looked back to the east, down toward the crater, I realized I couldn't see it. I could see the rim around it, the visitor center next to it. But I couldn't see into the crater. It was covered with a cloud lid.

I finally started to trust in my judgment and believe maybe I was in the right place at the right time. And that was before I began to record what the sunset sounded like—the crunching of footsteps on the red cinder, children laughing, people speaking a variety of accents and languages, a few members of one family softly singing a devotional chant.

I asked them if they'd mind if I recorded them, then ended up joining them to watch the sun set. I thought about how many of my memories of the first sunrise involved the company of Lili and Carol. I had watched a lot of sunsets and sunrises by myself since then, and as much as I appreciated that contemplative solitude, I liked the idea of watching this one with people.

It was a large family, four generations, some originally from Haiti. They looked like a poster family for what the park service kept talking about needing in the future. Visitors that weren't just aging white baby boomers like me. Minorities and kids.

The family included two adorable little kids, a ten-year-old brother and his little sister.

I ended up chatting with their dad. He was in his early forties,

dreadlocks, a warm smile. We were talking about hiking in the crater when out of the corner of his eye he saw his son almost run into
something.

"Watch your head, Denali," he said.

"His name is Denali?" I said. "Like the mountain?"

"Yes," he said.

We talked about Denali, the name and the mountain. I explained how I had planned to go to Denali National Park this year
with Mom—and how, when I didn't go, somehow a place I had
never been to took on added significance.

I hadn't made it to Denali. But on the last day, a boy named Denali was running around my feet.

"I'd like to take him there someday," his dad said. "We'll see."

"What was the chant you did earlier?" I asked.

"There are several powerful mantras in Hinduism," he said.
"The gayatri mantra is one of the more powerful ones. I could loosely
translate, but I'd do a very poor job of it. It's a chant my wife heard
during the birth of both of our kids, and it's one that we sang to my
mom as she was dying."

I thought about when Mom was dying. One of her girlfriends,
a younger woman she met while walking dogs, had come to the
house. Along with a friend and a guitar, they sang to her. I could
only remember one song they sang—"Here Comes the Sun"—
partly because when they sang it, it was monsoon season. In the
distance, a wall of rain was approaching, rolling across the desert,
blocking the sun, perfuming the landscape, giving life.

Now I was in this desert in the sky, above the clouds.

"Oh, there it goes!" said one of the women, pointing at the sun.
"Yay!"

They applauded, watched for a few more minutes, and then began to head to their cars. One of the women said they did this every
year, that I should join them again in the future—"and go to
Denali," she added.

Denali's dad lingered, softly singing the mantra he had sung for births and deaths, before turning to me and saying: "All right, brother."

"Thank you," I said, sticking out my hand.

"Nah, give me a hug, man," he said. "Have a good journey."

It wasn't until later that I learned Moriba Jah—Dr. Moriba Jah—had been involved in some remarkable journeys. He helped NASA land rovers on Mars. He now was the lead for the Air Force Research Laboratory's Advanced Sciences and Technology Research Institute for Astronautics. Or as he put it in his Twitter bio: "Attempting to embrace the concept that The Source Is Infinite. My day job is to understand and predict the behavior of objects in space."

I stayed until the summit area was almost empty. All that remained of the sun was a tiny bit of orange on a very distant horizon, beneath a patch of light blue sky that gradually turned darker and darker.

It felt like this sunset lasted far longer than most, like the sun was honoring its age-old agreement with the boy who lassoed it for his mother.

Then it was gone, but certainly not forgotten.

Two decades after Mark Twain left here, he wrote a letter to a friend in Hawaii that began, "The house is full of carpenters and decorators; whereas, what we really need here, is an incendiary. If the house would only burn down, we would pack up the cubs and fly to the isles of the blest, and shut ourselves up in the healing solitudes of the crater of Haleakalā and get a good rest; for the mails do not intrude there, nor yet the telephone and the telegraph."

The "healing solitudes" still existed on Haleakalā. I could vouch for that. But if the year taught me anything, it was that they still exist all over America. Yes, they're dwindling and under constant attack. But they're out there.

They can be found in deserts and rain forests, canyons and islands, the stars and the sun. They can be found on the way to the bottom of the Grand Canyon and the top of Half Dome. They can be found in a seventeen-ton boulder in a Pennsylvania field and a stone in a child's hand. They can be found in a boy named Denali and a girl named Mia.

They even can be found in New York City.

None of this is a given. Not today, certainly not tomorrow.

But when the sun disappeared, I took comfort in thinking it wasn't an end or a beginning. It was merely a continuation of the eternal grand show. It is always sunrise somewhere. And in less than eight hours, the sun's light would be reaching a mountain in Maine.

EPILOGUE: AFTER SUNSET

*T*his is just my national parks story. There are, of course, millions like it. Stories about people lost, places that remain and how the two are intertwined.

After the year, I sometimes thought back to a trip I made before it all began, before I knew Mom was dying, before I realized just how much my national parks story—nearly everyone's national parks story—involves a love not only of these places, but of the people we've shared them with.

Two months before the first sunrise, I went to Walpole, New Hampshire, home of Florentine Films, to meet with Dayton Duncan, the writer who suggested to his longtime friend and collaborator, Ken Burns, that they do a documentary about America's national parks.

With streets lined with sparkling white buildings, Walpole feels like a quintessential New England town, a Bedford Falls come to life. And when I met Duncan for coffee at Burdick's, the town in *It's a Wonderful Life* came up during our conversation. He said that his friendship with Burns started with having two things in common: They both read the Declaration of Independence to their children every Fourth of July, and they both considered *It's a Wonderful Life* to be their favorite film.

While working on *The National Parks: America's Best Idea,* they talked about how that movie related to their documentary. When

George Bailey gets his wish and he never was born, the town becomes Pottersville, the girl becomes a tramp, the wife becomes an
old maid, the brother dies as a child. If our national parks never had
been born . . .

"What would the rim of the Grand Canyon be right now?" he
said. "It would be lined with trophy homes. And you and I, unless
we knew one of the owners of those homes, would never have the
glorious experience of standing there. Yosemite Valley would be a
gated community with a beautiful golf course, thirty-six holes in
the valley there, a par-3 with Half Dome as the backdrop. The Everglades would be shopping centers and housing tracts. Yellowstone
would be Geyser World."

I thought about that often during the year, not only when I was
in a park but when I came home and saw what was hanging on the
family room wall: a framed *It's a Wonderful Life* movie poster my
wife gave me as a wedding present.

But it was another part of that conversation in Walpole that I
kept coming back to after the year. I asked Duncan a question I'm
sure he has heard countless times, a question I asked others throughout the year: What is your favorite national park?

He said that when they were working on the documentary, he
had two answers. The first was that his favorite was whichever park
he was in at the moment. "Which was both flippant and true," he
said. The second answer was Glacier. Not because its beauty trumps
all others, but because of the time he had spent there with his wife,
Dianne, and children.

And then there was Grand Teton National Park and Jenny Lake.

He first went there in the summer of 1959. He was about to turn
ten. The previous winter his mother had decided they were going
to take a long-distance family vacation. They borrowed an old car
from his grandmother, a trailer from a neighbor, and camping equipment from friends. And they hit the road.

"I can almost remember that trip day by day," he said. "I don't
know exactly why that it is, but it must have something to do with

that it was all foreign territory to me. When you go into a new land or foreign place, your senses are heightened."

He remembers the car breaking down at the Badlands, stopping at Wall Drug, going to Custer's Battlefield (as it was known then), seeing bears and bison at Yellowstone, sleeping on the sand next to the Green River in Dinosaur National Monument, and camping at Jenny Lake.

"My mother to her dying day would get a little misty-eyed talking about that view across Jenny Lake," he said. "When I took my kids to Dinosaur National Monument, I took them to the place where we slept on the sand. All that rushed back to me. I was nine years old again. . . . There is this confluence of time and memory that, for me at least, is overpowering."

He recalled taking his children back to the small town in Iowa where he grew up. The field where his mother used to pitch to him has been replaced by a music center. Where he used to play, there now are apartments. His childhood house is gone, a parking lot in its place. He can point to these spots and tell his children what used to be there. But he can go back to the Grand Tetons, stand at Jenny Lake, and in the same spot where his mother held his hand, hold his own child's hand and feel like he has somehow warped time.

"It's not just timelessness in the geological sense," he said. "It's a timelessness that's very personal. You feel like you're touching something that is as close to eternity as you might be able to experience."

He laughed.

"It starts to sound a little squishy, I know," he said. "But there's a reason the big national parks were preserved in the first place. They are so overwhelmingly powerful, so transcendent that even a nation that was as intent as any nation has ever been of subduing nature and the continent in as little time as possible—even that nation had to stop and say, 'Maybe in this place we won't do all those things.'"

MY FAVORITE NATIONAL park? Maybe Redwood, because of that first trip as a child and the last trip with Mom. Maybe Grand Canyon, because it keeps pulling me back. Maybe Denali, because it represents the places I haven't been to yet but take comfort in knowing are still there.

But two years after my year in the national parks, my favorite one was the one I was in at that moment: Cumberland Island National Seashore.

Mia was twelve, the age Mom told each of her four grandchildren she would take them on an adventure.

I felt like I owed it to Mom and to Mia to plan something. I had visions of some big adventure to some faraway park. But life got in the way and in the end I settled on a trip to Cumberland Island that spring.

At first I felt guilty about this. Getting to Cumberland Island involved a one-hour drive from our driveway to St. Marys, Georgia, followed by a forty-five-minute ferry ride.

But the more I thought about it, the more I liked it. I was giving Mia a gift that Mom and Dad repeatedly gave me, one I often needed to remind myself about. An appreciation of my own backyard.

There are larger barrier islands on America's East Coast. Most of them have bridges leading to paved roads and so-called civilization. Cumberland Island is about eighteen miles long and between one-half and three miles wide. Its forty square miles include 9,800 wilderness acres. It's surrounded by the ocean to the east; rivers, sounds, and marshes to the west, north, and south.

The island's two-hundred-year-old main road is a single sandy lane framed by natural arches, the canopy of moss-covered oaks.

It's a place with a rich, quirky, and ongoing human history, sort of *America's Best Idea* meets *Midnight in the Garden of Good and Evil.*

It's a place where the wildlife includes loggerhead sea turtles, great horned owls, pileated woodpeckers, oystercatchers, terns, armadillos, hogs, and—what most visitors hope to see—feral horses that have roamed the island for centuries.

When you leave Cumberland Island, part of you wants to tell everyone about it. Part of you wants to tell no one.

Toni and I spent our twentieth anniversary there, riding bikes up to the Plum Orchard Mansion and having a picnic lunch on the porch. I went there several times with Mom. When Mia turned twelve, it felt right to take her there.

Or at least it felt right to me.

As Toni and I prepared for the trip, Mia made it quite clear that she was dreading it. Dreading the ferry ride, dreading camping, dreading being a short walk from miles and miles of undeveloped beach. On the drive to Georgia, she said she was jealous of her cousins in Missouri.

"They don't have to go to the beach," she said.

If I had given Mia the option, she would have stayed home. As we started the trip, that was starting to sound like a good idea to me too. Screw it, I thought more than once.

I knew some of it was anxiety. I could relate, to a certain degree. I remembered starting many a day at middle school doubled over in the bathroom, my stomach feeling like someone was twisting it in knots. I didn't even really know why this happened, just that it did—and that it didn't happen when I got outside, climbed a rock, went for a hike, or swam in a lake.

I could not have imagined doing some of the things Mia routinely did—like getting up on stage, reciting lines, singing a solo, or, God forbid, trying to dance. So I tried to be understanding when she seemed frightened by the things that would have excited me when I was twelve. Like a ferry ride.

Once we were onboard, she actually seemed to enjoy it, partly because they served soda inside. After we docked, we listened to a mandatory ranger talk for campers—I glanced at Mia when the ranger mentioned venomous snakes—and picked out a site. No. 8.

As we wheeled carts loaded with our duffel bags, a tent, and a cooler to our campsite, Mia continued to complain. When we got to the campsite, she complained about the tiny flying bugs. Once the tent was up, she climbed into it and let out a yell when she heard something land on top of it.

"What was that?" she said.

It was a leaf.

I stood there thinking, Where did I go wrong? For that matter, where did Mom and Dad go right? How did they make trips like this turn out so well? Or did they? I vaguely remember moments of my sisters and me fighting, of bugs and rain, of being tired, hot, cold, and scared.

Toni and I told Mia we were going to the beach. We walked through perhaps my favorite collection of oaks anywhere, their limbs wildly twisted. Mia paid no attention to the trees. But when we got off the boardwalk and into the thick sand, we passed some horse poop and her mood instantly improved. Not because she was excited about the possibility of seeing some of the island's horses. Merely because she was a middle schooler, and as such, was amused by horse poop. It wasn't bison poop, but it would do.

When we stepped onto the beach, there were the most people I had ever seen on it at one time: about a dozen, mostly directly in front of us. To the left there was nothing but miles of empty beach. To the right, there was more empty beach—except for four horses in the distance.

We decided to head toward the horses. Mia picked up the pace. She did some cartwheels. She stopped, excited about finding some snake-shaped bones in the sand. She took some pictures. After watching the horses from a safe distance, she found a stick and started drawing in the sand. An obstacle course. Just as we had done when we went to the redwoods, our last family trip with Nana.

She asked Toni and me to do the course with her. Again and again.

"Let's go back to the campsite," we eventually said.

"Why?" she said. "I'm having fun here."

She begged to stay a little longer.

Okay, we said, ten more minutes.

She picked up a stick again. "Don't look," she said.

Toni and I turned and looked at the ocean. Sandpipers skittered along the shoreline. The late afternoon sun was at our backs. Toni took my hand. There was the sound of the surf and a slight breeze carrying the scent of the island. I took a deep breath, wishing there was a way to bottle this moment so I could pull it out whenever one of us needed it.

"Okay, you can look now," Mia said.

I turned around and saw what she had written.

When I was growing up and we went to a beach, Dad inevitably would write messages in the sand, typically in haiku.

Mia never met my dad. None of the grandchildren did. But they all watched Nana continue this tradition of beach poetry. When we were at the redwoods and spent a chilly day at the beach, exploring the tide pools and climbing on rocks, Mom started writing haiku and Mia joined in.

That had made me smile. But this? This made me forget what it took to get to this moment. This made me remember why we were here. And this made me think Cumberland Island will forever be one of my favorite parks.

I was standing on the beach that Mia did not want to be on a couple of hours earlier, but now didn't want to leave, looking at what she had written in the sand.

Nana
By Mia Woods
I miss you Nana
I wish you were here with us
We love you so much

ACKNOWLEDGMENTS

I'm indebted to so many people for so many reasons. But I have to start by giving thanks to Mom and Dad for taking me to the parks and giving me a love of rocks and rivers, stars and starfish, stories and storytellers.

To my sisters, Lisa Woods and Beth Lemke, for everything they did while Mom was dying and for continuing to do something that would make Mom and Dad happy—gather with family in beautiful places.

To my wife, Toni, for all of her support since we first met thirty years ago when I was editing her copy at the University of Missouri, for enduring my ups and downs during five years of working on this book, for always believing in me, for being a better editor for me than I ever was for her, and for allowing me to share my love of the parks with her.

To my daughter, Mia, for going with me to my idea of the happiest places on earth.

To Abe Valenzuela and his family for embracing my mom—and for helping us let go of her.

To Mom's group of friends for showing me what true friendship means. (I won't name them all, for fear of leaving some out.) To Alison Harrington and Tucson's Southside Presbyterian Church for their love and support of my mom.

I owe an enormous thanks to the Society of Professional

Journalists and the Pulliam family for the Eugene C. Pulliam Fellowship for Editorial Writing, an award that allowed me to work on my dream assignment and, as it turned out, spend stretches of time in Tucson with my mom.

To Mary Kelli Palka, Marilyn Young, Frank Denton, and Kurt Caywood—editors at *The Florida Times-Union* who allowed me to take two sabbaticals, one for the fellowship year and another to work on the book.

Thanks to Gail Ross, my agent, and the Ross Yoon Agency for seeing promise in my story. To Steve Inskeep for suggesting, at the end of an interview with him about his book *Jacksonland,* that I contact Gail.

To Laurie Chittenden, my editor, for her love of the parks and memories of family road trips—experiences that gave us an instant connection and led to her and Thomas Dunne Books taking a chance on me and my book.

To Silvio Cavaceppi for letting me use his cabin on the Suwannee River and to John Atchison for renting his house on Big Talbot Island—two serene spots in North Florida where I finished the original manuscript.

To Chris and Cindy Burns for letting me hole up in their garage apartment while trying to cut fifty-four thousand words from that original manuscript.

To my colleagues for constantly making me proud to work alongside them. To Mike Marino for helping me brainstorm before, during, and after the year. To Glenn Guzzo for helping me to get started writing and for reading everything once I finished.

After winning the fellowship, I quickly realized that it not only allowed me to travel to America's national parks, but it also gave me the excuse to spend time with people who work in them. I have always admired and envied park rangers. Working on this only punctuated that.

Thanks to all the National Park Service employees, past and

present, who shared some of their time, passion, and expertise, starting in Washington, D.C., with Director Jonathan Jarvis, David Barna, and Jeffrey Olson and continuing throughout the year and across the country with park service staff, retirees, affiliates, and volunteers, including (but hardly limited to): Darla Sidles, Don Swann, and all the staff at the Saguaro National Park western district visitor center; Barbara Goodman, Craig Morris, Daniel Tardona, and John Whitehurst at Timucuan Ecological and Historic Preserve; Candace Tinkler and Keith Bensen at Redwood National and State Parks; John Kelly and Sheridan Steele at Acadia National Park; Mike Jester, Christopher Ziegler, and Tracy Ziegler at Dry Tortugas National Park; former Dry Tortugas chief ranger Wayne Landrum and his wife, Kathy, at their house on Big Pine Key, Florida; Lee Whittlesey, Dave Hallac, Rick Wallen, and Bob Hamilton at Yellowstone National Park; Dave Taft, John Warren, John Lincoln Hallowell, Colleen Sorbera, Dan Parker, and Anthony Sadasiva at Gateway National Recreation Area; Dave Uberuaga, Maureen Oltrogge, and Kim Besom at Grand Canyon National Park and former ranger Bruce Aiken at his art studio in Flagstaff, Arizona; Shelton Johnson, Jesse McGahey, and Linda Eade at Yosemite National Park; Jeffrey Reinbold, Brendan Wilson, Barbara Black, Kathie Shaffer, and Donna Glessner at Flight 93 National Memorial; Leonard Pearlstine and Erik Stabenau at Everglades National Park; Barb Maynes at Olympic National Park; David Harrington and Sharon Small at Little Bighorn Battlefield National Monument; Fred Boyles at Cumberland Island National Seashore; Denali climbing ranger Brandon Latham; Tef Rodeffer at the Western Archeological and Conservation Center; Matt Brown and Nan Cabatbat at Haleakalā National Park.

Thanks to the Grand Canyon River Guides Association for allowing me to spend a weekend hanging out with a bunch of people who are passionate about the Colorado River.

To the National Parks Conservation Association staff in

Washington, D.C., and in regional offices around the country, not only for their help during my year but also for what NPCA has been doing every year since 1919.

To Kasi Craddock of the Buffalo Field Campaign for spending a day driving me around the West Yellowstone area, giving me one side of the bison debate. And to rancher Druska Kinkie for inviting me into her home north of Yellowstone the next day and giving me the other side of the debate. As was the case with much I gathered during the year, these stories didn't make it into the book. But I am grateful to them and everyone who gave me their time.

Thanks to Barbara Uberuaga for adding a plate to the table when her husband, superintendent at the Grand Canyon, called to say he was bringing a guest home for dinner.

To Joe Butler and the staff at Black Creek Outfitters, particularly Mathew Rini, for helping me prepare for trips during the year—and dream about future ones.

To Gordon Hempton for sharing his yurt and making me, for better and worse, constantly think about the sounds around me.

To Ross Zimmerman for taking me to Wasson Peak and a trail where an echo of his son persists.

To the Guadagno family for making me feel like a part of their family.

Thanks to all the fellow park visitors I met along the way. People like Helmut and Flo Kuhnen, campground neighbors in Yosemite who invited me to their site for probably the best dinner of the year.

To the friends—David DeLong, Chris Burns, and Mark Schnorr—who tagged along for parts of my year in the parks and helped me in more ways than they'll ever know.

To the friend who read the column I wrote after Mom died—about how Byrd Baylor was right, everybody needs a rock—and mailed me a heavy package. When I opened it, I found a rock that was slightly larger than a baseball and fit neatly into my hand, as if made for it. An attached note read: "The kids and I were on a beach recently, and I found two rocks out of the thousands that seemed to speak to me. I am sending you one in celebration of your mom, my mom's life, and as a reminder of our friendship." That rock is still on my desk. And it still speaks to me every so often.

To Lili Pew and Carol Bult, who were married in 2015, for showing me Acadia and sharing a New Year's sunrise.

To Dayton Duncan for not only spending hours talking about the parks over coffee-turned-lunch in Walpole, New Hampshire, but also for writing and producing *America's Best Idea*. The 2009 documentary inspired many Americans to return to the parks, and I'm sure to a certain degree sparked my idea for a book about the future of the parks.

To Willie Browne, a man I never met but think of often. As I was working on this book, I sometimes went to my nearest national park site, the Timucuan Ecological and Historic Preserve, and walked the Willie Browne Trail.

"Mr. Willie," as he was known, called these North Florida woods home for nearly all of his eighty years. In a time when we were sending men to the moon, he was still living in a one-room cabin without running water, a Model T battery powering a single light bulb. When he died in 1970, he barely had enough money to pay for a funeral, headstone, and chain-link fence around a modest family cemetery.

He could've been rich. As Jacksonville grew, the land he lived on—hundreds of acres of woods and marsh and waterfront bluffs—became worth millions of dollars. But, as he once said, "Money can't buy me happiness, and this place makes me happy."

He never married and didn't have children. So the year before he died, he decided he wanted this place to forever make other people happy. He signed a deed to make his land become our land. He did so with a stipulation about what should be done with the land when he was gone. Nothing.

Decades later, when one of the park rangers leads walks on the Willie Browne Trail, telling people about the man and his gift, he likes to stop talking and just listen as they pass the Browne cemetery. Because inevitably, he says, people whisper something—something I echoed when I walked the trail shortly after finishing this book.

Thank you, Mr. Willie.